Praise for *Stop the 401(k) Rip-*

"This book should spur an entire new industry of 401(k) police [because of its statement] that every 401(k) plan should be rated on how efficiently it is being run for the employee...This is just too important an issue to be ignored."

—Len Reinhart
President of Lockwood Advisors (an affiliate of Pershing)
Past President of Smith Barney Consulting Group

"The retirement dreams of millions of baby boomers ride on their 401(k) plan. And as David Loeper so clearly and passionately illustrates, too many of the nation's 401(k) plans are costly, inefficient clunkers. Fortunately, there is a way out, and Loeper's book provides us a great map."

—Evan Cooper
Senior Managing Editor of Investment News

"If you want to know what's lurking inside of your 401(k), read this book."

—John F. Wasik
author of The Merchant of Power
Bloomberg.com news columnist

"This book explains how to tell if your 401(k) is run in the best interest of financial professionals or of employees. It is required reading for those who oversee company retirement plans and for employees who intend to keep a larger slice of their own investment return."

—Parker Payson
Executive Vice President of Employee Fiduciary Corp.

"A lot has been written about the excessive costs charged by many 401(k) plans. David Loeper's new book shows plan participants how to actually do something about these costs. I highly recommend this handy and very readable book."

—W. Scott Simon, J.D., CFP®, AIFA®
author of The Prudent Investor Act: A Guide to Understanding

Stop the 401(k) Rip-off!

Eliminate Costly Hidden Fees to Improve Your Life

David B. Loeper, CIMA®, CIMC®

BridgewayBooks

Stop the 401(k) Rip-off!: Eliminate Costly Hidden Fees to Improve Your Life
Published by Bridgeway Books
P.O. BOX 80107
Austin, Texas 78758

For more information about our books, please write to us, call 512.478.2028, or visit our website at www.bridgewaybooks.net.

Library of Congress Control Number: 2007933860

ISBN-13: 978-1-934454-10-7 (hardcover)
ISBN-10: 1-934454-10-9 (hardcover)
ISBN-13: 978-1-934454-07-7 (paperback)
ISBN-10: 1-934454-07-9 (paperback)

Disclaimer: The information contained in this book is the sole opinion of the author and is designed to provide accurate, dependable information in regard to the specific subject matter covered. It is provided with the understanding that the content herein is not to be deemed as investment advisory, legal, financial, tax, or other professional services for any specific reader by the author and that the publisher is not engaged in any such services. Readers should retain the services of a competent professional to advise them on any aspects covered within the content. Third party data and other information sources cited, used, referenced or otherwise relied upon in this book are believed to be reliable, but are not guaranteed by the publisher or author.

10 9 8 7 6 5 4 3 2

This book is dedicated to my children, Brian and Megan. I am incredibly proud of both of you for the unique personal qualities you possess. Remember, it is your life and to be happy you need to fearlessly pursue your passions. You have but one life and it is up to you to make the most of it. Don't let anyone push you around or tell you how you should live YOUR life!

"I swear by my life, and my love of it, that I will not live for the sake of another man, nor ask another to live for the sake of mine."
—Ayn Rand, *Atlas Shrugged*

TABLE OF CONTENTS

Preface   xi

Acknowledgements   xvii

Introduction—The Five Steps YOU Can Take   xix

Chapter One   **1**

Step One—Understanding the REAL and HIDDEN 401(k) Expenses You Pay

Chapter Two   **17**

Deeply Hidden Expenses

Chapter Three   **25**

The Price to Your Lifestyle of Needless Expenses

Chapter Four   **39**

Step Two—Complaining without Complaining

Chapter Five   **47**

Step Three—Rallying Your Troops

Chapter Six   **53**

Step Four—What Happens If My Employer Ignores Us?

Chapter Seven   **61**

Step Five—Now That My 401(k) Is Fixed, How Can I Make the Most of My Life?

Chapter Eight   **72**

Resources, Investment Selection, Asset Allocation, Tools, and Advice

Appendix A—Lifestyle Prices of Excessive 401(k) Expenses   105

Appendix B—Sample 401(k) Participant Statement   171

Appendix C—Sample Summary Annual Report   175

Appendix D—Sample Annual Form 5500 Report   177

Index   195

PREFACE

Over the last twenty years or so, there has been a major shift in the retirement plans that companies offer their employees. Your parents were probably covered by a *pension plan* (specifically, a defined benefit pension plan) where the company *guaranteed* a certain fixed lifetime income (the "defined benefit"). Upon retirement, this would provide an ongoing retirement paycheck throughout their life. Such plans have become less and less popular among employers because **the guaranteed benefits cost the company a lot of money.**

Employers have increasingly switched to 401(k) plans, which transfer the risk of the ultimate retirement benefit (along with most of the other expenses) to employees. Such plans have been around for quite some time but were initially not very popular. Employers loved the 401(k) plans, though, because instead of the employer guaranteeing a specific benefit (and paying for 100% of the cost of the benefit as in many older pension plans) *the employer could move both the costs and risk to their employees.* Despite this, 401(k) plans gained in popularity among employees as well, influenced partially by the high market returns some of the mutual funds experienced. Also, many companies that previously could not have afforded the cost or risk of a traditional pension plan could afford to offer a 401(k) plan, since the employees carried the burden of most expenses and all of the risk. Thus, many small companies that never would have had any retirement plan at all started 401(k) plans in an attempt to compete with larger employers' benefit plans. Even though the employee was assuming 100% of the investment risk, 100% of the retirement benefit risk, and, in many cases, most of the cost in the form of annual contributions (most 401(k) plans have some matching contribution by the employer), the flexibility of these plans made them attractive to some employees.

There is nothing wrong with an employer trying to reduce their share of the costs of retirement benefits by moving to these plans. After all, if your employer doesn't pay attention to their costs, they won't be in business for long! Such retirement benefit plans are offered by employers in order to be competitive in recruiting talent and having employees perceive a positive benefit to encourage them to stay with the company. Therefore, your employer's goal is to offer the greatest benefit *as perceived by employees and recruits at the lowest cost to the company.* This is Economics 101. A 401(k) plan fits the bill perfectly today, because employees view them in a positive light while generally bearing most of the costs and risks and saving the company a mountain of expenses.

As mentioned, when 401(k) plans first came out, they were not viewed as positively by employees as they are today. Many large companies were slow to move to 401(k) plans because of the revolt from employees. That might be hard to imagine today when it is expected that a company will offer a 401(k) plan, and such plans are normally viewed as a positive benefit to employees. But, back when most employees were covered by pension plans, the companies that attempted to switch to a 401(k) plan often froze the benefits in their existing pension plans and offered employees these new 401(k) plans instead. As you might imagine, these employers experienced a fair number of complaints from their employees. At the time, the existing employees covered by the old pension plan realized that with the new 401(k) they were taking on the investment risk, the benefit risk, and most of the cost and expenses. It seemed like a rip-off when compared to the old pension plan in which the employer carried all of the risks and expense.

However, over time, more and more employers were able to pull off this switch, and as new people entered the work force, who never had a pension plan guarantee, the 401(k) became an expected, popular benefit. Also, remember that because the cost and risk to the employer is practically nothing, or at least very small relative to older types of retirement plans, many more companies that would not have offered any retirement plan at all under previous rules now found themselves in a position to offer a retirement plan to their employees.

So that is where we are today. There is over $3 trillion in 401(k) plans covering more than 47 million employees. Odds are that you, and if married, your spouse or both of you participate in such plans. More than 500,000 employers offer these plans, meaning that a retirement benefit program is no longer just for large public companies as was generally the case in the past. There are less than 6,000 public companies in the USA, which means that more than 98% of these 401(k) plans are offered by smaller, privately held companies.

Over the last 20 years, employers have been able to dramatically reduce their benefit costs and risks, transfer most of these to their employees, and they have done so with their employees generally being happy about it! If you are happy, if the person sitting in the cube or office next to you is happy, and your employer is happy, shouldn't we just all lock arms and sing "Kumbaya?"

The Rip-off YOU CAN FIX

Complacency and the general euphoria employers and employees alike have with their 401(k) plans have created a massive opportunity for product vendors to excessively profit *from your retirement savings*.

This is not someone crying wolf. A study by the Center for Retirement Research at Boston College noted, "The bottom line is that over the period 1988–2004 defined benefit plans outperformed 401(k) plans by one percentage point. This outcome occurred despite the fact that 401(k) plans held a higher portion of their assets in equities during the bull market of the 1990s."[1]

Since you are bearing all of the risks in your 401(k), what does this 1% cost YOU? All things being equal, except this extra 1% cost, you may be surprised to find the price to your lifestyle is HUGE.

For example, if you are forty years old with $75,000 in your 401(k) plan, and you are earning $50,000 a year, contributing 10% with a 50% match by your employer, and planning on retiring at age 65 with the hope of a $32,000 annual retirement income, this 1% excess expense can cost you any one of the following:

1) A 90% chance that this excess cost will reduce your retirement fund at age 65 by $100,000 to $700,000
2) Working three more years to age 68
3) Working an extra hour every day for 25 years until age 65
4) Living on 22% less than you desired ($25,000 instead of $32,000)
5) Accepting a 72% greater chance of outliving your resources (31% versus 18%)
6) Increasing your annual savings by 80% from $5,000 (10%) to $9,000 (18%)

---

1 Alicia H. Munneli, "Investment Returns: Defined Benefit vs. 401(k) Plans" (Brief 52, Center for Retirement Research , Boston College, September 2006).

There is a reason why you are bearing this burden, and it DOES NOT generally have to do with your employer saving money on the costs of offering the 401(k) plan. Your employer wants you to perceive a positive benefit from the 401(k) plan they offer. If you and your neighbor in the next cube both perceive the 401(k) plan as an attractive benefit, then your employer has done their job, **even if you are getting "taken" to the tune of more than $100,000!**

FIXING THIS IS UP TO YOU!

How would you spend an extra $4,000 a year for the next twenty-five years? How much more secure would your retirement be with an extra $100,000 or more? How much more time could you spend at your family dinner table if you could *work an hour less each day*? What would you do in retirement with an extra $7,000 every year? What would you do in retirement if you could retire three years earlier? THIS is the price of complacency to many 401(k) participants.

In the old days of defined benefit plans, your employer assumed the burden of all of the risks and all of the expenses, and those employers that still offer such plans still carry that burden. Back then, and today as well, employers who accepted the risks and carried the expense of a defined benefit plan bore a huge incentive to reduce the costs, because THEY would get the benefit of doing so. The benefit they promised was fixed, the variable of the COST of that benefit *saved the company* money. THEY could avoid increasing THEIR contribution for your benefit by 80% if they saved 1% in expense. That might just be the reason, or at least part of the reason, that such plans outperform 401(k) plans by 1% a year.

In a 401(k) plan, because YOU bear this expense, your employer has little motivation to shop for a better deal if you and your associates are content, even though they probably should be looking for that better deal in their role of a "prudent fiduciary." The vendors of plans in this market have no reason to compete on fees **since practically no one is complaining about them**.

A study by the Government Accountability Office, commissioned by Congressman George Miller of California, reported that in 2005, despite 47 million people being covered by 401(k) plans, the Labor Department only received TEN complaints about fees.[2] If you aren't complaining, and no one else in your company is complaining, and if your employer really doesn't care as long as you are happy with the plan, your employer isn't going to bear even the tiny cost of shopping for a better deal.

Your 401(k) plan is probably one of your most important future sources of financial security. This book makes it easy for you to **take the five steps needed to add more than $100,000 to your retirement nest egg without taking more risk or saving more money.** This can allow you to improve your lifestyle, increase your benefits, identify the hidden costs, and improve your standing within your company by proactively helping your employer to take needed action.

There is no reason, other than the price of this book (a free extra copy is available for your benefits or human resources department) and a little bit of your time, why you can't capture the opportunity to improve your lifestyle, reduce how much you need to save, retire earlier, or work less. **Isn't $100,000 worth a few hours of your time?**

---

2 U.S. Government Accountability Office, Private Pensions: Changes Needed to Provide 401(k) Plan Participants and the Department of Labor Better Information on Fees, GAO-07-2,1November 2006, 21.

ACKNOWLEDGEMENTS

Writing acknowledgements, to me, is perhaps the hardest thing to write, because we are a product of all of the people we know. How do you thank everyone that has helped make you who you are? Of course I need to thank all the people of Financeware, Inc., that have each made a contribution to this book either directly or indirectly. Special thanks need to go to George Chamberlin and Brandy Nelson for their countless hours of edits and coordination of this project. We have a great team of people that truly care about helping people making the most of their lives, and they do so with unbridled passion. They live as role models for others by consistently acting with unquestioning integrity. Jerry, Travis, Christopher, TJ, Elliott, Joe, Will, Jeremy, RJ, Bridget, Bill, and, of course, my executive committee partners Bob and Karen have all made huge direct contributions to this book. Thank you all for your patience, objectivity, and coaching and for understanding how to help us to help others.

Of course, I have to thank all of my former associates from my "Wheat First" days that are now, or were, part of Wachovia Securities. These associates had the courage to challenge conventional wisdom and risk being different to serve clients better. I have to credit Dave Monday, Mark Staples, Danny Ludeman, Jim Donley, Marshall Wishnack, and, of course, the late James Wheat, a blind man who had more vision than all of us put together. Respect should be earned, not given, and every one of these people have earned mine. I consider each of them heroes in his own way.

There are a handful of people in the industry I have to thank, because they too have truly earned my respect by their actions and courage. People like Len Reinhart, Frank Campanale, Bob Schnibbe, Ron Surz, and Don Tabone have all contributed greatly to my knowledge, and their willingness to have rational debate on numerous topics have helped me immensely.

I have to thank Dawn & Jim Loeper, who were kind enough to give this a read and provide some valuable feedback. Also, Donna Wells, who helped to make my normal pontification understandable, is due credit for her enormous contribution.

A big part of understanding expenses came from Parker Payson of Employee Fiduciary Corp., whose expertise in ferreting out hidden expenses was invaluable in helping to identify the hidden costs.

I have to thank my late father, Kenneth A. Loeper, for teaching me "not to let anyone push me around." Without that skill ingrained in my brain, I would have never had the courage to face the attacks of the industry groups that hate having their apple cart upset. Also, my mother, Anna, for teaching me that the biggest responsibility we have in raising children is teaching them to be respectable people of integrity who can take care of themselves.

Finally, I want to thank the late Ayn Rand. Whether you like her or not, you have to respect her passion for and vision of a hero or heroine, so often demonstrated in her novels. The abstracts of her concepts, living a moral life and acting with integrity, helped me to understand and express why I am what I am. Who is John Galt?

INTRODUCTION

The Five Steps YOU Can Take

What do you need to do to add more than $100,000 to your retirement nest egg? In this section, I will outline the five simple steps you can take, and each step is covered in detail in the following chapters. The first step is to figure out what you really are paying in expenses in your 401(k) plan and the price of those expenses to your lifestyle.

Not all 401(k) plans have excessive fees, but if the company you work for has less than 1,000 employees, the odds are high that you are paying them. I wish figuring out what you are really paying could be as easy as reading your 401(k) statement and looking for expenses, but unfortunately, that isn't the case.

That doesn't mean that it is impossible to figure out. It really isn't that hard IF you know where to look. The first step is getting your arms around where to look for the hidden expenses you are paying so that you can truly identify your real costs. Once you know where to find your real expenses, it is easy to figure out how much of those expenses you are paying.

Chapter 1 covers this expense discovery process in an easy, step-by-step fashion that will enable you to understand how much you are really paying and to do so in a manner that doesn't require an advanced degree in mathematics, or even much time or effort. With just thirty minutes and a calculator or spreadsheet, you will know what you are really paying, or at least most of the expenses that are required to be accessible to you by law.

Chapter 2 covers the myriad of expenses that you might be paying but that are not legally required to be disclosed to you. These expenses can be very large and could actually be far more than the expenses discovered in chapter 1. While discovering many of these expenses requires some additional cooperation from your company that goes above and beyond the legal obligation they have, it might still be possible to find them. Some of these will be easier to discover than others, and in some cases, it might even be easier to calculate your share of these expenses than those discovered in chapter 1. In other cases, the best you will be able to come up with is an estimate, but at least knowing these other expenses exist will help you to gain a sense of what you might be paying.

It might be a good idea to have some aspirin nearby in case you have a heart attack once you see all of your real costs from chapters 1 and 2.

In chapter 3, you will figure out whether the expenses you discovered using the approach in chapters 1 and 2 make enough difference for you to continue with the rest of the steps. Maybe after the first thirty minutes you invested in uncovering expenses you found out that your 401(k) expenses are only 0.75% a year, or just a tad higher than they should be. If you are close to retirement anyway, it might not be worthwhile to look into it any further, because the effect is so small. Chapter 3 will expose when it isn't worth further effort.

However, our introductory example showed how a typical forty-year-old middle-class participant (with $75,000 in their 401(k) and saving $5,000 a year) had a 90% chance of adding anywhere from $100,000 to more than $700,000 to their retirement fund by finishing the steps in this book. In reality, the cost savings and benefits could be far greater. Chapter 3 will show some examples of the price to your lifestyle at various ages and contribution levels so you can see if it is worth going any further. You will also see what the benefits might be and how you can get free help to figure out the advantage of executing the remaining steps.

Chapter 4 introduces the second step in the process: Complaining Without Sounding Like a Complainer. Let's assume you, like millions of other Americans, find out that it is worthwhile to take the next step because your 401(k) plan is costing you absurd amounts of excess fees. You also will have discovered that these excess fees carry a huge cost to the lifestyle you want to live. Knowing these costs exist isn't going to change things unless you take action. You might view yourself as just a cog in the company wheel, and you don't want to "make waves" with those in command. But, there are ways to correct these expenses, and, instead of being viewed as a complainer, you might actually end up being viewed as a hero in the eyes of both your bosses and your coworkers. This chapter gives you all of the secrets to fix your retirement plan in a positive and proactive manner.

The third step in the process—rallying your troops—is the subject of chapter 5. After discovering your expenses were way too high and were materially affecting your quality of life in step 1, you took step 2 and proactively and positively brought it to your employer's attention. Having done this, what can you do when, as is often the case, nothing is done about the problem?

Step 3 is required when the distractions of day-to-day business have the "powers that be" in your company complacently ignoring your initial attempt to highlight the problem of excess expenses. While we would like to sell more books, because we are donating the profits of this book to charity, we give you a no cost way to help your fellow associates and coworkers join in your rally to get your employer to spend a few hours working on this problem. Your associates also will be protected from being viewed as complainers, and it generally will not take more than an email and a brief discussion over the water cooler to encourage a few of your coworkers to help in the cause. Your one voice may not be enough, but if your employer receives just a couple of additional questions from other employees, it is likely your employer will wake up and take notice. If they hear one complaint, they might assume you are the only one who cares. If the employer hears three or more complaints or questions, they will assume there might be many others who have not yet complained. At this point the employer may become concerned that they are losing the positive benefit they are trying to create by sponsoring the 401(k) plan, and they might take action to solve the problem.

In chapter 6, we move on to step 4—What Happens if My Employer Ignores Us? This step is the course of last resort for those of you who already completed steps 1 through 3. If you have figured out that your expenses are far too high, if the price to your life of these expenses is too great, if you and your associates have let your employer know about these expenses and where to go to for a solution and nothing happens, it is time to take more drastic action.

While several lawsuits have been filed against employers that ignore their fiduciary obligations, there is an easier and less disruptive way to solve the problem that will bring in the government on your side as an added bonus. The government exists only because you pay taxes to fund their activities, so this course of action, while drastic and unnecessary in most cases and a bit more adversarial than the teamwork methods shown in prior steps, might be the only way for you to get your employer to wake up and fix the problem.

Specifics are provided in chapter 6 that explain some of the terminology of ERISA (Employee Retirement Income Security Act), where to go, how to remain anonymous, and what you should say to put the fear of government intervention to work for your retirement. Finally, we will also explore how to overcome one of the most common defenses for using overpriced investments (past performance, or performance track records) and what the real facts are about fund ratings and track records.

The fifth and final step—Making the Most of Your Life—is covered in chapter 7. You have spent a few hours taking the steps needed to get your employer to fix your overly expensive 401(k) plan, and it worked! Your expenses now are reasonable, and the options this creates to improve your lifestyle are vast. Should you:

- Save less money?
- Plan on retiring earlier?
- Work fewer hours?
- Add a travel budget to your plan for retirement?
- Take less investment risk so that market gyrations still let you sleep at night?
- Take the vacation of your dreams?
- Leave a bequest to your church or school?
- Buy the new sports car you have always dreamed about?
- Pay off credit card bills?
- Send your child to a private school?
- Build an addition on your house?
- Help your elderly parents improve their lifestyle?
- Upgrade the way you pursue your hobby?
- Buy a vacation home?

While this list of options just scratches the surface of the choices you have, if your 401(k) is costing you too much, then executing the five steps will enable some (maybe many) of your dreams for a better life to confidently become a reality. While it may seem too good to be true, any one of these goals (or any others you might have that are not on the list) might be achievable if you can move the expenses of your 401(k) to *your* pocket, instead of an investment product vendor's pocket.

THIS IS WHY IT IS SO IMPORTANT FOR YOU TO TAKE THE STEPS NEEDED TO IMPROVE YOUR 401(k)!

You might be skeptical that saving 1% in expenses in your 401(k) could produce options like these to improve your lifestyle. A quick calculation for our sample middle-class American with $75,000 in their 401(k) would infer that the benefit of saving 1% in fees is only worth $750 a year. But remember that this person is contributing 10% of their income ($5,000 a year), and their employer is matching an additional $2,500 so that the $75,000 balance will likely accumulate to far more money in the coming year. In fact, if he earns 7% on his $75,000, a year later his 401(k) would be worth $87,750. His investment may have grown by 7% but his excess fees grew from $750 to $877! That is a **16.9% increase in fees!!!**

Think about the way compound interest works. In ten or twenty years, your 401(k) could easily be worth $250,000 to over a $1,000,000! An extra 1% expense at that point **could cost you $2,500 to over $10,000 a year!** If your fees are growing by more than twice the rate you are growing your investments, this will clearly compound into some serious money!

Of course, investments will go up and down over time, and your contributions each year will become a smaller percentage of your total account balances. There are a lot of uncertainties in the markets, your goals, what you personally value, and also a lot of choices of how you can "spend the dividend" you get by taking the five steps needed to fix your 401(k).

Step 5 walks you through the process that you and your spouse or partner can go through to figure out how and on what you can confidently use the "expense saving dividend" benefit of your repaired 401(k). Without this step, you really won't realize the benefits of the first steps you took to get your 401(k) fixed.

Your assets (and their expenses), allocation choices, goals, dreams, priorities, and how you personally value each of these items are inextricably connected. The bottom line is that while you may have fixed the problem of paying needless expenses by taking the first four steps, you may still be saving too much, working too long, vacationing too little, or merely compromising something you value to achieve something you do not value as much. The real payoff comes from making informed choices about what makes the most sense for what you personally value.

How do you know if you are making an informed choice? How do you choose an asset allocation strategy? How can you tell whether your advisor is conflicted or is helping you make the most of your life? What questions should you ask? How can you select investments that avoid needless expenses and risk? Fixing the expenses in your 401(k) is not going to improve your life if the advice you get is conflicted, you have a poor asset allocation, or you choose investments that expose you to unnecessary risks.

Finally, to truly make the most of your life, this initial process of making informed choices cannot be a one time event. To make the most of your life it needs to become continuous process responding to the changes in your life, your values, your priorities, and the markets. We call this continuous life relative advice "Wealthcare" and how it works and the benefits to improving your lifestyle are explored along with several helpful tools enabling you to implement choices in chapter 8. Fixing your 401(k) may be a one time event, but making the most of the only life you have should be a continuous process.

CHAPTER ONE

Step One—Understanding the REAL and HIDDEN 401(k) Expenses You Pay

Most Americans either do not know what they are paying within their 401(k) or think they aren't paying anything. While it is absurd to think this, all one has to do is look at the typical 401(k) statement produced for each participant, and it becomes easy to see why so many people have no idea what they are paying **or often don't even realize there are any expenses!** THE TYPICAL 401(k) STATEMENT EFFECTIVELY HIDES FEES YOU PAY FROM YOU! Believe it or not, this is legal! It may not be ethical, but it is legal.

I've included a copy of one of my own 401(k) statements in appendix B so you can see every little detailed disclosure. Your statement probably looks pretty similar. This was the standard statement that came from the Principal Group (our company's former 401(k) vendor before I fixed my company's plan, which is how I know that far lower cost alternatives are available). The Principal Group is no small outfit and can afford to do decent record keeping. According to *Pensions & Investment Age,* the Principal Group had over 2.7 million participants getting similar statements from over 32,000 different sponsoring companies. Think about this. The number of companies whose 401(k) plan provides this sort of statement is FIVE TIMES the number of all public companies in the USA!

But, if one were so possessed to look beyond the first page of my statement (figure 1) that shows the bottom line of what any participant is interested in (i.e., how much money you have), where would one search for expenses? How about the details of the statement entitled "account activity?"

1

Figure 1 Cover page of a 401(k) statement—The bottom line

The account activity section of my statement supposedly details the financial activities and even has a column heading that includes the word "expenses" (table 1).

ACCOUNT ACTIVITY BY INVESTMENT OPTION AS OF 12/31/2005

INVESTMENT ADVISOR	INVESTMENT OPTION	Beginning Balance	Additions/ Transfers In[1]	*Net Earnings	Withdrawals/ Expenses/ Transfers Out[2]	Ending Balance
	Moderate					
Principal Global Investors	Total Market Stk Idx Sep Acct+	$79,413.38	$14,875.12	$4,338.57	$0.00	$98,627.07
	Dynamic					
Principal Global Investors	Diversified Intl Sep Acct+	$13,069.14	$2,274.95	$3,515.85	$0.00	$18,859.94
Principal Global Investors	Intl Emerging Mkts Sep Acct+	$2,048.72	$349.93	$801.80	$0.00	$3,200.45
TOTALS		$94,531.24	$17,500.00	$8,656.22	$0.00	$120,687.46

Detailed transaction activity is available on the web at www.principal.com.

[1]May include deposits and transfers.

*Net earnings reflect plan expenses as well as the timing and amount of deposits to the account.

[2]May include withdrawals, transfers, and expenses.

Table 1 Account activity section of a statement—Note the column entitled "Withdrawals/Expenses/Transfers Out"

IS IT ANY WONDER SOME PEOPLE THINK THEY HAVE NO EXPENSES?

Here I am reviewing what on the surface appears to be a detailed accounting of my 401(k) balances. I see beginning values. I observe $17,500 in additions (my contribution plus my employer's match). I see that *Net Earnings* has a little asterisk, which in the financial services industry in general and particularly in 401(k) plans, means "we are trying to hide something from you." If I read the footnote, it clears things up perfectly for me. Well, not so much. All it says is that the net earnings reflect plan expenses as well as—

Let's get this straight! I have a column that says "net earnings" (footnoted as net of expenses) which means they are mixing up returns with expenses even though they have another column where they could easily break out the expenses.

That expense column is footnoted too, this time with the number two. Like an asterisk, anything footnoted is likely to mean someone is attempting to hide something from you, because few people read footnotes. **Read the footnote**. All it says is that it *may include* the same things that are listed in the column heading! I guess it *may exclude* it, too, since it says ZERO.

Because the numbers in the expense column are zeros, it appears as though there are no expenses. Look at my full statement in appendix B, or better yet, look at your own 401(k) statement and see if yours is equally misleading. You are probably one of the millions of Americans who receives a misleading statement that has only zeroes in the expense column of your statement.

Maybe I'm not your average Joe and I know those funds that I invest in have expense ratios. They might be "no load" which in today's world often means that the fund doesn't confiscate a big chunk of YOUR money from you all at once up-front. Instead, often such "no loads" will take a little bit at a time forever and try to hide it from you unless you look for it. So, I keep paging through my statement and sure enough there is a page that shows me information about all of the alternatives in my 401(k) plan (table 2*)*.

INVESTMENT PERFORMANCE THROUGH 12/31/2005

While past performance does not predict future results, this section helps you compare investment options. This history shows the rate of return that would have been earned from a sum of money invested on the first day of the period and left until the last day of the period, with no other transactions. Returns marked with an asterisk (*) reflect performance since the inception date of the investment option. Returns shown for periods of less than one year are not annualized. All returns displayed here are after Total Investment Expense, but before any plan expenses, of the investment option.

INVESTMENT ADVISOR	INVESTMENT OPTION	YTD	Last Calendar Quarter	1 Yr	3 Yr	5 Yr	10 Yr or *Since Inception	Inception Date	NAV/ Unit Value
	Stable								
	Guaranteed 5 year	3.95	---	---	---	---	---	---	---
Principal Global Investors	Money Market Sep Acct+	2.72	0.87	2.72	1.45	1.96	3.64	12/10/1980	45.3369531
	Conservative								
Principal Global Investors	Bond and Mtg Sep Acct+	2.48	0.62	2.48	4.12	6.04	6.30	02/01/1983	735.7602015
	Moderate								
American Century Inv. Mgmt.	LgCap Value II SA+	5.83	1.61	5.83	---	---	*5.81	12/31/2004	10.5826814
Principal Global Investors	Lg Cap Stk Idx Sep Acct+	4.58	2.00	4.58	13.99	0.16	8.66	01/01/1990	47.0805293
Principal Global Investors	Total Market Stk Idx Sep Acct+	5.33	2.03	5.33	14.83	1.05	*1.81	09/28/1999	11.1817384
	Aggressive								
American Century Inv. Mgmt.	LgCap Growth II Sep Acct+	4.58	3.31	4.58	12.91	-2.63	*-2.62	12/29/2000	8.7541287
Mazama Capital Management	SmCap Growth III Sep Acct+	12.50	8.04	12.50	---	---	*13.31	06/01/2004	12.1930230
Mellon Equity	MidCap Growth I Sep Acct+	13.43	4.18	13.43	20.43	-5.15	*-10.49	12/31/1999	19.6066484
Principal Global Investors	Mid-Cap Stk Idx Sep Acct+	12.20	3.23	12.20	20.63	8.11	*10.90	08/31/1999	19.2818973
Principal Global Investors	Small Co Growth Sep Acct+	4.35	2.64	4.35	22.22	1.61	6.00	06/01/1995	19.2785040
Principal Global Investors	Sm-Cap Stk Idx Sep Acct+	7.29	0.29	7.29	21.89	10.27	*11.66	08/31/1999	20.1305345
	Dynamic								
Principal Global Investors	Diversified Intl Sep Acct+	24.14	5.75	24.14	26.17	5.16	8.53	05/20/1987	49.3574051
Principal Global Investors	Intl Emerging Mkts Sep Acct+	35.09	7.54	35.09	38.94	18.87	11.99	01/01/1995	33.3525171

These results are for the investment options selected by your company's plan, and may be different from the results for other plans.
+For more information about this investment option, including its full name, please visit The Principal Retirement Service Center® at www.principal.com or call assistance from a retirement specialist.
The Guaranteed Interest Account rate is as of the statement effective date.

Table 2 A section of the 401(k) statement showing investment options

See if you can find what expenses are in this section. YOU CAN'T BE-CAUSE EXPENSES ARE ONCE AGAIN NOT SHOWN! If you scan this closely for the words "expense" or "expenses" you will observe that the last sentence in the introductory paragraph says, "**All returns displayed here are after Total Investment Expense, but before any plan expenses of the investment option.**"

So here again, **they are hiding expenses in the returns**. They are also tipping you off, though, that there may be other expenses, *because these returns are before plan expenses.* This helps defend them from class action lawsuits, because if you and your coworkers try to sue them for their misleading participant statement they can claim that they said there were other expenses. As far as you can tell from my statement (and probably yours, too) it looks as though I'm paying ZERO in expenses.

I had just over $120,000 in this plan as of this statement date. Want to venture a guess as to what my REAL expenses were? Hint: They WERE NOT ZERO!

MY annual expense for the next year, based on just my current balances would be: $1,566! THIS IS A LOT DIFFERENT THAN ZERO!!!

You should note that 82% of my allocation was in a Total Market Index Fund, which according to the 401(k) website had 0.31% in annual expenses. How did my total expenses end up at $1,566 or almost 1.3%? I'll show you how to figure it out. It is unlikely that your statement is going to be of much value in doing so, because as we have seen, it is standard practice to hide the fees from appearing on your statement. And it is legal, but in my opinion it is NOT ethical.

How to find your REAL expenses

If your statement isn't showing your expenses, you are probably wondering how you will figure out what you are really paying. You have a couple of choices.

Option 1—Find your expense ratio

If you are anxious to quickly determine your costs, you can usually get the answer for at least some of your expenses by just taking a few minutes to go to your 401(k) website and look for the **expense ratio** for each fund you own. It may be shown in a table of performance information like table 2 but with an additional column entitled either "Expense Ratio" or "Total Investment Expense." There may be links to other websites like Morningstar.com that will show you the expense ratio of your fund. You may even have a fact sheet from your original enrollment materials that summarizes this information, or such a sheet may come with your quarterly or annual statement that includes the expense ratios. As a last resort, if you can't find this information in any of those places, you can look up each fund you own on a website like Morningstar.com or Yahoo! Finance.

The expense ratio will be reflected as an annual percentage expense like 0.85% or 1.25%, etc. For each fund you look up, record the expense ratio next to the balance you own of that fund on your statement (figure 2). See, the statement is useful for something! How long this process takes, whether ten minutes or twenty minutes, is somewhat dependent on the number of funds you have to research and how deeply the information is hidden from you.

ACCOUNT ACTIVITY BY INVESTMENT OPTION AS OF 12/31/2005						
INVESTMENT ADVISOR	INVESTMENT OPTION	Beginning Balance	Additions/ Transfers In¹	*Net Earnings	Withdrawals/ Expenses/ Transfers Out²	Ending Balance
	Moderate					
Principal Global Investors	Total Market Stk Idx Sep Acct+	$79,413.38	$14,875.12	$4,338.57	$0.00	$98,627.07
	Dynamic					
Principal Global Investors	Diversified Intl Sep Acct+	$13,069.14	$2,274.95	$3,515.85	$0.00	$18,859.94
Principal Global Investors	Intl Emerging Mkts Sep Acct+	$2,048.72	$349.93	$801.80	$0.00	$3,200.45
TOTALS		$94,531.24	$17,500.00	$8,656.22	$0.00	$120,687.46

Your Research: 0.31%, 1.06%, 1.51%

Detailed transaction activity is available on the web at www.principal.com.

¹May include deposits and transfers.

*Net earnings reflect plan expenses as well as the timing and amount of deposits to the account.

²May include withdrawals, transfers, and expenses.

Figure 2 Recording the expense ratio for each fund you own based on your research

Your Research:
0.31% = $305
1.06% = $199
1.51% = $48

ACCOUNT ACTIVITY BY INVESTMENT OPTION AS OF 12/31/2005

INVESTMENT ADVISOR	INVESTMENT OPTION	Beginning Balance	Additions/ Transfers In[1]	Net Earnings[3]	Withdrawals/ Expenses/ Transfers Out[2]	Ending Balance
	Moderate					
Principal Global Investors	Total Market Stk Idx Sep Acct+	$79,413.38	$14,875.12	$4,338.57	$0.00	$98,627.07
	Dynamic					
Principal Global Investors	Diversified Intl Sep Acct+	$13,069.14	$2,274.95	$3,515.85	$0.00	$18,859.94
Principal Global Investors	Intl Emerging Mkts Sep Acct+	$2,048.72	$349.93	$801.80	$0.00	$3,200.45
TOTALS		$94,531.24	$17,500.00	$8,656.22	$0.00	$120,687.46

Detailed transaction activity is available on the web at www.principal.com.

[1]May include deposits and transfers.

[3]Net earnings reflect plan expenses as well as the timing and amount of deposits to the account.

[2]May include withdrawals, transfers, and expenses.

Figure 3 Calculating the dollar cost of your expense ratios

ACCOUNT ACTIVITY BY INVESTMENT OPTION AS OF 12/31/2005

INVESTMENT ADVISOR	INVESTMENT OPTION	Beginning Balance	Additions/ Transfers In[1]	[3]Net Earnings	Withdrawals/ Expenses/ Transfers Out[2]	Ending Balance
	Moderate					
Principal Global Investors	Total Market Stk Idx Sep Acct+	$79,413.38	$14,875.12	$4,338.57	$0.00	$98,627.07
	Dynamic					
Principal Global Investors	Diversified Intl Sep Acct+	$13,069.14	$2,274.95	$3,515.85	$0.00	$18,859.94
Principal Global Investors	Intl Emerging Mkts Sep Acct+	$2,048.72	$349.93	$801.80	$0.00	$3,200.45
TOTALS		$94,531.24	$17,500.00	$8,656.22	$0.00	$120,687.46

Detailed transaction activity is available on the web at www.principal.com.

[1]May include deposits and transfers.

[3]Net earnings reflect plan expenses as well as the timing and amount of deposits to the account.

[2]May include withdrawals, transfers, and expenses.

Your Research:

0.31% = $305
1.06% = $199
1.51% = $48
0.45% = $552
($552/$120,687)

Figure 4 Calculating the combined expense ratios

10

Once you know the expense ratio for each of your funds, use a calculator, or drop the information into a spreadsheet, and multiply the expense ratio by your ending balance as shown in figure 3.

Finally, to figure how your expenses are combined based on your fund selection, add the dollar amount of the expenses for all of the funds as above, and divide by your total ending balance (figure 4).

Now, this figure does not tell you ALL of your expenses, it just shows some of the expenses that may be hidden within the funds. **It specifically DOES NOT show you the "plan expenses" as that little footnote we saw earlier made mention.**

Unless you diligently file away every scrap of information you get, in order to calculate your real total expenses (at least those that are required by law to be accessible to you), you will need to contact your human resources department, controller, payroll, or some other person within your company who provides you with your 401(k) information. The expense ratios we have looked at are merely a portion of what you are likely paying.

The additional statement you are looking for is something you get every year but never pay attention to it since it doesn't show you anything specifically about your balances. It is normally called something like, "Summary Annual Report" and it may expose some HUGE expenses.

Since you are probably going to have to contact your human resources or benefits department anyway, the second option might be easier for you if you have the patience to wait for them to respond.

Option 2—Let Human Resources Do Some of the Work for You

If you have the patience to wait for a response from your HR/benefits department, the easiest way to understand your costs is to let them collect the information you need to figure it out.

First, make a copy of the page showing the balances of each of your funds from one of your statements, or print out your fund holdings from your 401(k) website. Then, attach a note that says something similar to the following:

```
To: Human Resources Dept.
From: MY NAME
Re: My 401(k)

Dear NAME:


    I've been doing some retirement planning and I'm
trying to get an understanding of the expenses I am in-
curring in my 401(k) plan.
    I was wondering if you could provide me with two
things:
    What are the expense ratios of the funds I own?
(statement of balances attached)
    Please provide me with a copy of the Summary Annual
Report for the plan.
    Thank you for your prompt attention to this matter.


Sincerely,
My Name
```

Depending on the size of your company and how well you know your benefits department staff, you can obviously make the note more personal and less formal. The bottom line is that you should get two things back from them. The first is the expense ratios of your funds (you will still need to take the steps shown in option 1 to calculate the dollar cost of those ratios, but at least you won't have to look it up). The other is a document that looks something like figure 5.

SUMMARY ANNUAL REPORT

This is a summary of the annual report for

FIN ███████████ INC. 401(K) PLAN

EIN ██ 040████

for January 1, 2005, through December 31, 2005. The annual report has been filed with the Employee Benefits Security Administration, as required under the Employee Retirement Income Security Act of 1974 (ERISA).

BASIC FINANCIAL STATEMENT

Benefits under the plan are provided by a combination of funding arrangements. Plan expenses were $46,230. These expenses included $0 in administrative expenses and $34,926 in benefits paid to participants and beneficiaries, and $11,304 in other expenses. A total of 25 persons were participants in or beneficiaries of the plan at the end of the plan year, although not all of these persons had yet earned the right to receive benefits.

The value of plan assets, after subtracting liabilities of the plan, was $1,341,870 as of December 31, 2005, compared to $1,013,895 as of January 1, 2005. During the plan year, the plan experienced an increase in its net assets of $327,975. This increase includes unrealized appreciation or depreciation in the value of the plan assets; that is, the difference between the value of plan's assets at the end of the year and the value of the assets at the beginning of the year or cost of assets acquired during the year. The plan had total income of $374,205, including employer contributions of $42,614, employee contributions of $221,624, gains of $0, from the sale of assets, and earnings from investments of $109,967.

YOUR RIGHTS TO ADDITIONAL INFORMATION

Figure 5 Summary Annual Report

You already get this statement once a year, but you probably do not pay any attention to it, because it does NOT APPEAR to have any information about your particular situation. But on closer inspection, you will find that it does. In the Basic Financial Statement you can discover how much you are paying beyond the expense ratios, but it requires a little addition, subtraction, multiplication, and division.

First, start at the second paragraph and look for some numbers. Take the plan expenses (in this case, $46,230) and subtract the amount of benefits paid (in this case, $34,926). The difference between these two dollar amounts is either going to show up in "administrative expenses" (in this case, $0) or in "other expenses" (in this case, $11,304). It does not make any difference how much falls into either category. The bottom line is that you need to take the total expenses and subtract the benefits paid.

This amount could possibly be zero, and it could be a HUGE amount depending on your plan, side deals for what is called "revenue sharing," and other factors. Revenue sharing is a kickback to the plan to help make up for the excessive fees you pay in the form of the expense ratios. In fact, it is possible that it could even be a negative number if there are a lot of funds providing these kickbacks. We will discuss these more later. The bottom line is that the expense *will* show up somewhere, if you look for it.

In this plan's case, the difference between the plan expenses and benefits paid was $11,304. The next step is to figure out *how much of that you paid*. To calculate this number, take the $11,304 and divide by the total plan value (in this case $1,341,870, which is found at the beginning of the third paragraph showing the value of the plan at the end of the year). This number ($11,304 divided by $1,341,870) is 0.84% in this example. Depending on your plan and the revenue sharing side deals, it could be 0% (possibly even negative, but not likely) or it could be 2% or more.

However, the bottom line is that *this percentage is in addition* to your fund expense ratios. So in my case, in calculating my real total expense, I had to add to my total fund expenses of $552 (figure 4) and an additional expense shown only in this report of $1,014 (0.84% multiplied by my total account balance of $120,687). Therefore, my *total real expense* was $1,566 ($522 in expense ratios, plus $1,014 in plan expenses) or about 1.3% in assets.

Considering that 82% of my portfolio is in a total market index fund, **that is a lot of fees! It is 1% more than the expense ratio of my fund!**

Quirks you might discover

In the example of my plan, the expense ratios overall were not that excessive (0.45%), because I was using a relatively low-cost index fund for most of the portfolio. But, the other expenses were chewing up a lot of my retirement money—almost twice the amount of my investment expense.

Don't be surprised if your expense ratios are much higher than mine, for it is very common to have expense ratios of 0.75% to over 2.0%. As previously mentioned, in many cases the funds with the higher expenses have another legal, but potentially unethical practice of kicking back some of their excessive fees in a practice known as "revenue sharing." **These kickbacks take the excess fees YOU PAY from your fund selection and use YOUR MONEY to pay for EVERYONE ELSE'S costs.** Yes, this is legal. No, I do not think it is ethical. No, it isn't disclosed to you anywhere. No, your employer may not even know about it.

If you have expense ratios of 0.75% or more, it is likely that your other expenses in the Summary Annual Report will be at least partially or completely defrayed by these kickbacks. This is just swapping money from one bucket into another. In my case, it could have just as easily shown my fund expenses at 0.84% instead of 0.45% and my Summary Annual Report might have shown "other" expenses of 0.45% instead of 0.84%.

Also, do not be surprised if your plan expenses, the sum of your expense ratios and the other expenses in your Summary Annual Report, total more than 2.0% in the calculation. I've seen plans with more than $5 million in assets paying more than that, and for smaller companies it is more likely to be the norm. THAT DOESN'T MEAN YOU HAVE TO PAY THAT PRICE!

Paying for your boss's retirement

If you are one of the unlucky millions of people out there who go through this exercise only to discover your expense ratios are high, but the plan administration and other expenses are relative low in the plan Summary Annual Report, you could be funding your boss's retirement, or at least the retirement of the person in the next cube.

Say you have $100,000 in your 401(k) and you discover that your expense ratios total 1.5% a year. You also discover that in your plan's Summary Annual Report, the difference between total expenses and benefits paid was zero. (It is possible, by the way, for this difference to be even less than zero, and this will still work in the calculation. You just add the "negative expense" percentage of the total plan expenses against your expense ratio thus reducing your total expense. For example, -0.25% + 2.50% = 2.25%.)

If your expenses are in this range, there is likely a 0.25% to 0.35% kickback (known as a "revenue share") that everyone in your company benefits from! You are such a nice guy!

Here's how it works: For each fund offered to participants, there will be some higher cost funds with big kickbacks and some funds that do not offer any kickbacks (usually funds with expenses of 0.40% or less). The kickbacks, or revenue shares, are not normally disclosed to you, and they may not even be well disclosed to your company. **You DO NOT get the benefit of those higher expenses in proportion to what you paid in expense.** Instead, everyone (your boss included) gets the benefit of you selecting expensive funds. The kickbacks from the expensive funds are used to defray the overall cost of operation of the whole plan, and **EVERYONE in your company shares proportionately based on their balance, even if they didn't use ANY of the expensive funds that generate these kickbacks.**

If your plan just consisted of you and your boss, and you selected these expensive funds for your $100,000, but your boss selected lower cost funds without the revenue share for his $1,000,000 balance, you would, in essence, be making a contribution to your boss's retirement fund of $318 a year. This amount is determined by which funds you select. Expensive funds **charge you personally for these excess expenses, and then they are shared as kickbacks with everyone else in the 401(k) plan.** The amount that is shared back to others is not based on what the other people paid but instead it is based on their proportion of the total plan balances. Yes, this is legal, too! It is unethical in my opinion, but it is legal.

If you are like the vast majority of Americans, you will find that your expenses are likely to be over 0.75% or more, perhaps much more. If they are less than 0.75%, read chapter 2 to see if you are paying expenses that are even harder to discover than the ones that are required to be disclosed to you.

CHAPTER TWO

Deeply Hidden Expenses

You might think finding out what you are paying in your 401(k) shouldn't take as much effort as was outlined in chapter 1. In reality, those are the easy expenses to find. Many in Congress and the Labor Department would concur with you that understanding what you are paying should not be that difficult. In fact, as of this writing, the Department of Labor is seeking comments on new disclosure rules, and I have spoken with a couple of congressional aids that are working on some proposals as well.

It gets worse, though. Not only does it take some effort to figure out your expenses as outlined in chapter 1, but **that effort only exposes the expenses that are legally required to be accessible to you under current law.** Chapter 1 only showed you a small portion of the potential total expenses you may be paying. Thus, if your chapter 1 exercise showed your expenses at 0.75% a year or less, it is critical to your lifestyle to try to discover some of these more deeply hidden charges. **It is quite possible these other charges may total 2%, 3%, or even 4% a year or more!**

Before you jump into all of these potentially deeply hidden expenses, keep in mind that if you already found out that your 401(k) was too expensive in step 1, the simple point is that your 401(k) is too costly. If it is too costly by 1% or 2% in annual fees, you need to take the steps to get it fixed. If you already know your 401(k) is too expensive, you can skip this chapter and move on to the next chapter to learn the steps needed to fix the problem. If you are unsure of whether your 401(k) is too expensive, you may want to see if you can discover whether you are paying some of the fees outlined here.

Since there are not any generally easily accessible documents that are required to be provided to you for these other fees, you will definitely need help from the person in your company that knows the most about your 401(k) plan. I will outline each one of these fees, explain how and where it is charged, and show what kinds of documents you might be able to access to discover the costs.

Wrap fees

A wrap program account is sold by a broker or consultant and could have three or four different money managers that each manage different portfolios for participants to select for their 401(k). Each of these portfolios might have different charges and different break points that must be reached to achieve lower fee levels.

A wrap fee is charged on these accounts and is generally a combined investment advisory fee that is bundled with brokerage commissions and custody services. It may provide for discretionary portfolio management services, asset allocation advice, performance reporting (normally only to the trustees), investment manager selection, due diligence and brokerage executions (trades), or any subset of these services. It is very common for these fees to be 2 to 2.5% a year or more on accounts of less than $250,000. The fees generally scale down as the account size increases, but it is not uncommon for these wrap fees to exceed 1.0% even for an account that is $5 million or more.

What constitutes an account? It could be that a broker/consultant sold the trustees on the wrap program where three or four different money managers are selected to manage different portfolios for participants (like you) to select for their 401(k) elections. EACH of these alternatives might have different charges and different break points that must be reached to achieve "lower" fee levels.

There are additional twists on these wrap fees. In some cases, the broker or consultant charges a lower wrap fee but buys mutual funds with additional expense ratios instead of using independent or proprietary money managers. There are even accounts called Multi-Discipline Accounts (MDAs) or Multi-Manager Accounts (MMAs) where multiple money managers each manage a piece of the overall account.

In many cases, wrap account fees can easily total 1.0% to 3% a year. **Also, it is not common that these expenses would be disclosed to you.** The way a wrap account is often accounted for is by opening up a brokerage account for each portfolio alternative, and the wrap expenses of the portfolio come right out of the account. The administrator or record keeper just tracks how much of each portfolio a participant owns and pays no attention to the fees. In essence, the fees come right out of the investment return.

If you have any investment selections that are not specific mutual funds with tick symbols but are instead just an investment selection called "Conservative Growth" or "Moderate" or something similar, ask your benefits department person if that portfolio is in a wrap account, and see if you can find out who is managing it. You might also ask to obtain a copy of the investment advisory agreement that will outline the fee schedule for the advisory and brokerage services, although it will probably exclude mutual fund expense ratios if it is a mutual fund wrap program.

Mortality and expense (M&E) charges

A large percentage of 401(k) plans are sold by insurance companies and thus have a nice little trick they can play with your retirement assets. In addition to the fund expense ratios and administration charges we discussed in chapter 1, insurance companies tack on this additional contract charge, which is charged directly against your investment earnings, and is not part of your normally disclosed investment expense or administration expenses outlined in chapter 1.

What does it buy you? Well, being offered by an insurance company, you might suspect that it buys you life insurance. It does a little at least. Often, the extra M&E fee you are paying on all of your retirement assets (sometimes "stable value accounts" do not have a separate M&E fee) buys you insurance so that if you die before you retire, the insurance company guarantees your beneficiaries will be paid what you put in. In essence, they guarantee your beneficiaries will get at least a zero percent return. There are a lot of complicated and often expensive bells and whistles that insurance companies can tack on to your account for this guarantee, some of which might be valuable to you, and some that are a complete waste of money for what you are trying to achieve. The Securities and Exchange Commission (SEC) has an excellent website that explains many of these issues at www.sec.gov/investor/pubs/varannty.htm. You probably want to know what this guarantee might cost you.

According to Don Taylor, Ph.D., CFA who wrote an article about this at Bankrate.com, the average M&E charge is 1.15% in variable annuities.[3] Some companies have far lower M&E charges (I haven't seen any less than 0.28%), and some are far higher. Keep in mind, though, that these charges are in addition to your fund expenses and administration expenses.

3 Don Taylor, Ph.D., CFA, "Are Annuities a Worthwhile Investment Option?" Bankrate.com, http://www.bankrate.com/brinkadv/news/DrDon/20020411a.asp.

The best way to find out about these costs is to contact your benefits/ HR department and ask if your 401(k) is provided by an insurance company. Tell them you are doing some retirement planning and you need to understand the contract charges like M&E and surrender charges.

Surrender charges

While we are on the topic of insurance company fees, I should discuss surrender fees. These fees are, in essence, penalties charged against your balances if you redeem the assets during some specified period of time—often years. They are conditional, one-time fees, so at least these expenses are not a continuous drag on your account balances. However, it is possible that if you redeem an investment, or roll over your account, you might be subject to this penalty of 1%, 2%, 3%, or more.

Similarly, some mutual funds have a fee known as a redemption fee or a contingent deferred sales charge (CDSC), which is charged against your investment if you liquidate the investment before some specified time has passed. Sometimes these fees are waived for retirement plans, but that isn't always the case.

You will probably need the help of your company's benefits/human resources staff to discover these fees, because they are rarely disclosed to participants in any of the normal reporting you receive.

Fund of fund fees and lifecycle fund fees

Not to be outdone in the hiding fees game, the mutual fund industry has created a neat little trick to hide their expenses from you. They create a "new fund" that owns other funds and tacks on what appears to be a very small additional expense ratio. When you look up the information on this new fund, the expenses appear very low, maybe 0.10% a year or less. But, unless you look for it (look at the top holdings of the fund) you would never know that you are paying an additional 0.5% to 2.0% a year in fees within the funds that this fund owns. Sound confusing? It is. In essence, the fund company can increase their sales of expensive funds by packaging them up and using them as investments in other funds that have lower expense ratios. Nice trick, huh? You own the fund that owns the other funds, but the expense ratio of your fund looks low despite it owning a bunch of expensive funds!

This is a common practice in many lifecycle and target funds. Go to one of the mutual fund websites on any fund you have that appears to have a low or reasonable expense ratio. Then find out what the top holdings are. If they are other mutual funds, you have to look up the expenses for each fund your fund holds to figure out what you really are paying. If the top holdings are individual stocks or bonds instead of other mutual funds, you aren't paying additional expense ratios of funds, but there is another expense you need to be aware of that can cost you a lot. (Recently enacted regulations require funds to disclose these "Acquired Fund Fees & Expenses" or AFFE in the prospectus.)

Other hidden mutual fund expenses

The total expense ratio of a mutual fund will include the management, administrative, 12b-1 (distribution) fees, and the like that are charged under contract directly against the fund assets. We have already discussed how to find your funds' expense ratios. But, there are potentially significant other expenses, and you will not find these in the prospectus of most mutual funds. These other expenses are usually only available in a document called "Statement of Additional Information" (SAI) that is not required to be given to you.

Mutual funds buy and sell stocks and bonds just like you might do in a self directed brokerage account, and all holders of the mutual fund own pieces, or shares, of the account. Also, just like you, the mutual fund must pay brokerage firms commissions on the trades they make in the mutual fund's brokerage account. **These commissions are not part of the expense ratio.**

It is a painful process to find these expenses, because (a) getting your hands on the SAI isn't the easiest thing to do, since it isn't required to be given to you, and (b) once you get it, you have to dig through the document and do some math to figure out the expense.

In the SAI, the commissions will not be disclosed as an annual percentage of value like expense ratios. Instead, buried in the document there will be a section that states commissions paid. There may be a few sections broken into different categories (commissions paid for research, etc.), and you will have to add up all of these expenses. It will say something similar to the following:

2004 Commissions Paid:

Directed Brokerage:	$856,757
Prime Brokers:	$120,000
Total:	$976,757

This number obviously doesn't tell you a lot. You may even need to first add them together yourself. The next step is to divide this by the total value of the fund, which is another number you have to dig up. Say the total assets of the fund were $600 million, and the commissions totaled $976,756. That would mean that in addition to this fund's expense ratio, the fund had additional undisclosed expenses of 1.62% ($976,756/$600,000,000). If the fund had $1.2 billion in assets, these additional expenses would be 0.81%. For many index funds and exchange traded funds (ETFs), these expenses will total less than 0.05% annually, some even less than 0.01%. However, it is quite common for an active fund to have these additional hidden expenses total 0.20% to over 1.00% a year. According to a study done by the Zero Alpha Group, the typical **actively managed mutual fund** averaged 0.48% in these other hidden expenses annually.

Your benefits or HR person will not be able to help you discover these expenses nor will many of the fund-rating websites. In most cases, you will need to search for the SAI on the website of the actual mutual fund you own. In some cases, it won't be available on the website either, and you will be forced to just accept it as an unknown. You could also write or fax the mutual fund company and request a copy of the SAI for the fund you own.

Money market "spreads"—Banks get to hide fees too!

In my company's repaired 401(k), one of the investment alternatives is a riskless investment. It is a federal money market fund (symbol VMFXX). As of this writing, it has a yield of 5.08% and has an expense ratio of 0.29%. The yield is net of that expense. Let's compare this to the current yield of a ninety-day Treasury bill. The two types of investments have about equal risk. Both have daily liquidity and practically no interest rate risk. The current yield on the Treasury bill is 4.61%. My money market 401(k) cash balances are earning 0.47% more than the ninety-day Treasury bill, net of the expense of the fund.

As part of my brokerage account at Schwab, there is a Schwab interest bearing bank account with "no fees" that I use for my paycheck direct deposit, bill paying, etc. This "no fee" bank account has a current yield of 4.25%. Now think about this. Because it is a bank account, they can call it "no fee," but why wouldn't Schwab invest my money the same way Vanguard does and get the gross return that Vanguard produces (5.08% PLUS the 0.29% expense, totaling 5.37%) and pocket the difference from what they are paying me (4.25%)? Schwab would get to make the 1.00%+ difference.

Well, that "no fee" bank account is doing EXACTLY that. Money market accounts, interest bearing checking accounts, stable value funds, etc. all might have "no fees" and can legally get away with saying that. But in reality the spread between what they earn and what they pay you can easily be 1–3% or more. If you have a brokerage account, find out what the yield is on your cash. Don't be surprised if it is 2% less than what a ninety-day Treasury bill is paying. It might not be disclosed to you as a fee, but if your portfolio allocation is 10% in cash, that spread can cost your whole portfolio 0.20% a year in additional hidden expenses.

That "no fee" stable value fund from the insurance company (with a 1% surrender fee!?) that is paying 4.5% is costing you 0.58% a year relative to what other riskless choices are in the marketplace. Don't ignore this hidden cost. The vendors are counting on you to not worry about it, but you should. There is no reason you cannot earn competitively high yields on cash balances.

"Float"

The last of these hidden costs is perhaps the easiest for you to discover. "Float" is interest earned on someone else's money while you are processing transactions for them or waiting for transactions to clear. Think about what happens when you get your paycheck from the company's perspective. The company deposits your net pay into your bank account, and your bank probably credits it the same day, maybe one day later to get one day of "float," and the money is then available to you. While that is going on with your payroll, the company also makes a deposit for your 401(k) with the vendor of your plan. They get the money the same time you do. When does it get invested in your fund selections? The next day? A few days later? A week later? Two weeks? A month?

The rules on this in ERISA (Employee Retirement Income Security Act) are very weak as well as many other areas that are covered more in chapter 6. There is no requirement for how quickly your money is invested other than "as soon as administratively practical," and some 401(k) vendors are not finding it very practical to get around to it on a timely basis. During the time between your payroll and when the money is actually invested in your 401(k) selections, **the vendor gets to keep any interest earned on your money!** While most of the vendors do process your deferrals within a day or two, I have seen some that can take as long as 30 days! For a company of our size and contribution levels, this "float" with a vendor that drags their feet like this could cost us more than the administration expenses!

To find out if you are paying this expense, simply look at the time between payroll and the dates your contributions are actually credited to your 401(k) plan on your vendor's website. If it is more than a few days, you have a legitimate gripe, and this delay may explain why the administration expenses you found in chapter 1 were lower than otherwise anticipated.

If you went through the steps in chapter 1, discovered your expenses were not excessive, hunted down some of these deeply hidden expenses, and still discovered that your expenses are in line, congratulations! You are not being ripped off!

Regardless of whether your plan needs fixing or not, you still have to make the best choices about what you value and how to maximize the lifestyle benefit of having a cost effective 401(k) plan. If this is the case, you can skip chapters 4, 5, and 6. But, if your expenses are excessive, it is critical to your lifestyle that you take the steps needed to fix your 401(k) plan.

CHAPTER THREE

The Price to Your Lifestyle of Needless Expenses

If you are within three years of retiring or found your real total expenses were 0.75% annually or less, you can skip to chapter 7, "How Can I Make The Most of My Life?" However, if your expenses were more than 1% or maybe even 2% or if you are not at the brink of retirement (and even if you are near retirement) the effect of the choices you still have might make it worthwhile for you to read this chapter. If you are contributing to a 401(k) plan and are saving for retirement in five, ten, even twenty years, there are some key concepts we will address in this chapter that may help you understand the cost of these expenses to your life.

What are those costs? Appendix A provides a series of examples of the costs to your lifestyle of these hidden expenses in your 401(k). Whether it means saving hundreds or even thousands of dollars more each year until you retire, spending less once you reach retirement, or even putting off retirement for one, two, or more years beyond age 65, these unnecessary expenses cost you something in your life, and this book will help you to put your finger on that cost.

You will rightly ask how we can forecast what the cost of these expenses may be, and that is the point of the discussion that follows. To understand the costs, we first need to know what you might be able to accomplish in your life, what you might value in your retirement, and what you are willing to do towards that goal. You are already contributing to a 401(k) plan, and you make those savings because you want to have money to spend during your retirement and a lifestyle you can enjoy.

The tables in appendix A show what a person of various ages might already have saved and what they are contributing each year. That is only a part of the picture, though, since how the money is invested in the plan—stocks, bonds, or cash—and the level of spending once a person retires are a part of the mix as well. The examples examine how much one might spend in retirement given a particular combination of these factors and at varying levels of expense. The higher the expense charged in a 401(k) plan, the more something else must give, whether it is the age at which one retires, the amount one saves, or the spending level during retirement.

Why is that so? Let's begin with the markets.

Uncertainty is CERTAIN

You may have figured out your "savings shortfall" using a retirement calculator sponsored by your friendly 401(k) vendor who profits from you sacrificing your life by scaring you into saving too much. Perhaps you have a financial planner who examines in excruciating detail your spending budget on pet food, your cable bill, your insurance policies, etc., and produces a one hundred page document planning the rest of your life for you. Often they will proceed by attempting to guilt or coerce you to stick with this long-term plan despite your goals, priorities, and changes in the markets since they created the plan.

No one knows what the markets will do over any period of time. Some today will argue that returns will be lower in the future because of one reason or another. Others will argue that they can beat the market, because the gambles they made in the past worked and it is evidenced in their long-term track record, as if a lucky slot machine player has figured out how to beat the odds. Study after study has shown that past performance is not an indication of future results.

We did a study comparing the very top 5% performing mutual funds for the three years ending March 2003. By March 2007, slightly more than 54% of those very top performers from 2003 performed well below their best matching index. In fact, as of March 2007, slightly more than 54% *of all funds* underperformed their best matching benchmark. It made no statistical difference whether they were a top performer in the past or not. This concept is why the NASD (National Association of Securities Dealers) requires the statement, "Past performance is not necessarily an indication of future results." It is true! The reality is that there is an enormous amount of uncertainty in the two main factors that can affect you that neither you nor your advisor can control.

Remember that sample forty-year-old with $75,000 in his 401(k) plan, saving 10% of his $50,000 income a year with an employer match of 50%? Assuming an allocation of 80% to stocks, the rest in bonds and cash, and a very reasonable 0.50% in expenses, historically the sample person's twenty-five years of accumulation produced a retirement fund at age 65 of anywhere from $1,084,000 (market returns of 1950–1974) to over $5 million (1975–1999)! That's just based on actual historical returns for this portfolio going back to 1926 *in the order they occurred*. If we used the same historical returns and just randomly mixed up the order of when they occurred, the range of uncertainty of the future expands from $134,000 to over $25 million! Of course, the markets may produce results that we have not yet seen that would just further expand this range of uncertainty.

Again, the only uncertainties represented by this are of the markets, and they are obviously highly uncertain. And they are uncertain in two ways. First, the overall long-term compound return of the markets in the future (i.e., stocks, bonds, or cash) is uncertain. Second, how that overall return happens, (i.e., *when* big returns or losses will happen) is unknowable but can impact your lifestyle profoundly. This *when* part can produce surprising results.

For our sample 401(k) participant, the worst actual historical result in terms of dollars in the retirement fund at age 65 was the period of 1950–1974, when this person ended up with $1,084,000. The portfolio allocation, rebalanced annually, produced a compound return over this period of 8.83%. But, there were a lot of twenty-five-year historical periods when the allocation produced a lower long-term compound return yet still produced a larger retirement fund in terms of dollars. This happened because of the uncertainty of the **timing of returns, or *when* different returns occurred**. The graph and table that follow provide an example of how Great Depression Era compound returns were lower overall for the whole twenty-five year period, but for THIS SAMPLE CLIENT, the timing of *when* bear and bull markets happened and how much money he had invested during those periods produced **more money** in the retirement fund despite these lower Depression Era returns.

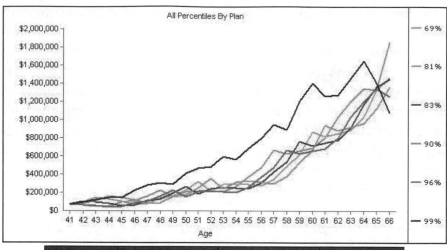

Percentile	Ending Value	Market Period	Return
69	$1,858,731	1930-1954	8.55%
81	$1,468,026	1927-1951	8.10%
83	$1,448,878	1928-1952	7.52%
90	$1,360,253	1926-1950	7.80%
96	$1,256,409	1929-1953	6.19%
99	$1,084,733	1950-1974	8.83%

Figure 6 Higher returns can produce lower values

For some reason, people seem to be perplexed by this reality of uncertainty, but the cause of this is really quite simple. In the Crash of '29 and the Depression Era, markets in which our sample 401(k) participant would have lost half of his portfolio value over a few years, he didn't have much money invested. If the portfolio was only $50,000 to $100,000 when he experienced the 50% declines, the cost to his retirement fund of this decline in dollar terms was only $25,000 to $50,000. Yet, the 99th percentile result during the 1950–1974 period experienced a decline not at the beginning when our sample participant had lower balances, but just before he was about to retire, after he accumulated nearly $1,600,000! It only takes a 3.1% decline to cost you $50,000 when you have a $1.6 million portfolio. The bear market of 1973–1974 hurt his portfolio to the tune of nearly 30%, which was not as bad as the Depression Era, but it cost him more than $400,000 because of the timing!

So, the markets are highly uncertain in two ways that no one can control. The *overall* long-term compound return AND *when* various high or low returns happen **are *both certain to be uncertain* and this can dramatically affect your life**.

Those little retirement savings calculators that tell you how much to save assuming some rate of return are therefore VERY misleading. You know the ones I'm talking about. You input your starting balance, how much you save each year, how long you are accumulating and it uses some assumed rate of return to calculate how much money you will have at retirement. The problem is that the risk of *when* various returns happen is ignored in such analysis. Remember, IT IS CERTAIN that you WILL NOT receive the same return each year.

You might think the assumed rate is close enough, but it is not. Look at how misleading such an analysis can be. In the example that follows, I calculated a projection of the future values for our sample middle class 401(k) participant using the simple assumption of 10% a year, which is certain to not happen! Notice how smooth the line is experiencing neither bull or bear markets.

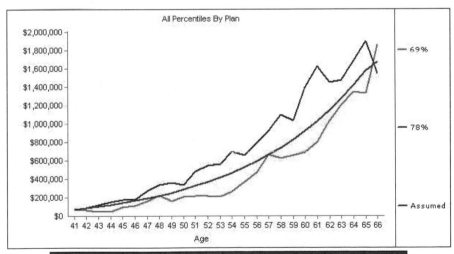

Percentile	Ending Value	Market Period	Return
69	$1,858,731	1930-1954	8.55%
77	$1,672,925	assumed return	10.00%
78	$1,548,591	1949-1973	10.37%

Figure 7 Comparison of a simple return assumption to real market returns

That assumed return produced *an ending value less* than 77 percent of all actual historical market periods. What is more interesting though is the effect of this timing of *when* returns happen. The period of 1930–1954 produced a compound return that was almost 1.5% less per year than the return I had assumed in the calculator, but lucky timing of a bull market just as the sample participant was approaching retirement (when he had accumulated a lot of money) had him soar past the assumed return ending value by nearly $200,000! A lower return but yet a higher portfolio value: the effect of *when*.

Conversely, unlucky timing of a bear market as he approached retirement in the 1949–1973 period cost him a fortune, and he ended up short of the assumed result (at a certain 10%) by more than $120,000, despite compounding at a higher return. A higher return yet lower portfolio value: again the effect of *when*.

Do not trust anyone's projections!

The truth of the matter is that these uncertainties are real, and there is nothing you can do about them except pay attention to the changes as they happen. A recent fad in the financial services industry is to run computer simulations of this uncertainty effect, but how it is normally used doesn't give you particularly useful information. In the following example, I simulated 25,000 years of investing for our sample 401(k) participant, just randomly ordering historical market returns for 1,000 twenty-five-year periods. All it tells us is that if nothing changes in this person's plan—income, savings, and the like—for the next twenty-five years, there is a 96% chance they will end up with a 401(k) balance of somewhere between $373,000 and $7 Million. You probably don't need a calculator to tell you that. I bet you knew it already!

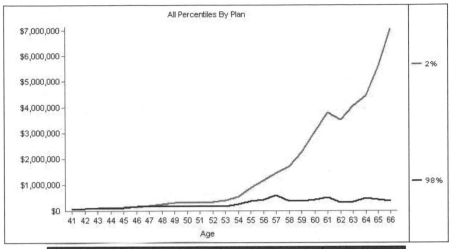

Percentile	Ending Value	Market Period	Return
2	$7,055,083	Simulated	16.95%
98	$373,673	Simulated	2.74%

Figure 8 Range of simulated results

Of course, there are more uncertainties than those in the financial markets, but we will deal with those concerns later on in chapter 7.

Soup lines and scare tactics

Have you noticed another Great Depression lately? Look out your window and see if you can find any soup lines forming. If there were a Great Depression, do you think you might cut back your spending a little? Are you sincerely afraid of another Great Depression happening anytime soon, or even in your lifetime?

IF you don't see any soup lines and IF you are not currently living your life as if there is another Great Depression looming on the horizon (although it IS possible), **DO NOT treat your retirement fund and your lifestyle AS IF the Great Depression has already arrived.**

Most of the product vendors (salespeople) will run some kind of retirement planner for you. Some may even use the simulation technique illustrated above to show you the odds of "success." What they don't tell you is the reason they use "conservative assumptions" or attempt to get you to the "highest probability of success through simulation tools" is for **their success, not yours**!

That conservative return assumption of say 7% that is suggested to you in that little online retirement planning tool and that ignores uncertainty, would project a value for our sample 401(k) participant that is worse than any historical period going back to 1926! Why would they do this? They can scare you into saving more so they get more fees!

What about that advisor who showed you a simulation that got you to 95% "success" (his, not yours!) to accumulate a $1,000,000 retirement fund, and all it took to achieve this confidence level was tripling your annual savings? He probably said you had a "savings shortfall" or a "gap" in retirement funding. He probably even positioned it that you might want to even consider saving a bit more to avoid some of that 5% chance of "failure."

Did your friendly advisor also tell you that if it were 1929 and you followed his advice you would have ended up with an extra $1,500,000 above the $1 million you were targeting despite the Crash of '29 and Great Depression? Is that how afraid you are of a depression and crash? Was that your goal? Are you really willing to triple your savings for the next 25 years and make all of the compromises to your lifestyle because you are *that* terrified of a depression?

My company creates the math engines and capital market research for thousands of financial advisors and their firms to run this type of analysis, and we try to get firms and their advisors to use them ethically. Recently though, I was in a meeting where we were discussing the fact that a firm requested us to try to rig the mathematics to always get people scared into saving more so that the firm could get more fees and assets from their clients. That firm is no longer a client of ours.

While the uncertainty is vast, and it is possible that you are not saving enough or may be spending too much, it is also possible that you are saving too much, spending too little, or taking more investment risk than is needed for *what you personally value*. We call this "needless sacrifice."

Uncertainty is manageable but not controllable

The statement above may appear as if it is a contradiction. You cannot control *what* the long-term results of the markets will be, nor can you control *when* high or low returns will happen. If you don't believe me, ask your advisor if he can control when a bull or bear market will occur. What **you can do** is tweak the choices in your lifestyle to constantly keep the odds tilted in your favor but avoid the needless sacrifice to your lifestyle of living your life now as if a depression existed. If it comes, you may have to reduce your spending, so you should monitor the effect of the markets' continuous future uncertainty on your life. Instead of reducing spending, though, you have other choices that can work in poor markets. You might increase your portfolio risk, although mentally this is hard to do when a bear market has prices low, or compromise some other goal like a portion of an estate goal, delay buying the boat, etc.

The financial product vendors would have you think that it is not possible to save too much money. However, as a rational being, you know compromising your lifestyle by tripling what you save each year to accumulate 250% of your targeted retirement fund value in a Crash of '29 and Great Depression environment is probably too conservative and a needless sacrifice to your lifestyle. You could also wash used aluminum foil if you really are that concerned about another depression.

So, how do you take this vast uncertainty and make it manageable? First, while there is *some* remote chance of these wide extremes occurring, they are unlikely. Do you really care if there is a 2% chance of accumulating more than $7 million or a 20% chance of having more than $3 million? Certainly you aren't going to live your life expecting these remote extremes to occur. More importantly, if your portfolio were producing results like that, wouldn't it make sense to change your plan? All of that extra wealth would allow you to safely take less investment risk, increase your spending, retire earlier, gift more to your favorite charities, etc. All of these choices *should be exposed to you* long before your portfolio grows to such levels. So the reality is that it is highly unlikely that your portfolio would ever achieve those levels not just because the odds of it occurring are fairly low, but also, and more likely, because you would change what you are doing or planning on if such strong results occurred. **If you had an extra million or two lying around, wouldn't it change something in your life?** Do you really think you would stick to the long-term plan you created twenty years ago just to see if it worked?

Likewise, if the markets are very unkind and we have another Crash of '29 with the ensuing Great Depression, do you really think you would not alter your lifestyle a bit? Would you really continually spend your portfolio down to maintain what you planned on twenty years ago just to see if the odds were right? Would you still buy that boat, the new luxury car, and take the vacations you planned on when your neighbors are waiting in soup lines for food just to survive?

This is the problem with most online planning tools, many financial planners, and simulation tools. They calculate outcomes that *assume* no matter what happens you will *never* change your plans. Is that really the way you want to live your life? Do you really want to ignore opportunities to improve your lifestyle? Do you really want to risk financial ruin for the sake of sticking to a plan you made five, ten, or twenty years ago?

There is an easier way to strike a rational balance. You have X amount of resources and Y amount of goals. The markets are highly uncertain, and you have some chance of winning the market lottery, which would enable larger, sooner, or more goals. Likewise, the markets may be unkind, and there is a risk that it wouldn't be safe to leave the Y goals unchanged in the face of unfortunate timing or results.

The simulation techniques that are available (but typically not used in a manner where they provide any value to you) can help you actually figure out *when* you *should* change your Y goals *because* of what happened to your X resources. If we think about the vast range of outcomes that may occur assuming no changes or response to what is happening in the markets, there is an area where we can calculate that things are "safe enough" meaning that there is *neither* too much uncertainty nor needless sacrifice. We would want this area to have the balance tipped sufficiently in our favor, enabling us to live the life we planned on, **despite severe** overall long term market results or very unfortunate timing of market results. If we could calculate this range (and we can) we would then know *if* we should be spending more, increasing goals, taking less risk, moving goals sooner, or, when we should prudently tweak goals downward, delay them a bit or move up the risk scale a notch.

The Comfort Zone

All of the analysis shown in the tables in appendix A is based on this critical notion of avoiding too much uncertainty and needless sacrifice. We call it the comfort zone, because it continuously considers all of the future uncertainty of the markets as it relates to your resources and goals. It keeps the odds tilted in your favor, considering bad timing of bull and bear markets or bad overall results, yet identifies when you are needlessly compromising your lifestyle and when continuing with an old plan without adjustment is too risky. Used correctly, the comfort zone can continuously and confidently guide you through the best choices about how to live your life without needless sacrifice or unnecessary investment risk.

To simplify the thousands of simulated returns and make them uncomplicated enough to understand in these terms is easy. It takes those thousands upon thousands of potential results to rationally assess your confidence, and we can reduce those results to a simple scale that we need to keep in balance. If the scale is in balance, the choices about what we are planning for our goals and overall exposure to the risk of the markets keeps the odds tilted sufficiently in our favor so we can be comfortable.

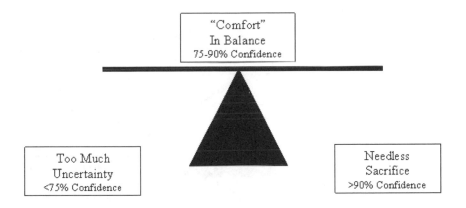

Figure 9 The comfort zone

This does not imply that we have eliminated *any chance* of needing to make adjustments in the future. It merely means that, without paying attention to what is going on in the markets, you could still likely survive the worst historical markets like the Crash of '29 and Great Depression without adjusting your goals. We wouldn't recommend ignoring the effect of that kind of a market on your resources, but in planning your life priorities in a balanced, rational fashion, it should be conservative enough and enable you to avoid needless sacrifice to your lifestyle.

All of the prices to a person's lifestyle of the excess 401(k) expenses illustrated in the tables in appendix A are based on having this rational, comfortable balance. In essence, they provide examples of what the lifestyle price is with the burden of excess 401(k) expense.

It is possible that the simulations of market results may expose that you are indeed living your life as if the Crash of '29 were happening now and the Great Depression is about to follow. We call this "needless sacrifice" because these simulations are really far more severe than what we have ever experienced in the last 80 or so years. If a set of choices for your goals falls into the sacrifice zone, you are needlessly sacrificing your lifestyle. You may be accepting more investment risk than is needed, saving more money than necessary, spending too little, or waiting too long for your goals and dreams. Such excess conservatism in how you are living your life can tip the scale out of balance.

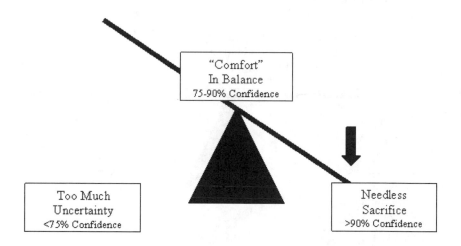

Figure 10 The impact of needless sacrifice

Finally, your ideal dreams and goals and your desire to avoid as much investment risk as possible might combine into something that is asking more of the markets than they are likely to produce. The scale again tips out of balance, suggesting you should consider delaying and/or altering some goals, perhaps saving more, or taking a bit more investment risk in attempting to achieve a bit more investment return.

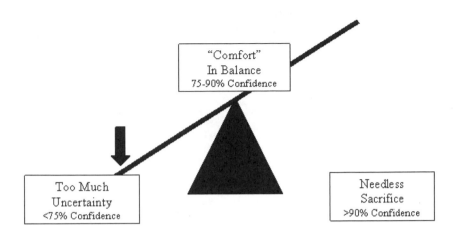

Figure 11 Too much uncertainty

For all of the complicated jargon that can come out of investment simulations, the main question that you should be concerned about is: **Are you in balance? Are you avoiding too much uncertainty? Are you avoiding needless sacrifice** to your lifestyle?

As we mentioned at the beginning of this chapter, appendix A presents a series of tables that will give you examples of the price of excessive 401(k) fees, in terms of one's lifestyle, while maintaining this balance. These are only examples, and if you want to find out what the **real cost is to your life,** you can use a free trial of the simulation tools we offer financial advisors (at wealthcarecapital.com) or call our toll-free number (1-866-261-0849), and our staff will be happy to analyze it for you for free.

To get an idea of what your excess 401(k) fees are costing you, the tables in appendix A lay out various ages, rates of saving, retirement income desires, asset allocations, etc. You can probably find a table that is reasonably similar to your circumstances and discover the corresponding price to your lifestyle of the excess fees you are paying.

Remember, even if you are in a very small company and your employer needs to pass on all or most of the cost of your plan, if you are paying more than 0.75% a year in expenses, it **is probably excessive**. If your expenses are 1.25%, look at the tables that show the effect of an excess fee of 0.50%. If your current 401(k) expenses are 1.75%, look at the tables that show the effect of an excess 1%. If you would like to improve your 401(k) plan and avoid the effect of these excess fees to your lifestyle, then move on to the next chapter, and we will show you how you can easily start the process to fix your 401(k) plan. If you don't sort out your 401(k) expenses, no one else is likely to do it.

CHAPTER FOUR

STEP TWO—Complaining without Complaining

You spent time uncovering what you are really paying in your 401(k) plan and discovered it was more than the 0.75% a year that should be your maximum cost. (Chapter 8 will show you why you shouldn't need to pay any more). You found the price to your lifestyle in the tables in appendix A and determined that it is worth fixing this problem. But you aren't in charge of selecting the 401(k) for your company, so what can you do?

First, you probably do not want to be viewed as a complainer. Second, you cannot assume that whoever is in charge of selecting your 401(k) plan is necessarily aware of these expenses or knows where they can go to find the lower cost alternatives. Your company may be larger and may have a benefits department, and **you will need their help** if you are going to resolve the problem. Remember, whoever in your company selected your 401(k) plan probably has some pride in the work he or she did to create it, so it is likely this person will be a bit defensive. Also, please keep in mind that most 401(k) plans have the revenue sharing kickbacks that are poorly disclosed, if disclosed at all. The chances are very high that the person or people in your company who are responsible for the company 401(k) plan are unaware these side deals are confiscating money from *their* retirement savings, too!

You will also need to understand how 401(k) plans are sold to companies if you are going to effectively solve the problem. The top ten providers of 401(k) plans, in terms of number of companies or plan sponsors, account for over 300,000 plans or more than half of all 401(k) plans. At some point, maybe several years ago, your company probably didn't have a 401(k) plan. An insurance agent or broker probably sold the executives in your company on the notion that they should offer a 401(k) plan to be competitive. This agent or broker most likely also told the decision maker that offering such a plan would cost the company nothing or practically nothing, so it made sense to give the option to employees. In all probability, the agent or broker probably put together a proposal that included a selection of over-priced funds or variable annuities (the proposal didn't say these were over-priced) that showed your employer that the company expense for administering the plan would be somewhere from $10,000 a year all the way down to zero if the plan were large enough in terms of assets. The agent or broker may have also encouraged a matching contribution.

So, the person you need to talk to about your 401(k) may well think the plan is in good shape even if it is not. This person could well believe that there is a wide selection of funds available, which is a good thing (despite the available funds being mostly excessively expensive ones). The cost of administration charged to the company is probably zero by now. (By the way, it is possible the cost of administration is charged against the earnings in your account—not disclosed anywhere except in the Summary Annual Report—so it might be that the company has never paid for any of the cost of the plan.) Other employees aren't complaining about the 401(k) and generally have a positive view of the plan. The "powers that be" probably feel like they have done a good job.

Yet in your analysis from previous chapters, you see the expenses that you—not the company—are paying are 1.0%, 1.5%, or 2.0% a year or more. These costs are far more than are needed, but the last person who will tell your employer the costs are too high is the insurance agent or broker who sold the plan to the company—an agent or broker who is getting a commission of 0.30% to 0.90% a year on *your* retirement assets. Even if your employer questions the 401(k) salesperson about the expenses, this agent or broker likely will come up with some story about the great services he or she offers (like annual seminars where you get all that personal attention—NOT!), their brilliant fund selection and how what is important is the return net after fees, not the total fees paid. What the agent or broker won't say is that the brilliant fund selection is always in retrospect (past performance, which is not an indication of future results) and he clearly will not be able to explain why lower cost alternatives are simply not offered (the reason these alternatives are not offered is because the agent or broker can't get paid his or her 0.30% to 0.90% on assets for showing up at a meeting once a year to sell the over priced funds).

Here are the facts:
1. Expenses are 100% certain, but past performance is not necessarily an indication of future results.

2. Plan administration (the record keeping fees) is not a cost that is tied to the plan assets; it is based on the number of participants. It is a bookkeeping function in which there are several independent vendors not tied to financial products that provide the 401(k) website, record keeping, participant statements, and various employer services such as testing, compliance, and government form filings. For those independent firms that do not conflict themselves with side deals from the investment product vendors, the cost shouldn't be any more than $25 a year per participant with an annual minimum of about $1,500 a year for the *whole company.*

3. Globally diversified portfolios can be assembled from low-cost funds that do not have investment minimums, redemption fees, deferred sales charges, or commissions. Our recommended portfolios can be found in chapter 8, but you can see that nearly everyone's risk tolerance and reward objective can be met with these portfolios of funds with expenses ranging from 0.09%–0.17% a year.

4. Personalized custom advice and monitoring should be available as an option by choice, instead of charged against everyone, along with management of the portfolios for no more than 0.30% a year charged *only* to those who select it.

5. Custodial costs can be covered by several vendors for no more than 0.06% a year. Custodial costs are the bookkeeping charges by banks or brokerages to keep track of how many shares of what securities the plan owns, collects dividends, invests contributions, processes withdrawals, etc.

6. A self directed brokerage account option should be offered for all those who wish to play the game of gambling their retirement on outsmarting the markets. The additional cost of this option should be borne only by the participants who select it, and the only extra costs should be limited to the commissions (usually $12.95 or less) and excess fund fees (usually 0.50% or more) that they choose to pay when they select this option.

Let's take a look at what the real total expenses should be, based on what is available in the market. Say your company has 100 employees participating in the 401(k) plan. Also assume that the average participant has a 401(k) balance of $35,000, which means the total plan assets are $3,500,000. Remember, either the company or the employees may bear the expenses depending on how the company elects to structure the plan. Therefore, we will examine the total overall costs.

Record keeping/administration/testing/filings @ $25 a participant = $2,500	
Custody: @ 0.06% a year on $3,500,000	**= $2,100**
Investment expenses @ 0.17% on assets (most expensive portfolio)	**= $5,950**
TOTAL	**= $10,550**
TOTAL as % of assets	**= 0.30%**

How do I know these expenses are realistic? I know this because the 0.30% example above is more than our little company with only 25 participants and $1,800,000 in plan assets is paying. If we can have a plan with expenses this low, why can't you?

Don't tell me it is because of "other services." We have a powerful website that tracks our performance with daily valuations and details every single transaction. Participants can have 100% of their investments invested in a self-directed brokerage account if they want to play that game, and *only they* bear their own additional commission costs. There are 14 funds to select from, in addition to the 1,500 no-load funds in the self directed brokerage account, covering all macro asset classes, from large and small cap stocks to foreign stocks, real estate, short- and long-term bonds, cash, etc. Participants receive quarterly statements that actually disclose the real fees they are paying. Pre-designed professionally constructed portfolios are available to cover nearly everyone's time horizon and risk tolerance. And, if any participant wants a personally designed, managed, monitored, and continuously revised Wealthcare plan covering all of their life goals and assets, it is available for only an additional cost of 0.25% to 0.35% a year, keeping the maximum possible cost at 0.65% a year or less. How does this stack up against your 401(k)? **If we can do this, so can your company!**

Assuming the company pays for nothing and charges back all expenses to employees in the form of the hidden charge against your returns disclosed in the Summary Annual Report, the typical employee with a $35,000 balance would be paying $105.50 a year, or 0.30%. In our company, the employer is paying for the record keeping and custody fees, which is only $2,600 a year *for our entire company* versus the $9,000 extra our previous vendor was charging. The participant is only paying the investment expense between 0.09% and 0.17% depending on the selected portfolio.

What about the advice? Each participant in our company can get personal advice with an SEC registered advisor instead of a broker or insurance salesman for *free*. If a participant wants the investment advisor to continuously manage and monitor the portfolio and personal Wealthcare plan that is based on the participant's own goals and priorities, the participant *can optionally* select to hire the advisor to provide this service for 0.25 to 0.35% charged *only to those participants who select it*. Doing so would raise the total expense to the employee participant to a maximum of 0.65% a year if the company is paying for nothing. If the company is paying for administrative costs, the participant is paying less than 0.50% with custom, personalized continuous life advice even while using the most expensive portfolio that is continuously, professionally managed.

How do these expenses compare to what you are paying now? Do you have any alternatives in your current plan that could reduce your expenses to these levels while maintaining global diversification across major asset classes? Some of the custodians that are not conflicted—unlike the primary vendors with their army of salesmen—offer over 33,000 different funds to select from, probably all of the funds in your plan, PLUS the lower cost alternatives generally available that you can't currently access.

Step one in getting your employer to look at this is a nonthreatening hand written note to your benefits/human resources/payroll department. You need to address it to whatever area or person in your company who has the most responsibility for your 401(k). If your company is very small, it might even be to your CEO or CFO.

Positioning the note as a follow up to your initial inquiry about the expenses can be helpful as it may help dialogue to proceed, which is exactly what you need to happen.

In your note, you do not want to focus on the fact that the expenses are too high. What you merely want to do is establish that you have figured out the expenses and you wonder if there is any way some of the lower cost alternatives can be made available. Handling it in this manner will potentially trigger your employer to contact the 401(k) plan vendor.

Something like the sample message that follows is a good way to start.

To: Human Resources Dept.
From: MY NAME
Re: My 401(k)

Dear NAME:

Thank you so much for providing me the information
I requested about our 401(k) plan. It was very helpful
in my retirement planning efforts.

One thing that I discovered in my personal situation
that I thought I would share with you is that the funds
I previously selected had annual expenses of ____%. I
ran across the enclosed book, and it shows that any company can offer funds with expenses ranging from 0.09%
a year to 0.17% a year. Reducing my expenses to those
levels would save me a lot of money over time. Plus, of
all of the alternatives we offer in our plan, none of
them are close to these expenses, and many are four to
ten times the expense. I thought I'd share a copy of the
book with you in hopes you might be able to find a way
to offer some of these lower expense alternatives too.

Thanks Again!

Sincerely,
My Name

Put yourself in the shoes of the person who receives this note. This isn't a letter of complaint—it is a "thank you note." You are even giving the person a gift of this book. This human resources person likely will not be offended and may even send you a thank you note back for sending the book. However, the human resources person probably won't read the book. He or she will most likely assume you calculated something wrong. In addition, he or she will probably *mistakenly think that the cost to the company* of offering lower cost funds is going to be very high, because those funds don't offer the kickbacks the current expensive funds have.

You are but one voice in the company, and the odds are NONE of your associates has done their homework on the expenses. Even less likely is that one of your coworkers also sent this book to the powers in your company who control the options you are offered in your 401(k) plan.

There is a chance that whomever you sent the book to will read it, research the truth behind all of the hidden side deals, and actually start the work to offer the lowest cost alternatives that will benefit everyone in the company. The odds of that are low.

I would suggest, about thirty days after delivering the book, that you drop off a follow up email to the person to whom you sent it, simply asking her if she enjoyed the book. If the human resources person indicates she read it but checked with the vendor, and those lower cost options aren't available in your plan, you will need to move on to the next chapter. If her response is that she hasn't gotten around to reading the book yet but plans to do so soon, you may want to follow up just one more time in another sixty days or so.

Remember, if your expenses are too high in your 401(k), the odds are that you are in a smaller company and these smaller companies are the ones where employees are harmed the most by the excess fees. These smaller companies simply are not large enough to have a full-time, dedicated staff in place to spend the time to do the homework and get past all of the salespeople to find the best alternatives. In all likelihood, the human resources staff really is trying to do the best they can with the time available from their other responsibilities to devote to the company's 401(k) plan. YOU NEED TO REMEMBER THIS when you are interacting with the human resources representative. While you might know the truth and have done the homework, it is reasonable for this person to assume that since no one else has mentioned it, and the time she spent on it was obviously the best attempt, the *assumption* will be that there really isn't a problem.

You also need to remember this is the retirement plan for the human resources representative, too. You might have an opportunity to even meet with this person. I'd suggest taking some sticky notes to flag sections of this book you want to point out to her. I'd also be prepared to go over the homework you did on your own expenses and highlight the sections of this book that explain how to calculate expenses.

But in the end, you will probably need some additional help. The next chapter covers how you can recruit allies to your cause of saving your own and your coworkers' retirements. This is how you can be the hero!

CHAPTER FIVE

STEP THREE—Rallying Your Troops

You did your homework. Your expenses are excessive in your 401(k). The price to your lifestyle is material. You told the "powers that be" and even gave them this book. Yet, nothing happens. Do not be surprised about this.

Human nature is an interesting thing. When the people in charge initially hear from you, they are starting with the assumption they have done a great job and that only one person in the company even is questioning the expenses. And those in charge are right. They did the best job they could and odds are you are the ONLY associate in the company who has mentioned a word about it. It is a good thing you handled it in a professional manner.

Yet, you know (and could very well be the only person in the company who knows) that you could easily lower your expenses by 0.50% to 1.00% a year or more if the company would just spend a few hours to work on it. You also know saving the excess expenses could buy you years of extra retirement, enable you to spend thousands more a year, take far less investment risk, etc., without jeopardizing your retirement.

An interesting aspect of human nature is the *added weight* we give to recent events (like performance records, we can't go back in time to actually earn that track record!). Maybe the cause of this goes back deep into our evolution? For example, perhaps we have this trait because it helped us to survive by first looking for water in the last place we found it? Yet, part of our nature is *to also discount* the significance of single random observations. Just because we experience one driver cutting us off on our commute home from work, we do not materially alter our driving habits going forward in anticipation of many other motorists doing so. We assume that "<u>driver</u>" was an idiot, not attentive, or distracted. Yet if we were cut off three times on the way home, we change the assumption from that "<u>driver</u>" to a new more expansive conceptual assumption that "*drivers*" in this town are *generally* rude, aggressive or not attentive.

These same human traits apply with your friends in human resources. They will likely assume your inquiry about fees is a single random event and will discount it just like they discount being cut off <u>once</u> on their commute home. However, their assumption about *employees of the company in general* may turn into this broader concept of many employees having concerns if they experience just a few more observations. This is particularly true IF it happens near the same point in time.

So, the person in human resources basically ignored your homework and feedback because of her assumption. What is interesting is how *her assumption* completely flips to the reverse if she receives just two or three more similar observations from other employees. The human resources person will change her perspective from the dismissive "only one person had a concern" to the perspective of "I've already heard from three people about this, so there must be many more." If two more people in your company did their homework and sent the book to the same person (this is critical) and that person is someone with the power to effect change (it must be) then the assumption this person makes flips from you being the only one concerned about it to wondering "how many more are concerned since I've already heard from three people".

To fix your 401(k) plan you are likely going to need some help because of the assumption the "powers that be" will make about your lone comment. You need to get at least one, and probably no more than four, to help you in your cause to improve your lives.

These other employees—your helpers—won't need to buy the book, but it wouldn't hurt if they did and personally forwarded an extra copy on to the "powers that be." It isn't necessary, though. We didn't write this book to sell a million copies (the profits go to charity) and we want to make it easy for you to accomplish your goals. To this end, we have included in this book three extra postage paid cards that will automatically send a free copy of this book to your person in benefits or human resources that you are targeting. Give them to your helpers, and make sure they fill it out and drop them in the mail. We will take care of sending the book to whomever you are targeting for free. But before this can happen, you will need to recruit your troops.

You probably will not want to go into detail about your personal circumstances and information with your coworkers. That is understandable, and it isn't necessary in order to accomplish your objective. You will, however, need one, two, maybe up to four of your coworkers to get concerned enough to trigger an inquiry to the right person in your company who has some influence over the decision. There are a couple of options as to how you can accomplish this.

Water cooler/lunch room/happy hour with peers

A great way to start the conversation with your associates in these environments is to simply say, "Have you guys ever figured out how much *we* are paying in our 401(k) plan?" Continue with, "I picked up this book that explains how to figure it out, contacted *(NAME)* in human resources and found out that I am paying $_____ a year that never shows up on my statement." Then, to get their response going you can say, "I don't know what you are paying, and I bet you probably don't really know either, since I discovered that *there are tons of hidden fees* that are never shown to us but that are coming from our accounts. I also found out that there are options out there that could reduce our costs by half."

At this point in the conversation, you need to wait and see who cares enough about their future and their lifestyle to be concerned about it. There will be plenty of skeptics who say things like their statements show the expenses as zero (like mine did despite the $1,500 a year I was paying—you might want to bring that up), that their brilliant market timing is what is more important, that they picked some incredible fund, or that the person in human resources wouldn't hide the fees from them. These people are not candidates to help you fix the problem, so don't waste anymore time on them. **Their complacency is why everyone is happy despite getting burned with massive, needless expense.**

However, you might find a few people who are objective enough to want to learn about the facts. These folks may say something like, "Hidden fees? I thought our 401(k) was free," or "Really? I didn't think I was paying anything. Where did you find out about this?" There is even a chance that someone might say something like, "What hidden fees?"

These are your targets for recruiting your troops. If you know these associates well enough, you might not be uncomfortable showing them the research you did, but it isn't necessary in most cases. While your troops might want your copy of this book to figure out their own individual expenses, it really isn't needed since you have already identified the excess expenses. All they really need to know is what they can do to help in the cause of lowering the expenses that every employee in your company is paying.

The best way to position this issue with the potential recruits is, "What have you got to lose by getting the company to look for a better deal on our plan?" Tell them you have already shown the "powers that be" the excessive expenses and all this person needs is a little nudge to get her to look into more cost effective options.

Alternatively, if you are lucky enough to get more than three troops, then have *one of them* send an email to the appropriate person each Wednesday for a month with a link to this book's website that says, "I thought you might find this of interest, because I'm sure you are as concerned about our 401(k) expenses as I am." It is necessary to change the phrasing a bit each week so the recipient doesn't think it is spam or get annoyed by the repetition. If you don't use email in your company, print out the page from the website and have your troops send it in interoffice mail with a hand written note.

How's that for easy? After you and your troops send this book several times and after your contact gets either a book, email, or hand written note every week for a month, there is a good chance that she will change her viewpoint.

Subordinates and immediate superiors

You may have someone who reports to you who hopefully respects your opinion. You might be this person's supervisor or manager. Also, you may have a supervisor or manager whom you report to. Depending on how close the relationship is, these are good candidates to add to the cause.

If you supervise staff, you may be able to bring up these excessive expenses and encourage the staff to help the cause. Have one or more of them email you or send a note asking about the expenses and forward it to the person you contacted originally. A nice way to get their attention on this is to say something like, "I'm forwarding you this message from one of my staff about our 401(k) expenses, because I wonder if this might be a human resources issue or perhaps a risk to the company if it is not handled appropriately. Please provide me some guidance as to the best way to handle this, because I completely understand the employee's perspective."

If you have a good relationship with your supervisor, she can be a great ally in your cause. It may not be over the water cooler, in the lunch room, or at happy hour, but the next time you have a positive meeting with your manager, you might ask if you can bring up an unrelated topic about which you have a "great deal of personal concern."

Unless your supervisor does not have time for you—and if that's the case, wait until she does—she is likely to say, "Sure! What is on your mind?" It is important that you handle this appropriately. You don't want to be viewed as a complainer, nor do you want to get the person you contacted in HR/benefits in trouble.

If you have your manager's attention, remember that she probably carries more credibility with the HR/benefits department than you do, and getting your boss on your side is very valuable. She might view this as an opportunity to move up in the company and will have you to thank for it. So use your supervisor appropriately to help your cause. This might help you move up too!

When dealing with your management, you will need to have more ammunition than your own research or this book. Fortunately, there is a ton of information available, and your knowledge of it will, at a minimum, impress your supervisor.

Start out by saying something like, "I know this isn't really my responsibility or even yours for that matter, but I feel an ethical obligation to share something I am concerned about with management." This statement will get 100% of your supervisor's attention. You have a 95% chance she will forget about what was preoccupying her and will truly listen to what you have to say. When your manager says, "Please, tell me about it," you will need to strike quickly, briefly, and succinctly without attacking your potential friend in human resources/benefits.

You can respond with, "I'm sure you are aware of the Congressional Investigations about excessive fees in 401(k) plans and the study from the Government Accountability Office. I'm sure senior management has also kept you abreast of the Department of Labor's investigations and proposals to change disclosure rules." Then continue with, "I actually calculated that I am personally paying $_____ a year for my 401(k). I researched it some, found a book on the topic, and forwarded a copy to Jerri in HR. It showed that I am easily paying an excess _____% a year on my assets. I think Jerri is too busy with other things to focus on this. While I'd personally like to have a more cost efficient 401(k) plan, what concerns me more is that the company might be at risk from the Labor Department if nothing is done about this."

Unless your supervisor is a complete idiot, she will pay attention to this and will contact the person in HR/benefits that you originally contacted (and possibly her supervisor too). Again, look at the wording. You positioned the issue not as a complaint but as a concern for the company, and the company is legitimately at risk. There is an opportunity for both you and your supervisor to become heroes, and that can't be a bad thing.

After assembling your troops, be it peers, subordinates or supervisors, there is still a chance that nothing will get done about your company's 401(k) problem. It might be because <u>you targeted the wrong person</u> in HR/benefits/payroll. If they were not the type of person who was going to do anything about it in the first place, despite the help of your troops, the problem might not get fixed.

Or maybe you are in a very small company and the CEO/CFO/owner is more worried about immediate business issues than what you are paying in your 401(k). **It is important to your future lifestyle and your career that you are empathetic to their situation.** Don't let that stop you. The next chapter outlines what is needed when your troops, subordinates and supervisors are ignored. It is more drastic, but it may be necessary in the face of such disregard for the facts by "the powers that be."

CHAPTER SIX

STEP FOUR—What Happens If My Employer Ignores Us?

If you and your troops targeted the wrong person and that person was not in a position to effect a change in your 401(k), you might need to retry step three with your troops, targeting someone more senior in the organization. If, after a couple of attempts you still do not see any action, your last resort is step four.

Pension plans, profit sharing plans and 401(k) plans are all regulated by the U.S. Department of Labor. The Labor Department enforces the myriad of rules that were born and continue to expand from a 1974 piece of legislation known as "**E**mployee **R**etirement **I**ncome **S**ecurity **A**ct" (ERISA). The laws derived from this act are intended to protect employees' retirement funds.

Among the many provisions of the legislation are definitions for who is a "fiduciary" for a retirement plan and the type of conduct that constitutes actions of a "prudent fiduciary."

There are provisions that prevent "self dealing" by fiduciaries and requirements that the assets of a retirement plan be handled in a manner for the "sole benefit of participants."

Fiduciaries are also required to make sure that investments are "diversified" and that they "avoid any investment risk *unless it is clearly prudent* to do otherwise."

Finally, there is even a provision that covers expenses. Unfortunately, it was worded rather weakly and how it has been interpreted in actual cases has not provided much protection for employees or the security of their retirement income. The provision relating to expenses only states that "expenses must be reasonable." Even this loose statement is offered further wiggle room by the addition of a provision saying "reasonable expenses relative to the overall services being provided."

You and I might interpret "reasonable" in very different ways. Go back to the expense ratios for the funds your plan has available that you collected in step one. See if your plan offered a "Large Cap Stock or S&P500

Index Fund" regardless of whether you happened to own it or not. What was the expense ratio? Was it 0.25% a year? How about 0.30% or 0.50%? Was it 0.07% a year? THAT is the expense ratio of the Fidelity Spartan S&P500 Index fund (symbol FSMAX). This fund has no sales load, no redemption fees, and no 12b-1 fees. It does have a $100,000 initial investment minimum, but that minimum is for your WHOLE COMPANY and not for individual employees. Even a company with only $500,000 in assets in their 401(k) would probably have $100,000 in large cap stocks and could meet the minimum. There is another S&P500 Index Fund offered by TIAA-CREF that has expenses of 0.08% a year that has no minimum investment amount required.

What is Reasonable?

What are the expenses for your company's S&P500 Index Fund or Large Cap Index Fund in your 401(k)? Is it "reasonable" to pay three to six times as much for the same thing?

Paying $75,000 for a Camry?

We are not talking about the difference between a Lexus and a Camry. We are talking about paying $75,000 for a Camry when you can get the exact same car for around $21,000! That doesn't seem "reasonable" to me, and it probably doesn't seem reasonable to you, either.

If you really want to get steamed, look at your fund selections for "International Stocks" and find the lowest cost offering. In my broken 401(k) plan, I was paying 1.06% a year. Now international investing does cost a bit more, but there are international index funds that are available with no loads, no minimums, no 12b-1 fees and no redemption fees for 0.15% a year or even less. Why would you pay 0.91% a year more (seven times as much) for the same thing? Is *that* reasonable?

Think about this! If you eventually accumulate $500,000 in your 401(k), that extra 0.91% a year in expense would be enough for you to make the payments on a Camry!

While no rational person could legitimately argue this is reasonable, there are two loopholes that are used to justify how much of your money is confiscated out of your retirement fund by these expenses.

Somehow, the case law has in practice come to measure "reasonable" not relative to what the same offering is available for in the marketplace, but instead it is measured by what the average expense is across the millions of plans that are over paying.

If I would have challenged the Principal Group for charging me seven times as much in expenses for owning the same thing, all their attorneys would have to do is go to Morningstar.com and show that the "category average" for "Foreign Large Blend" funds is 1.55% a year and therefore their 1.06% a year is "reasonable." The ERISA standard for expenses has been interpreted so that your employer (a fiduciary) *does not have to find the lowest expenses*, only that they are *reasonable* under this lame interpretation. So much for the "Employee Retirement Income Security Act" protecting your retirement! When it comes to expenses, ERISA should stand for "**E**mployees **R**ipped-off **I**ncreasingly by **S**uspicious **A**ccounting."

I had mentioned earlier that my company provides mathematical engines and capital market research for the financial services industry. One of the services we offer is a rating system for funds that exposes aspects that the popular star gazing methods do not. Believe it or not, the popular ratings systems out there, for all practical purposes, do not measure some of the very basic concerns anyone should be looking at when considering funds for retirement.

For example, in the popular rating systems in the market, the prudent fiduciary standard of diversification is completely ignored and, in fact, to get a high rating it almost requires that the fund being rated is not well diversified.

Since expense is a certainty for the future, but past performance is not necessarily an indication of future results, you would think that expense would be part of the popular rating systems, but in most, it is not. The only impact where excess expenses normally would show up is if they are so extreme that they severely impact the short-term (i.e., 3–5 year) performance. With many funds making wild bets and thus not very diversified, an extra 1–2% of expense doesn't hit the radar in the ranking system over the short 3–5 year periods being measured. Hey, it's only your retirement we are talking about, right?

One would also think that the risk of underperforming would be part of the measurement of ranking. If one or two months of some lucky returns made a three or five year return very high, but the fund had below market returns in many or most months, you would think this generally poor performance would show up in the rankings, but once again, it is usually ignored.

These are obvious basic measurements that are easy to calculate yet many of the popular, so-called "objective" ratings systems ignore these basics in their rankings that any truly prudent fiduciary would consider. Obviously risk and return need to be measured as well, but with past performance not necessarily an indication of future results, shouldn't an investor have a bit more to go on?

I'll tell you a little secret. We came up with a grading system that exposes all of these factors and what you will discover is **that there are no free lunches out there.** Just like the popular systems that automatically slap five stars on any fund that happens to randomly fall in the top 10% for risk adjusted return, we set a standard to be a grade of D if the fund's expenses are more than 50% higher than the lowest 10% of expense ratios. A total of 63% (more than 9,000 funds) of all of the 14,300 funds available in our database are charging at least 50% higher expenses or more. **A total of 3,307 funds earned an F because they were charging expenses 300% OR MORE** greater than the lowest 10% of funds. Some of these F rated funds in our system were five star funds in the popular, objective systems! So much for expenses being part of the typical rating system!

If you would like to look up your funds on this retirement grading scale, go to Fundgrades.com to see how your funds look from a retirement perspective. This will help you to see whether you are making a big gamble by not being diversified or taking a big risk of underperforming.

What this discussion of the fund-ranking systems means to you, though, is that lawsuits are not a good option for you, not just because bringing a lawsuit against your employer would not do much for your career, but also because the loose interpretation of what constitutes a "reasonable" expense has too many loopholes in it for you to win. Besides, all you really want is to have your 401(k) plan fixed, you don't want your friend in human resources/benefits to get in trouble.

The other loophole that makes it even more difficult to win a case is this notion of "expenses in the context of the overall services being provided." Most plans that have less than $5–$10 million in assets are sold to your employer by either an insurance agent or broker. In all likelihood, they are not doing a whole lot for the commissions they are earning on your retirement fund. On small plans of less than $1 million in total investment assets, it isn't uncommon for the agent or broker to earn 0.30% to 0.90% each year on your assets. What do they do for this?

While some of these agents or brokers offer to provide personal consultation and advice to participants, more likely than not they "help" the employer figure out which funds to offer in your 401(k) and give a speech once or twice a year. Now, do you perceive a conflict of interest in this? The agents or brokers are paid more in commissions for offering more expensive funds. And, even if they are not paid directly for the funds used, there is an indirect benefit of making the plan an easier sale to the employer if they recommend funds that offer those kickbacks (revenue sharing) because the cost of administration and record keeping to the company will be lower.

If your friend in human resources/benefits asks the 401(k) salesperson (again, usually an insurance agent or broker) if the company could offer one of these far less expensive funds (i.e., a Camry for a Camry price), the agent or broker has an easy defense to protect their commissions. He or she will either say, "We don't offer that fund on our platform." Or perhaps, "We could offer it, but your administration expenses will be a lot higher."

Remember the total cost for administration, recording keeping, government filings, statements, website, etc., should be no more than $50 per employee a year and can easily be as little as $25 a year with an annual company-wide minimum of $1,500. But, these agents and brokers need to get their commissions, so what they do is package the administration cost to be much higher and use expensive funds with kickbacks to bring the costs back in line. My company's plan, before we fixed it, was being charged more than $500 a year per participant for administration. That is ten to twenty times the maximum amount it should—*and actually does*—cost the provider. If instead of offering expensive funds, we went to only the lowest cost fund options, either the company or the participants would have to pick up this additional administration cost, according to our salesperson.

These agents and brokers earn their commission somewhere, and this is the bait and switch method employed to protect it. And how is this used to help justify the notion of reasonable expenses? Well, their conflicted suggestions (many will not admit to being a fiduciary but your employer may be counting on them for "advice" regardless) for offering expensive funds to you is supposedly a "service" that is part of that "expenses relative to the total services provided."

More likely than not, you too have been to speeches these agents or brokers offer once a year or so. They will tell you the virtues of maximizing your 401(k) contributions (even to the point of needless sacrifice to your lifestyle), show you how their (expensive) funds have higher star ratings, talk about asset allocation and how "the risk of stocks lowers with time" and your retirement should be a long-term investment.

It is possible your agent or broker is spending less than ten hours a year working on your plan and a lot of that time is used to sell people on buying excessively expensive funds, not on providing the objective fiduciary type advice that you both expect and deserve.

If you are truly interested in finding out the commission your company's agent or broker is paid, you can request a copy of the Form 5500 from your employer that will disclose this information. The employer is obligated to provide it to you if you request it, but the employer has the right to charge you a fee to photo copy it for you. So much for disclosure—more hidden fees.

At the top of page two of Schedule A in Form 5500 (a copy of our company's Form 5500 is in appendix D), you will find out who was paid a commission, how much that commission was, and what they were paid in additional fees on top of the commission. In our case, our salesperson was making about $4,000 a year for basically showing up once a year to give a speech. Nice work if you can get it! His commissions and fees were about 0.40% based on the value of the plan at the beginning of the 2005 tax year (see our Form 5500 in the appendix D).

This agent or broker may be (as ours was) the nicest guy. He is just trying to earn a living, too. But neither the company nor employees should be paying for "advice" that is conflicted or be paying for it if they were not using his services (like me and many others). And companies and employees should clearly have the option to avoid the expense if they are not using the "service."

This is why in some circumstances you and your troops may need to take more drastic action. The agent or broker who sold your employer on your 401(k) plan has an advantage over all of you. If the people in HR/benefits pay attention to your inquiries, their first step will be to contact their 401(k) sales agent or broker. The <u>agent or broker</u> has a lot of experience in evading fee disclosure and spinning the story so they can avoid losing or reducing their commissions. The more drastic action in the face of this conflicted agent or broker (who is going to do everything they can to convince your employer things are not broken), is instead to actually contact the Labor Department. They are waiting for your call.

In all likelihood, based on the GAO and Boston College studies previously mentioned, it would be reasonable to assume that perhaps more than half of all 401(k) plans are charging participants excessive fees based on what is available in the marketplace. Yet, according to the Government Accountability Office study, the Labor Department only received TEN complaints in 2005.[4] This just shows how well these vendors (and sometimes employers) are hiding the fees from participants.

Contact the Labor Department

www.dol.gov or call 1-866-4-USA-DOL

Having received only ten complaints about 401(k) fees in 2005, the Labor Department is literally waiting for your call. <u>Before you place the call, be prepared.</u> The information you will need is not extensive (other than the familiarity with the key terms of ERISA we outlined in this chapter), but it will help if you have it handy when you contact them. First, you will need your employer's EIN (Employer Identification Number). This is on your W-2 you get at tax time, it may be on your payroll stub, or better yet, you can get the number from the Summary Annual Report you obtained in step one.

The next step you will need to be prepared for is the case you wish to make. It is best to phrase these issues in Labor Department jargon so they will take you seriously and know how to respond. You also need to have factual information that presents a strong case, regardless of whether it personally applies to you. The easiest case to make is to show the excessive fees you and your associates are paying for a Camry.

When the first person answers at the Labor Department (you may be on hold for a while because they are obviously taking calls on many things other than 401(k) fee complaints), simply state, "I would like to complain about the excessive fees in my 401(k) plan." In all likelihood, you will be transferred to another individual.

---

4 U.S. Government Accountability Office, Private Pensions: Changes Needed to Provide 401(k) Plan Participants and the Department of Labor Better Information on Fees, GAO-07-2,1November 2006, 21.

When you get to the right person, restate that you are calling to complain about the excessive fees in your 401(k) plan and you "do not think they meet the ERISA standard of being reasonable relative to the services being offered."

You may be asked why you think this. If so, tell them that fees charged for index funds are _____ times (e.g., 3–7 times) what other plans have available and the services your plan offers are less than what smaller companies provide at far less cost. Then tell them you contacted your employer about this, that several other associates in your company have done so as well, but the employer has not done anything about it to your knowledge, and you would like to seek "whistle blower" protection of your identity to protect you from any possible retaliation from your employer.

The Labor Department may ask for a lot of personal information about you. Provide it ONLY if you are given the assurance that your employer will not know you are the one who turned them in. If the person says they cannot provide you with that protection, ask to speak to a supervisor and repeat the process.

Remember, this step is intended only as a last resort. You and your troops should exhaust several attempts within your company before you take this step. But, if it is needed, do not be afraid to use it, as long as you are guaranteed protection by the Labor Department for having them research your company's 401(k) plan. The reality is, an investigation may be triggered, and it will take a lot of time. The Labor Department may start with merely a letter that only mentions an investigation about the fees in your company's plan. This, however, will trigger actions by your employer to seek out the lower cost alternatives available in the market, so by the time any serious investigation takes place, your 401(k) plan could very likely be fixed.

Finally, don't give up. You might be employed for the next ten, twenty, or more years, so in the first six months to a year, if all of these steps do not repair your 401(k), keep up the effort with your troops. Rally a few more. Eventually you can avoid the retirement rip-off.

But when you do get your 401(k) fixed, it will be all for nothing if you don't use it to improve your life. The next chapter will show you how to maximize the dividend you receive by repairing your 401(k) plan.

CHAPTER SEVEN

STEP FIVE—Now That My 401(k) Is Fixed, How Can I Make The Most of My Life?

If you looked at the tables in appendix A that show you the various prices to your lifestyle of excessive 401(k) fees, you may realize that there are several choices you can make in using your fixed 401(k) to improve your lifestyle.

Which options might you choose? Do you reduce equity exposure and portfolio risk so that you can sleep better at night? Do you reduce your savings to buy that new sports car you have always dreamed of or to send your child to private school? Do you retire earlier? Travel more in retirement? The choices are endless. A few are outlined in the introduction, and appendix A gives additional examples.

More Bait and Switch

Watch the television ads from various financial services firms. Many of them talk about "making the most of your life" and "achieving your dreams," but the question you should ask is whether the advertising is just an attempt to draw you in or is it actually WHAT they deliver? Odds are that these ads are only an attempt to draw you in, because I have witnessed *very few advisors who actually deliver* on the promise of *what their firms are advertising.*

As a twenty-plus year veteran of the financial services industry, I will tell you some secrets that the financial services industry does not want exposed:

1) Many advisors care more about the PRODUCTS they can put into your portfolio than how you can use your portfolio to achieve your dreams and goals.

2) Experts in the home office at major firms provide guidance to their "advisors" (salespeople), but a non-expert salesperson is normally

who is ultimately responsible for what is recommended to you. What is recommended frequently makes more sense to the advisor than for the client (if the advice is objectively evaluated).

3) Discussion by the advisor about your personal goals is frequently used only to package the advice into a more effective sales pitch for a portfolio they want to sell you. Often, there are more rational choices the advisor has ignored that could improve *both your portfolio AND your lifestyle.*

The financial services industry will deny this. Yet, the facts are on my side. Forget about the 30,000-plus advisors we have serviced in one form or another to validate our observation. Forget about our repeated attempts to get them to focus on actually delivering advice about making the most of your life since that is what their firms are advertising, and it is possible to actually deliver that. Forget about the "advisors" who completely evade the risk of underperforming the markets when they attempt to justify their high cost portfolio recommendations. Forget about the hundreds of rational and reasonably objective advisors who understand the contradictions, yet they still want to "add the sizzle to your portfolio," because they think you won't pay them anything "if they don't play the game."

You may be one of the lucky clients who has an advisor who is focused on your valued goals and is dedicated to helping you reach them. You may already be working with a Certified Wealthcare Analyst™ or an advisor who has adopted a somewhat similar process. If so, you may already be on the road to making the most of your life. Chances are, though, that your advisory relationship is something like one of the following:

Maybe you deal with a bank brokerage that just happens to recommend funds it runs. How is that for objective?

Maybe you deal with a discount brokerage firm that provides you with great personal service and recommends their own funds.

Maybe you deal with a no-load fund company that provides you with exceptional personalized service and consistently recommends their own funds.

Maybe you deal with a full service firm that recommends only investments they do not manage but still plays the game with your portfolio of accepting the real risk of underperformance in the hope of possibly (but likely marginally) superior results.

Maybe your advisor attempts to identify your tolerance for risk and proceeds to position you in a portfolio that is likely to experience it!

Maybe your advisor regularly monitors your performance and recommends new investments AFTER they have performed poorly. (The smart guy we hired got dumb, but here's a better smart guy based on his five year record—SO WHY DIDN'T THEY RECOMMEND HIM BEFORE WE HIRED THE GUY WHO BECAME DUMB?)

The reality is that Wall Street is the biggest casino in the world, and many advisors are paid for convincing you to play the game. They are good at it. They make money whether you win or not, just as real casinos do in poker games.

There are some fee-based advisors who will spin their gambling game by saying, "My interests are aligned with yours, because if your portfolio grows, my fees grow, but if your portfolio goes down, my fees go down." What if *your* interest is spending your portfolio to finance your retirement? Is the fee structure tied to the portfolio value aligned with your interests? The real interest many advisors have is to create an air of objectivity, but sell you on taking risks you have the choice to avoid, and getting you to sacrifice your lifestyle to maximize how much is invested, or being "played." If that doesn't sound like a casino, what does?

If I sound angry and frustrated, it is only because I am. I'm sure that there is a large market of gambling investors out there who want to play the games Wall Street is promoting. However, there probably is also a fairly large market of people who just want someone they can trust. Someone who will listen to what they are trying to achieve. Someone who is objective and not paid based on selling conflicted investment selections. Someone who can objectively advise them on the best choices for making the most of their lives. Someone who is an empathetic, objective, listener.

Unfortunately, the industry has few of these types of people because such skills contradict the coercion skills needed to sell you. Instead of empathetic, objective listeners, by and large the industry is populated with aggressive, conflicted talkers. Their brains just are not wired to deliver the services about your dreams and goals their firms shamelessly advertise.

The standard solution offered by the industry is their portfolio of products, NOT your goals or your dreams or the best choices among them.

How can you tell if your advisor is one of the few who MIGHT actually deliver?

If your advisor asks you your tolerance for risk WITHOUT asking if you prefer to take LESS risk, the advisor is a gambler, gambling with YOUR life, and not someone who will make the most of your dreams.

If your advisor asks you how much more you might be willing to save, WITHOUT asking how much you would like to reduce your savings, the advisor is focused on his pocket, NOT yours.

If your advisor never asked you whether you might be willing to delay retirement a year if it meant taking less investment risk, the advisor is selling you, not advising you.

Think about these few simple issues. To "make the most of your life" and "achieve your dreams" wouldn't you—and your advisor—by necessity need to understand your position on risk, savings, retirement, and the relative priorities about the choices among them based on what you value? The real reason most advisors do not ask about your life or your dreams is because what **you want** <u>conflicts</u> with *the Wall Street casino profiting from your gaming activities.*

Of course, there are advisors out there who do care about those specific issues and will ask you about saving less and taking less risk and all of these questions that matter to you. You may be able to find them simply by asking these types of questions and learning whether they are thinking about you and what you want to accomplish instead of about themselves or their products. Ask your friends, relatives and coworkers about their experiences with advisors and whether any of them have been asked about whether they would like to save less or take less investment risk. The answer will be revealing.

Earlier in the introduction, we outlined a short list of the choices that would be available to you if you were to get your 401(k) plan fixed.

- Save less money?
- Plan on retiring earlier?
- Work fewer hours?

- Add a travel budget to your plan for retirement?
- Take less investment risk so that market gyrations still let you sleep at night?
- Take the vacation of your dreams?
- Leave a bequest to your church or school?
- Buy the new sports car you have always dreamed about?
- Pay off credit card bills?
- Send your child to a private school?
- Build an addition on your house?
- Help your elderly parents improve their lifestyle?
- Upgrade the way you pursue your hobby?
- Buy a vacation home?

This is just a short list of options. You may have other goals in mind to pursue if you had the resources to do so. The tables in appendix A show you examples of some of these alternatives. But, to make the most of your life, you probably need some help in analyzing the choices because there are so many options and all of them have impacts—some major and some minor, it all depends.

For example, say that you have already accumulated $500,000 in your 401(k), you are three years away from retirement, you are saving $5,000 a year, and your 401(k) is just meant to supplement your retirement income above social security. Do you really think that the $15,000 you plan on saving over the next three years will make any difference? Contributing that amount over the next three years has only a 1% chance of making a difference.

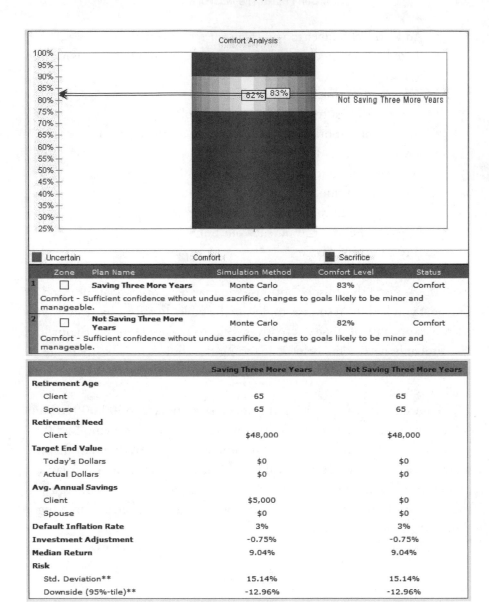

Figure 12 Comfort analysis of saving for three years before retirement versus no savings

However, for a person who has only $50,000 in a 401(k) and is twenty years away from retirement, not making the $5,000 a year contribution has a huge impact. Even discontinuing the contributions to the 401(k) for the next three years has a significant impact. This impact is illustrated in the savings example that follows.

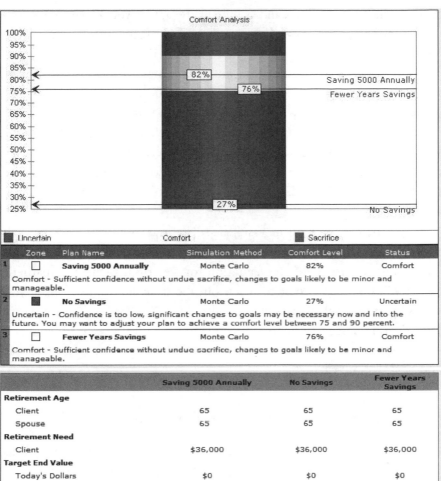

Figure 13 Comfort analysis of saving $5,000 a year,
saving for fewer years, and saving nothing

With so many options, the choices you have may seem overwhelming. There are myriads of possible other choices. Maybe you would reduce savings a bit, increase risk up a notch, but retire a little sooner. There are endless nuances and combinations and as long as the advice you are getting is from a vendor of products, these choices—about YOUR life—will in many cases be ignored.

I wish I could tell you that the answer for making the most of your life is simple. Well, it *is* simple if you know how. But, it takes an empathetic, objective listener to deliver that advice. It takes someone who is not conflicted and is paid for delivering *that* service instead of being paid for selling you on investments or paying ridiculous fees. Why does the industry tie fees to investments if they are giving you advice? Couldn't you implement the portfolio yourself but still get the advice? Ask if your advisor is willing to do that!

The choices you have are vast. The solution is easy if you have the right person with the right motivation servicing you. If you call our toll-free line, you can get a current recommendation for free from such an empathetic, objective listener. It is best to block off about an hour and to have your spouse/partner available as well. Just call 1-866-261-0849 and tell them you have the offer code "Retirement Rip-off" and they will create a free recommendation based on your newly repaired 401(k) and any other resources and goals you may have.

The Only Thing Constant Is Change

Remember in chapter 3 how, if all we did was randomize actual historical returns, our sample middle class participant had a 96% chance of accumulating a retirement fund of anywhere from $134,000 to $25 million? That means there is a 4% chance (or 1 in 25) that it would be outside of this range! Of course, as we mentioned, you would change your lifestyle long before either of these extremes presented themselves so they are purely theoretical.

But, since no one can control what the markets might do and the range of uncertainty is so vast even assuming that you just blindly stick with your plan regardless of what is going on, **maybe you should frequently pay attention to this uncertainty?**

Here again, the typical advisor in the industry will fall short. When you experience a severe bear market (which is bound to happen at some point in your life), instead of suggesting solutions that tweak your lifestyle choices to shift the odds back in your favor, the typical advisor will instead do every-

thing in their power to coerce you to "stick with your long term plan." They
will use guilt, if needed. They will remind you of the maximum risk you said
you could tolerate. They will pull out articles from "experts" demonstrating
that the average bear market only lasts twelve months (that means many of
them last LONGER).

What they are unlikely to do is tell you the choices you have, based
on what you personally value, to make some adjustments to your plan that
would move you back toward that comfortable balance *despite* the deprecia-
tion in your portfolios.

The reverse is true, as well. If you are lucky and end up with some very
strong markets, the advisor will be fat and happy, because his clients are, as
well. But, instead of advising you about the choices you have to take some
investment risk off the table (because you can now afford to do so) or tell
you to spend some more money (because you can afford to) he will likely
instead pat himself on the back for the lucky bull market that he just happened to be around for the ride.

Many advisors, instead of providing advice about what makes the most
sense for your life BECAUSE of what has been happening in the markets,
instead only report WHAT happened. **There is a big difference between
being an advisor and being a reporter.**

A reporter shows you what happened. He might even explain his the-
ory about why what happened, ummm, happened. But the fact is, NO
ONE **can change what happened**. So while looking at your returns relative to benchmarks might be interesting information, IT CANNOT BE
CHANGED. IT HAS ALREADY HAPPENED.

This is part of the game Wall Street plays in their casino. Like the casinos
do, Wall Street and their investment product vendors show advertisements
about you achieving dreams. Once they get you to the table though, they
stop measuring your dreams and goals and only provide you with a win/loss
statement of what happened. They call this a "performance report." You will
observe that the major things you are trying to achieve are not part of such
a report. There is no retirement income goal being monitored or measured.
Your desired retirement age isn't there either. Nor is your travel budget, your
new sports car, or your bequest to your church or other charity.

This performance report will show you that relative to all of the other
gamers in the Wall Street casino (either the market "benchmarks" or peer
group ranks of funds and managers) where your results fell. The advisor may

advise you to bet on a different horse since yours has been losing (the advisor won't take blame for this). Or, if your luck happened to be better than the other gamblers, the advisor will take credit for picking these winning "horses" (funds or money managers).

But, these advisors won't tell you that it is time for you to take risk off the table or spend more money because it makes sense to do so for what you are trying to achieve. These advisors won't tell you that it might be a good idea to plan on compromising some of your lower priority goals, or delay some of them for a while *because* of what happened in the markets.

But advisors should do all of these things if THAT is what you as a customer are seeking advice about from them. Their firms' ads sure make it sound like that is what the advisors will do. That is why I call it a bait and switch.

The Markets Are Not the Only Thing That Is Uncertain

Besides the uncertainty of the markets' behavior in how it might affect the lifestyle you are planning on, over your lifetime, your life goals and priorities will no doubt change as well. This is yet just one more reason why any financial planner's projection of how much money you might accumulate is useless. It is always based on numerous assumptions. There are assumptions about the behavior of the markets. Assumptions about how much you will save and what tax rates will be. There are assumptions about inflation, and assumptions about the goals you wish to achieve. Some may even include some assumptions about your priorities (although this is rare).

Do you know anyone who used to love their job, but their company was acquired, and now they do nothing but complain about how the culture has changed? Do you think that they might prioritize early retirement more in the face of this change?

Do you know anyone who has taken up a new hobby in the last ten years? Scuba diving? Flying? Photography? Woodworking? Gambling? All of these hobbies take money that would have never been accounted for in their lives and planning prior to the person actually engaging in the new activity.

What about the uncertainty of health? Do you know anyone who has been economically and, more importantly, emotionally affected by cancer? Heart disease? A car accident? Drug or alcohol addiction? Divorce? All of these are real uncertainties that might affect the choices and priorities you make in your life, despite all the insurance the broker sells you for some of these things.

The reality is your life is just as uncertain as the markets. Frankly, to many this uncertainty and how one can influence it by the choices they make is what makes life worth living. To others this uncertainty is a crippling fear that causes them to needlessly sacrifice the only life they do have.

If you live your life in crippling terror of everything that can go wrong, you won't benefit by fixing your 401(k) plan because the list of other things that can go wrong is as endless as the expenses that might occur. If you like playing the Wall Street casino game of worrying more about beating other players instead of making the most of your life, who cares if your 401(k) is too expensive because there will be an endless stream of new funds you with which you can "play."

But, if you are sick of the games, if you really want to strike a rational balance of the best choices in your life, if you wish to capitalize on the choices you have to improve your life, then I hope you take the steps outlined in this book to make your goals a reality.

CHAPTER EIGHT

Resources, Investment Selection, Asset Allocation, Tools and Advice

Investment Selection

This morning, as I sat down to write this last chapter, there was a promotion on CNBC announcing the appearance of a mutual fund manager who was rated "Five Stars" with a five-year compound return of over 35%. CNBC said it was definitely something I should listen to since this manager was an expert. What a great track record! He must be brilliant! Surely he will be my ticket to easy street!

Hold on a second. Before I get too excited about this unique opportunity, didn't I hear that past performance is not necessarily an indication of future results? Doesn't this sound familiar? This oft-cited phrase comes from the National Association of Securities Dealers (NASD). The NASD is the self-regulatory organization (not a government agency) that supposedly protects investors by making sure member firms abide by certain standards that protect the reputation of the securities peddling industry. All broker/dealers are members of the NASD. Thus, their primary regulators are themselves. These broker/dealers are not necessarily fiduciaries acting in your best interests. They are not necessarily acting as advisors. They are required to disclose to you that they are salespeople, not advisors, despite the misleading titles they give their employees (if you look at the fine print in your brokerage agreements you will find this disclosure of their myriads of conflicts). There are numerous rules that the industry—brokers/dealers—has come up with to "protect" investors, and the brokers/dealers all agree to abide by these rules so they can continue peddling securities.

The statement, "Past performance is not necessarily an indication of future results," is required by the NASD for those who sell securities and show performance records. Think about the statement. **If it is true, and you were an objective advisor instead of a salesman,** *why would you show past performance?* If it isn't an indication of future results, the record is meaningless. Hmmm. Yet, everyone is showing you their record. Sound like the casinos again?

As the CEO of a business, I get calls from "financial advisors" (securities peddlers) all the time. They normally go into how they have some fund, stock, partnership, etc., with a great track record that I should invest in. The conversation goes something like this:

"Mr. Loeper, George Salesman here with Fly By Night Brokerage. The last time we spoke *(note: normally we haven't spoken before, but it is more effective in their pitch to say that we have),* you said you would be interested in great investment ideas, and I have one for you today. The Acme Fund has a ten-year record of superior risk adjusted returns relative to the S&P500, and the same management team has been and is still in place."

At this point, my response goes something like this, "Are you saying that past performance is an indication of future results?"

Now, most product peddlers know that even their own industry would consider it a violation of regulations to imply past performance is an indication of future results, so they normally respond with something like, "There are no guarantees about any investment, but this team does have a great long-term record."

Now, to me, this sure sounds like they are at least implying that the performance record might be an indication of future results. When I have pushed them on this and asked, "Is past performance an indication of future results?"

They dutifully respond, "Not necessarily."

And I respond, "Then why should I care about it?"

They normally retort with something like, "While past performance is not necessarily an indication of future results, certainly you would want to work with a team that has a great long-term record. What else would you have to go on? We don't invest based on hunches around here, we need proven records!"

Can you perceive the contradiction in his statement? Flipped around outside of the salesman's spin on it, he is saying, "Track records are not reliable for choosing superior investments, but what you should pick are investments based on those unreliable track records."

We did a simple little study on this (there have been numerous academic and industry articles on the topic as well). As of the end of the first quarter of 2007, 54% of the 6,000 mutual funds that had been around since at least the first quarter of 2000 **materially underperformed** their best fit benchmark for the trailing three years (we eliminated funds that did not remotely fit any benchmark). That means that over half of the mutual funds performed well below their targets over the past three years.

We then went back to the first quarter of 2003 and found the top 5% of these 6,000 funds rated on their relative return to their best fit benchmark. These top rated funds all outperformed their benchmark by at least 50% of the volatility of the benchmark as of the end of the first quarter of 2003. However, when we looked at these funds four years later, 54% of those top rated funds *also materially underperformed* their benchmark for the trailing three years—THE SAME PERCENTAGE AS ALL FUNDS!

What does this show us? The fact that the top-rated funds were among the best in 2003 not only was no indication the funds would perform well in future years, but these top-rated funds underperformed just as often as all of the funds—low-rated or high-rated—that we tested. The track record had no apparent connection with how the fund would perform in later years.

But track records—no matter how unreliable—do make compelling sales pitches. Human nature wants to extrapolate what will happen (future tense) from what has *happened* (observe this is past tense) even if there is no evidence that the past is any indication of what is to come.

The reality is there is no free lunch that IS predictable. A track record is what happened to someone else's money, NOT YOURS, and IS NOT an indication of future results. It is an effective sales tool, though, since it preys on our innate desire to project forward past observations despite the disclosure that says we should ignore it.

If track records are useless, are there data elements that are more predictive? Perhaps. Certainly one would want to evaluate whether a fund under consideration for purchase is diversified or is making big, unpredictable bets with your money. We measure this by calculating a statistic called the *correlation coefficient*. Without getting into the detailed mathematics of this statistic, in essence it measures how directionally similar the performance is between two sets of returns, like a fund versus a benchmark. That is, if one return goes up, will the other return also rise at roughly the same rate? If so, then the returns may be said to be correlated.

Another data element that is more predictive of results is the subject of this book—expenses related to an investment. Expenses have surprising (or maybe not so surprising) relationships to results. If you think about this it makes sense because the expenses that are coming from your investment are a 100% certainty (unlike track records supposedly demonstrating skill on the part of fund managers). As a group, funds with high expense ratios are much less likely to perform at or above average than lower expense ratio funds. Likewise, a far smaller percentage of the low expense ratio funds end up with terrible performance than their higher priced competitors. Obviously this impact of expenses should not be ignored.

Risk and return records are not an indication of future results, but they probably should at least be observed so long as we do not excessively value the data. There is a means of evaluating these statistics relative to the best fit benchmark by combining this with correlation. Unfortunately, most of the rating services simply slap their ratings on a particular fund *relative to other "similar" funds*, without paying attention to the benchmark. The effect is that most rating systems ignore the risk relative to the benchmark or even the right benchmark, and **in fact the best way to get a high return rating for a fund is to have the fund misclassified into the wrong category.**

An example of how misleading these "peer group and universe ranks" can be might make this effect more obvious. One of the star gazing rating systems out there would classify a total market index fund (owns large, small, value and growth stocks) as "large cap blend" thereby throwing the fund into the same "universe" or "peer group" as the system would use to classify an S&P500 index fund that owns only large cap stocks. The two funds don't own the same stocks, but they are both index funds. Because the total market index fund owns small cap stocks and recently they have been doing well, the fund gets rated a 4 for large cap blend versus 3 for the S&P500 index fund. Fifteen years ago the total market index fund would have been rated a 2 instead of a 4 because the small cap stocks it owns underperformed. One fund isn't better than the other. They are different. The best way to get a good return rating and star gazing grade is to be misclassified into the wrong peer group!

One other data element or measure that one should consider in evaluating potential investments is "luck" in terms of frequency of consistently not screwing up. We call this "material underperformance risk," and we can measure it by looking at the best fit benchmark for the fund we want to examine, reducing the benchmark by a reasonable (like the lowest 10%) expense ratio and then seeing the percentage of the months where the fund underperformed by more than the reasonable expense. Clearly, if a fund more often than not underperforms by more than this reasonable expense yet has a good long term return grade, this combination of factors might suggest that one or two recent high performing months have "saved" the long term record.

FUNDGRADES.com

You can look up these grades as well as an overall grade that combines them all at Fundgrades.com. I will not tell you that this is predictive of a particular fund's future performance. However, using the overall grades here probably isn't as bad as looking at track records. Funds are graded on an A+ through F grade relative to the most appropriate benchmark (no misleading misclassification into peer groups) for both an overall grade and an examination of each of the criteria discussed above that we know expose some useful information.

While this grading system isn't predictive of which funds will be star performers, it might help you avoid some senseless risks. For example, nearly 75% of the honor roll funds from the Fundgrades.com grading routine, as determined based on 2003 data, ended up being rated average or above based on data through 2007. Likewise, 65% to 85% of the funds graded as D+ through F based on 2003 data remained below average when tested again in 2007.

While resources like Morningstar, Yahoo!, Google Finance, Lipper, etc., may provide you with a lot of interesting data, be careful about how much weight you give it. Peer groups can be very misleading for many reasons. Track records are not predictive, and it is impossible to discern whether the "great track records" boasted by a few funds were caused by skill or luck. Finally, even if you found someone with skill, you never know whether the "secret" of the method might be discovered by others, thus eliminating the advantage.

Asset Allocation

The main thing is to keep the main thing the main thing. Asset allocation is a main thing. I've written a number of whitepapers for the industry on the topic (go to Wealthcarecapital.com and click on the "Whitepapers" link) that you can review if you would like to learn more about this topic than we can cover here.

What's the main thing about asset allocation? The bottom line is the key drivers are going to be your allocation—of your investments—to stocks, bonds, and cash AND how well you are diversified in your selections for these asset classes. This element of diversification is the most misunderstood.

I've met people who think they are diversified in their portfolios because they bought the same sets of funds from three different brokerage firms. Diversification is based on what you own. If you do not own everything in the benchmark, in proportion to the weighting in the benchmark, then you are not completely diversified. In essence, you are making a bet. This is why index funds are so popular among objectivists that don't want to be sold. With many index funds (properly selected) you are getting a complete portfolio that is not making any bets against the benchmark.

Unfortunately, the securities peddling industry has taken these relatively pure, cost effective, and unbiased vehicles and packaged them into all kinds of products and services that defeat their purpose. There are advisors that will attempt to time the market and shift the weights in your allocation around in hopes of timing things correctly (while exposing you to the risk of timing everything incorrectly—a risk that you could have avoided).

There are portfolios of indexes that are not diversified at all, making huge bets on small cap, micro or value stocks, bets that subject you to risks you have the choice to avoid. All of these approaches are just a means of continuing to play in the Wall Street casino game.

The securities peddlers have even created and defined new "better" indices that "out perform" the old ones based on "long term track records." Don't buy this for a minute. It is hype. If it sounds too good to be true, it probably is, and it is likely going to cost you a lot of your hard earned savings to find that out.

Think about the 54% of the mutual funds that materially (not just by a little, but by a lot) underperformed their best fit benchmark as we mentioned above in our 2007 study. This is a little more than the advantage a casino has over you in roulette. Roulette is one of the biggest "take" games in the casino, which means it has the worst odds for the players. Yet, this is the same result as the entire mutual fund industry. The industry nonetheless seems to be able to spin it (pun intended) so you keep playing the game despite the disadvantage.

There were a couple of studies done by *Brinson, Beebower & Hood* that are often misquoted by the industry. What the studies showed was that 90%+ of the *variance* in investment returns is explained by your allocation to Stocks, Bonds & Cash. This means that less than 10% of the *variance* is explained by real estate, foreign, small cap, growth, value, alternative investments, etc. The way the industry usually misstates these studies, though, is to misquote them by saying, "90%+ of your *returns are due* to asset allocation" (subtext, the way our firm defines asset allocation). Observe they replaced *"variance is explained by"* with *"returns are due to"* which is a big deal if you understand the difference. You will also observe they do not normally disclose that the 90%+ was based on stocks, bonds, and cash. Instead, they will use this study to show why you need 10% in small cap value and 10% in small cap growth. Which, if you buy their mystical pie slices, is the exact same as 20% in small cap blend. The more pie slices the better, though! The better for the salesman and not the investor. The growth and value pieces of the whole **are not** diversified. By definition these securities peddlers, by splitting the whole into a variety of parts, are eliminating pieces of the more diversified whole.

Those pieces perform differently at different times. Everyone was selling an overweighting to the high performing growth piece in the '90's (which then blew up in the three year bear-market starting in 2000) and now these same securities peddlers are all pushing "value tilted" or "fundamentally weighted" portfolios, that, you guessed it, currently have GREAT TRACK RECORDS!

The odds of you or anyone outsmarting the markets are literally the same as winning a bet at the worst odds in any of a casino's table games. But many are tempted. The difference is that in the Wall Street Casino, they are tempted to play that game and make the bet with their retirement assets, not with a $500 entertainment budget.

Forget the hype. Don't take any more investment risk than makes sense for what you are trying to achieve. What follows is an easy to use, do it yourself, scoring model that shows you—based on your time horizon, risk tolerance, and liquidity needs—how to select a somewhat reasonable asset allocation. We designed it for 401(k) plans that want to offer participants an easy way to select a reasonable asset allocation since your asset allocation is one of the "main things."

INSTRUCTIONS: *Complete these eight questions, total the POINT VALUE scores from questions 1 & 2 for your TIME HORIZON score, and questions 3 through 8 for your RISK TOLERANCE score and find the intersection of these scores on the scoring model.*

TIME HORIZON

QUESTION #1 - Do you expect to begin withdrawing money (or borrowing) from your 401(k) account within the next 10 years? If so, how soon?

CHECK ONE Answer:

Answers	**Point Value**
_____ No	**15**
_____ Yes, within the next 2 years	**0**
_____ Yes, within the next 3-5 years	**5**
_____ Yes, within the next 6-7 years	**7**
_____ Yes, but not for at least 8-9 years	**10**

ENTER THE *POINT VALUE* FOR YOUR ANSWER: _____

QUESTION #2 - If and when you begin withdrawing (or borrowing) from your 401(k) account, over what period of time will the withdrawals last?

Answers	**Point Value**
_____ I will withdraw the entire account balance, all at once, for a specific goal	**0**
_____ Over a 1–3 year period, depleting most or all of the account	**1**
_____ Over a 4-7 year period, depleting most or all of the account	**3**
_____ For more than 7 years, depleting most or all of the account	**5**
_____ When I begin withdrawals, I expect to produce a **continuous income stream** without depleting the account	**16**
_____ I never plan to make withdrawals from this account	**20**

ENTER THE *POINT VALUE* FOR YOUR ANSWER: _____

ADD THE TOTAL POINT VALUE OF QUESTIONS #1 & #2 combined and ENTER HERE: _____

THIS IS YOUR TIME HORIZON SCORE TO BE USED LATER

RISK TOLERANCE

QUESTION #3- Inflation impacts the effective spending power of your money over time.

To design an appropriate portfolio for you, we need to understand your attitude about the trade-off between preserving spending power versus growing your assets <u>after</u> the effects of inflation.

Portfolios that are likely to preserve or increase spending power over long periods of time though, have higher volatility over shorter time periods.

Which best describes your attitude about accepting short-term risk relative to long- term growth?

<u>Answers</u>	<u>Point Value</u>
_____ Long-term maximum growth, in excess of inflation, is my primary objective even though the short-term risk will be very high.	**15**
_____ Long-term growth, in excess of inflation, is my primary objective, but I am NOT willing to accept extreme short-term risk.	**12**
_____ I desire a moderate balance between growth, in excess of inflation, and short-term risk.	**6**
_____ My primary objective is to avoid short-term risk even though it is likely that there will be little or no long-term growth in excess of inflation.	**0**

ENTER THE *POINT VALUE* FOR YOUR ANSWER: _____

QUESTION #4 - Investments that are likely to produce higher long-term average returns are also likely to have a greater chance of losing money. Also, for these types of investments, the magnitude of extreme losses increases as well. The table below demonstrates this trade-off between average return, the likelihood of losing money in any ONE YEAR, AND how extreme declines may be. Please select the portfolio that best balances these trade-offs between risk and return for you.

	Potential Average Return	Chance of Losing Money In Any ONE Year	Worst Year of 75 Years	Worst Year of 30 Years
Portfolio A	12.5%	1 In 3	-46%	-24%
Portfolio B	12.0%	1 in 4	-41%	-21%
Portfolio C	11.3%	1 in 5	-37%	-18%
Portfolio D	10.0%	1 in 6	-28%	-12%
Portfolio E	9.0%	1 in 7	-22%	-8%
Portfolio F	7.8%	1 in 8	-15%	-3%

Answers	Point Value
_____ PORTFOLIO A	20
_____ PORTFOLIO B	18
_____ PORTFOLIO C	12
_____ PORTFOLIO D	8
_____ PORTFOLIO E	5
_____ PORTFOLIO F	-20

ENTER THE *POINT VALUE* FOR YOUR ANSWER: _____

QUESTION #5 - Based on the information from the previous question, there is obviously a trade-off between risk and return. Which of the following best describes your attitude about this decision in balancing your desire to seek returns relative to the risk you can tolerate?

Answers	Point Value
_____ My primary goal is preservation of principal and risk avoidance. I will accept lower returns in an effort to avoid investment risk.	**0**
_____ I want to avoid risk, but will accept a relatively small amount to achieve a slightly higher return.	**5**
_____ I can tolerate a moderate amount of risk in an effort to achieve a moderate amount of growth.	**10**
_____ I want to achieve potentially high returns, and I am willing to accept the high amount of risk associated with this goal.	**15**

ENTER THE *POINT VALUE* FOR YOUR ANSWER: _____

QUESTION #6 - To achieve your investment objectives, it is important that you continue with your strategy even in periods of severe short-term price swings (volatility) as well as prolonged down markets. If your portfolio fell by 20% over a short period, assuming you still had several years before you needed the money, how do you think you would respond?

Answers	Point Value
_____ I would not make any changes since I anticipated this sort of volatility.	**15**
_____ I would want to reconsider my portfolio allocation, but if the overall market decline for portfolios like mine were similar, I would likely stick to my strategy.	**10**
_____ I would want to reconsider my portfolio allocation and cautiously adjust my portfolio toward more conservative investments over time.	**5**
_____ I would immediately move my investments to very safe and conservative alternatives.	**0**

ENTER THE *POINT VALUE* FOR YOUR ANSWER: _____

QUESTION #7 - The graph below shows a hypothetical potential range of returns over any twelve-month period of six model portfolio allocations. Please note that the highest median potential returns also have the greatest potential losses.

Which of these portfolios would you prefer to hold?

Answers	Point Value
____ PORTFOLIO F	-20
____ PORTFOLIO E	5
____ PORTFOLIO D	8
____ PORTFOLIO C	12
____ PORTFOLIO B	18
____ PORTFOLIO A	20

ENTER THE *POINT VALUE* FOR YOUR ANSWER: _____

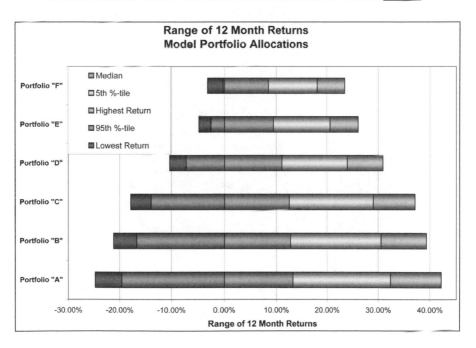

QUESTION #8 - To summarize your objectives, which statement below best describes your overall attitude between the trade-off between short-term risk and the possibility of achieving your long-term investment goal?

Answers	Point Value
_____ I can accept short-term losses to maximize the potential I will achieve long-term investment goals.	15
_____ I am equally concerned with avoiding short-term losses and meeting my long-term investment goals.	8
_____ Avoiding short-term losses is more important to me than achieving my long-term investment goals.	5

ENTER THE *POINT VALUE* FOR YOUR ANSWER: _____

SCORING:

Risk Tolerance Scoring—Enter the POINT VALUES for the following questions:

Question #	Point Value
#8	_____
#7	_____
#6	_____
#5	_____
#4	_____
#3	_____

YOUR TOTAL RISK SCORE: _____
(add the point values of questions #3-#8)

Enter Your TIME HORIZON SCORE (sum of point values from questions 1&2) FROM PAGE 2:

YOUR TIME HORIZON SCORE:_____

Find the Roman numeral that is at the intersection of your time horizon and risk scores.

Risk Tolerance			Time Horizon Score (Sum of #1 & #2)			
Score			< 7	7-12	13-20	>20
<	-	10	I	I	I	I
11	-	20	I	I	II	II
21	-	35	I	II	II	III
36	-	50	I	II	III	III
51	-	65	I	III	IV	IV
66	-	80	I	IV	IV	V
80	-	100	I	V	VI	VI

Portfolio #	I	II	III	IV	V	VI
Asset Allocation	Risk Averse	Balanced Income	Balanced	Balanced Growth	Growth	Aggressive Growth
Large Cap Stocks	17%	25%	33%	46%	46%	50%
Mid Cap Stocks	3%	5%	7%	9%	9%	10%
Small Cap Stocks	6%	9%	13%	16%	22%	25%
Foreign Stocks	4%	6%	7%	9%	13%	15%
Total Stock Exposure	30%	45%	60%	80%	90%	100%
Bonds	60%	50%	37%	18%	10%	0%
Cash Equivalents	10%	5%	3%	2%	0%	0%

SCORING MODEL

The scoring model and model portfolios are designed to help investors choose portfolios based on their time horizon and tolerance for risk. It does not include personal goals, priorities, or other assets, and you should consider contacting Wealthcare Capital Management to speak with one of our Wealthcare specialists to help you make better decisions about how your personal goals, choices, and priorities fit into your overall financial situation. There is no additional charge for this service unless you wish to have them manage assets *outside* of your 401(k) assets. Quarterly monitoring and consultation is included as well. Call our toll-free line (1-866-261-0849) and use the code word "Rip-off" to get your free analysis.

However, if you wish to use the scoring model, here is an example of how it works:

Assume **YOUR TIME HORIZON Score was 15**. That would mean you would be working with the green Time Horizon column of **13-20** because your score of 15 falls between **13-20**:

Risk Tolerance			Time Horizon Score (Sum of #1 & #2)			
Score			< 7	7-12	13-20	>20
<	-	10	I	I	I	I
11	-	20	I	I	II	II
21	-	35	I	II	II	III
36	-	50	I	II	*III*	III
51	-	65	I	III	IV	IV
66	-	80	I	IV	IV	V
80	-	100	I	V	VI	VI

Now, let's **assume your RISK TOLERANCE Score was 42**. That would mean you would be working with the pink risk tolerance row of **36-50** because 42 falls between **36-50**.

The correct model for these scores, based on the responses, would be Portfolio **III**- Balanced. It is the model that falls at the *intersection of the risk tolerance row and time horizon column*. Where do your scores place you? If you would like help, contact Wealthcare Capital Management at (1-866-261-0849) and their Wealthcare Specialists will be happy to assist you.

With all these people trying to beat the "market" and the odds of picking a winner worse than the typical roulette table odds, why do people play the game? Are you really a patient long term investor like the industry tells you that you should be?

Here's a long term record for you to ponder (not that it is indicative of future results). Our most basic "Growth Portfolio Allocation" is allocated 55% to large cap stocks, 35% to small cap stocks and 10% to Bonds. For the THIRTY YEARS ending in 2006, it returned 13.45% versus 12.47% for large cap stocks. In fact, this simple no-brainer allocation that anyone could manufacture from index funds out performs "the market" (i.e. large cap stocks or the S&P500) by quite a bit. The allocation is based on such simple, well-known "pieces of the markets" that we can measure it back to 1926.

There were 52 unique thirty-year periods between 1926 and 2006. This simple allocation outperformed the market in 48 of those 52 thirty-year periods. Understand the allocation did underperform the market by a small amount in 4 of those 52 periods. Those were:

Time Period	Our Growth Allocation	Large Cap Stocks ("the market")
1944–1973	11.88%	11.99%
1944–1974	10.05%	10.18%
1946–1975	9.88%	10.20%
1969–1998	12.46%	12.67%

In the other 48 thirty-year periods the simple Growth allocation you could (easily and cheaply) create, as described above, out performed the market on average by about 1%.

Also, the worst 30-year period for the growth allocation was 8.98% versus 8.47% for large cap stocks (both starting near the Crash of '29). The volatility of this portfolio, because of its broader diversification, despite exposure to more volatile small cap stocks, is about the same as a 100% large cap portfolio. The Growth portfolio allocation's worst year was 1931 when it declined by 41.48% versus the all large cap portfolio that lost 43.34% that year, so the risk is about the same between the two portfolios.

This does not mean this is the right portfolio for you. It just goes to show that a really impressive long term record is easy to create, but it does not make it predictive of future results.

As we mentioned earlier, it only makes sense to assume the risk level that makes sense for what you are trying to achieve. Even if you can tolerate more risk, why take it if it isn't needed for you to achieve what you personally value? The best way to determine this is to go through the Wealthcare process with someone who is not a commissioned salesperson but instead is an objective advisor. If you want to see what objective advice is like, call our toll free line (1-866-261-0849) and use the code word "Rip-OFF" for your free analysis.

So, while asset allocation is *a* main thing, your goals and priorities are still THE main thing. The reality is that it appears all the fiddling around with large, medium, and small pie slices is not really going to make any difference in your results. All the pieces and breakdowns of such an asset allocation will sound impressive and complicated, though.

For example, take a look at these two materially different allocations, and think about how hard it would be to actually perceive a difference between them based on the results over an eighty year investing lifetime.

	__Aggressive Portfolio__	__More Conservative__
Allocation:	60% Large/40% Small	55% Large/25% Small
		18% Bonds/2% Cash

Number of years in the last eighty years that performed:

Less than -30%:	3 ('30,'31, '37)	2 ('31 & '37)
Less than -1.55%:	20	19
Greater than +15%:	38	38
Between +15% & -1.55%:	22	23

Think about this whenever you talk to one of those advisors who boasts about his magical asset allocation based on a five, ten, or even twenty year record. The reality is that the markets themselves drive the majority of the results achieved and small shifts in the pieces did not then, and are not now, going to have a significant, predictable impact.

Unless you have too much money or your goals are extremely modest (maybe you have a goal shortage?) you can probably be best served by having a low-cost portfolio allocation that captures the market results instead of trying to bet on beating them.

We have six model portfolios ranging from a low risk (Risk Averse) portfolio with only 30% in stocks to a 100% stock portfolio (Aggressive Growth) that are all efficient and very inexpensive to construct. They are:

Six Model Portfolios:
I - **Risk Averse**, *low risk portfolio with income emphasis*

II - **Balanced Income**, *moderate risk blend of growth and income with income bias*

III - **Balanced**, *moderate risk with a balance between growth and income*

IV - **Balanced Growth**, *moderately high risk blend of growth and income with growth bias*

V - **Growth**, *high risk with growth emphasis*

VI - **Aggressive Growth**, *very high risk focused on growth*

Portfolio #	I	II	III	IV	V	VI
Asset Allocation	Risk Averse	Balanced Income	Balanced	Balanced Growth	Growth	Aggressive Growth
Large Cap Stocks	17%	25%	33%	46%	46%	50%
Mid Cap Stocks	3%	5%	7%	9%	9%	10%
Small Cap Stocks	6%	9%	13%	16%	22%	25%
Foreign Stocks	4%	6%	7%	9%	13%	15%
Total Stock Exposure	30%	45%	60%	80%	90%	100%
Bonds	60%	50%	37%	18%	10%	0%
Cash Equivalents	10%	5%	3%	2%	0%	0%

Figure 14 Wealthcare Capital Management 401(k) model portfolio asset allocations

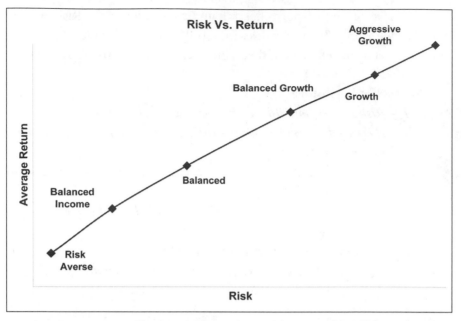

Figure 15 Annual risk versus return for Wealthcare portfolio allocations

Nearly anyone's financial goals can be met with one of these models. They are inexpensive and easy to construct, very tax-efficient (if done correctly due to the low turnover), and are not making bets against the markets, gambling on styles, or taking irrational risks.

"AGE" Based Investing and "Lifecycle" Funds

Be careful whenever you are investing based on someone else's rule of thumb. There are a myriad of "easy" ways to determine your allocation, but they almost always will end up being the wrong choice for you at some time in your life. Conventional wisdom says if you are younger, you should have more in stocks. In many cases this might make sense, but that does not mean it always will. What if you are terrified of market risk, and you have a large inheritance coming later in life that you can use to confidently fund your goals? WHY would you expose yourself to needless investment risk merely because Suze Orman says you are young and therefore should own more stocks?

Lifecycle or target funds are very similar. You choose a date now (better hope it doesn't change), and the fund automatically lowers your equity exposure over time as you approach that fixed date. It doesn't matter whether the automatic changes make sense for what you are trying to achieve. It doesn't matter that the fund will change the allocation at potentially the wrong time for your goals based on what is going on in the markets, the fund simply will change the allocation based on changes in the calendar without regard to whether it makes sense for you.

This *is not* how to make the most of your life, and the problems created by using such simple strategies—strategies that are ignoring goals you are personally trying to achieve and the reasons you value those goals—will likely cost your lifestyle far more than your excessive 401(k) fees.

Life Relative Allocation

The time to decrease your equity exposure and risk is when you can *afford* to do so for what you are trying to achieve. It might have to do with the passing of time, but a decrease in equity exposure might be indicated far sooner if you happen to have a "lucky" bull market result that occurs over a period of just a few short years. Such a market could enable you to confidently fund all those goals you personally value with far less equity exposure not because of the passing of time but precisely because of what happened in the markets. Lifecycle and target funds completely ignore this possibility and will continue exposing you to excessive risk you do not need to take.

The inverse can happen as well. Sometimes those past "wins" in the market lottery might have you rationally reducing your equity exposure over time, but if a particularly bad bear market occurs, it might make sense, even if you are older, to move up the risk scale a notch or two in order to maintain confidence in achieving the goals you value. Target funds, lifecycle funds, and age based allocations would have you doing the exact opposite. Just when it makes sense to increase your equity allocation a bit for the goals you are funding due to market changes, they all would have you reducing your equity exposure without regard to the markets or your goals.

Many financial advisors wrongly accuse our company of "passive" management. It is understandable, because from their *market relative gambling game* perspective, we are passive. We are not making timing or style bets. We do not attempt to forecast what the markets will do, and we always assume they are uncertain. We don't mislead people into thinking they will "beat the market" with us by using our track records of superior risk adjusted performance without regard to future performance (Remember, our Growth model allocation beat the S&P in 48 of 52 thirty-year periods, yet we do not advertise this in any brochure). The portfolios we recommend use passive indices, because these indices are inexpensive and tax efficient—two certainties we think one should capitalize on, if possible. We just don't take the risk of materially underperforming the strategic allocation that makes sense for your goals in hopes of *maybe* outperforming, but also *maybe* underperforming.

That doesn't mean your allocation won't change. We continuously manage the appropriate allocation for what you are trying to achieve. If you think about it, we actually provide far more customized services for clients. The Wall Street gamers, if they think the market is headed for a rally, will increase the equity exposure in all of their clients' portfolios regardless of whether that makes sense for their clients' goals. Sometimes such bets will pay off, and they will look like geniuses, but sometimes such gambles won't, and they will come up with excuses.

But you are a lot different than everyone else, and your allocation should be matched to what you are trying to achieve. We always assume the markets are constantly uncertain. We assume risk is always present. Wouldn't it make sense that for some clients, who may have been initially positioned very conservatively because of modest goals, we might advise them to increase their stock allocation a bit if their goals become less modest or the markets produced poor results that lowered their available resources?

At the same time, while we are advising those clients to move up a notch on the risk scale, might it not make sense that some clients might have other unplanned resources become available that perhaps would enable them to move down the risk scale a bit? **Neither** of these outcomes happen in the market relative casino on Wall Street. Increasing or decreasing equity exposure in that game isn't based on either of these client specific circumstances that might be present. Therefore, in the market relative game there are always some clients having their main investment decision of strategic asset allocation handled exactly the opposite of how it should be.

So we actively manage a client's strategic exposure as it matches their unique goals and changing market conditions and what that means to the client's confidence of exceeding their goals. To this end, we have two sets of specific portfolios that are very cost efficient. One set is constructed of low-cost index funds for use in 401(k) plans, and the other is a portfolio of exchange traded funds, or ETFs, that can be more tax efficient than mutual funds for taxable accounts. Both sets of portfolios own essentially the same securities in the same proportion, weighted the same.

The 401(k) portfolios are constructed as shown in the following figures.

Data Updated Through March 31, 2007

Wealthcare Capital Management - Backtested 401K Model Portfolio Asset Allocations

Data shown reflects characteristics and performance of underlying indices
(see accompanying page for important disclosure information)

Portfolio VI Aggressive Growth Portfolio

(backtesting inception date: January 1, 1981)

Asset Class (Modeled Index)	Asset Weighting
Large Cap Equity (S&P 500)	50.00%
Mid-Cap Equity (Russell Mid Cap Index)	10.00%
Small Cap Equity (Russell 2000)	25.00%
International Equity (EAFE - Europe, Austrialia, Far East)	15.00%
Fixed Income (Citigroup 7-10 Year Treasury)	0.00%
Cash (90 Day T-Bills)	0.00%

Annualized Model Portfolio Performance - Net of Estimated Fees*					
1 Year	*3 Year*	*5 Year*	*10 Year*	*20 Year*	*Since Inception*
11.22%	12.25%	9.24%	9.03%	10.07%	12.13%

Model Portfolio Standard Deviation (since inception January 1, 1981)	14.53%

Performance Statistics - Since Inception			
Highest 1 Month Return	12.44%	Lowest 1 Month Return	-23.02%
Highest 3 Month Return	23.08%	Lowest 3 Month Return	-29.01%
Highest 12 Month Return	65.69%	Lowest 12 Month Return	-25.25%

Estimated Portfolio Expense Ratio Using Index Mutual Funds:	0.0855%
Estimated TOTAL Expense with 30 BP Advisory Fee:	0.3855%

Portfolio V Growth Portfolio

(backtesting inception date: January 1, 1981)

Asset Class (Modeled Index)	Asset Weighting
Large Cap Equity (S&P 500)	46.00%
Mid-Cap Equity (Russell Mid Cap Index)	9.00%
Small Cap Equity (Russell 2000)	22.00%
International Equity (EAFE - Europe, Austrialia, Far East)	13.00%
Fixed Income (Citigroup 7-10 Year Treasury)	10.00%
Cash (90 Day T-Bills)	0.00%

Annualized Model Portfolio Performance - Net of Estimated Fees*					
1 Year	*3 Year*	*5 Year*	*10 Year*	*20 Year*	*Since Inception*
10.70%	11.16%	8.88%	8.89%	9.90%	11.93%

Model Portfolio Standard Deviation (since inception January 1, 1981)	13.20%

Performance Statistics - Since Inception			
Highest 1 Month Return	11.32%	Lowest 1 Month Return	-20.24%
Highest 3 Month Return	22.67%	Lowest 3 Month Return	-26.10%
Highest 12 Month Return	61.89%	Lowest 12 Month Return	-21.80%

Estimated Portfolio Expense Ratio Using Index Mutual Funds:	0.0945%
Estimated TOTAL Expense with 30 BP Advisory Fee:	0.3945%

Portfolio IV Balanced Growth Portfolio

(backtesting inception date: January 1, 1981)

Asset Class (Modeled Index)	Asset Weighting
Large Cap Equity (S&P 500)	46.00%
Mid-Cap Equity (Russell Mid Cap Index)	9.00%
Small Cap Equity (Russell 2000)	16.00%
International Equity (EAFE - Europe, Austrialia, Far East)	9.00%
Fixed Income (Citigroup 7-10 Year Treasury)	18.00%
Cash (90 Day T-Bills)	2.00%

Annualized Model Portfolio Performance - Net of Estimated Fees*					
1 Year	*3 Year*	*5 Year*	*10 Year*	*20 Year*	*Since Inception*
10.15%	9.89%	8.15%	8.59%	9.72%	11.66%

Model Portfolio Standard Deviation (since inception January 1, 1981)	11.89%

Performance Statistics - Since Inception			
Highest 1 Month Return	10.29%	Lowest 1 Month Return	-17.46%
Highest 3 Month Return	22.48%	Lowest 3 Month Return	-23.30%
Highest 12 Month Return	57.33%	Lowest 12 Month Return	-18.52%

Estimated Portfolio Expense Ratio Using Index Mutual Funds:	0.1039%
Estimated TOTAL Expense with 30 BP Advisory Fee:	0.4039%

Portfolio III Balanced Portfolio

(backtesting inception date: January 1, 1981)

Asset Class (Modeled Index)	Asset Weighting
Large Cap Equity (S&P 500)	33.00%
Mid-Cap Equity (Russell Mid Cap Index)	7.00%
Small Cap Equity (Russell 2000)	13.00%
International Equity (EAFE - Europe, Australia, Far East)	7.00%
Fixed Income (Citigroup 7-10 Year Treasury)	37.00%
Cash (90 Day T-Bills)	3.00%

Annualized Model Portfolio Performance - Net of Estimated Fees*					
1 Year	*3 Year*	*5 Year*	*10 Year*	*20 Year*	*Since Inception*
9.07%	7.97%	7.60%	8.17%	9.14%	11.07%
Model Portfolio Standard Deviation (since inception January 1, 1981)					9.51%

Performance Statistics - Since Inception			
Highest 1 Month Return	8.78%	Lowest 1 Month Return	-12.07%
Highest 3 Month Return	20.98%	Lowest 3 Month Return	-17.22%
Highest 12 Month Return	50.11%	Lowest 12 Month Return	-11.03%

Estimated Portfolio Expense Ratio Using Index Mutual Funds: 0.1249%
Estimated TOTAL Expense with 30 BP Advisory Fee: 0.4249%

Portfolio II Balanced Income Portfolio

(backtesting inception date: January 1, 1981)

Asset Class (Modeled Index)	Asset Weighting
Large Cap Equity (S&P 500)	25.00%
Mid-Cap Equity (Russell Mid Cap Index)	5.00%
Small Cap Equity (Russell 2000)	9.00%
International Equity (EAFE - Europe, Australia, Far East)	6.00%
Fixed Income (Citigroup 7-10 Year Treasury)	50.00%
Cash (90 Day T-Bills)	5.00%

Annualized Model Portfolio Performance - Net of Estimated Fees*					
1 Year	*3 Year*	*5 Year*	*10 Year*	*20 Year*	*Since Inception*
8.37%	6.52%	7.01%	7.66%	8.57%	10.50%
Model Portfolio Standard Deviation (since inception January 1, 1981)					7.91%

Performance Statistics - Since Inception			
Highest 1 Month Return	7.78%	Lowest 1 Month Return	-7.87%
Highest 3 Month Return	19.46%	Lowest 3 Month Return	-12.41%
Highest 12 Month Return	43.77%	Lowest 12 Month Return	-5.39%

Estimated Portfolio Expense Ratio Using Index Mutual Funds: 0.1422%
Estimated TOTAL Expense with 30 BP Advisory Fee: 0.4422%

Portfolio I Risk Averse Portfolio

(backtesting inception date: January 1, 1981)

Asset Class (Modeled Index)	Asset Weighting
Large Cap Equity (S&P 500)	17.00%
Mid-Cap Equity (Russell Mid Cap Index)	3.00%
Small Cap Equity (Russell 2000)	6.00%
International Equity (EAFE - Europe, Australia, Far East)	4.00%
Fixed Income (Citigroup 7-10 Year Treasury)	50.00%
Cash (90 Day T-Bills)	10.00%

Annualized Model Portfolio Performance - Net of Estimated Fees*					
1 Year	*3 Year*	*5 Year*	*10 Year*	*20 Year*	*Since Inception*
7.47%	5.03%	6.21%	7.00%	7.88%	9.76%
Model Portfolio Standard Deviation (since inception January 1, 1981)					6.59%

Performance Statistics - Since Inception			
Highest 1 Month Return	6.77%	Lowest 1 Month Return	-4.24%
Highest 3 Month Return	17.73%	Lowest 3 Month Return	-7.76%
Highest 12 Month Return	37.43%	Lowest 12 Month Return	-3.56%

Estimated Portfolio Expense Ratio Using Index Mutual Funds: 0.1621%
Estimated TOTAL Expense with 30 BP Advisory Fee: 0.4621%

Figure 16 Wealthcare Capital Management 401(k) model portfolio asset allocations

Representative Risk Versus Return Graphic

Annual Risk Versus Return - Wealthcare Portfolio Allocations
(Based on Monthly Underlying Index Total Return Data for the Period 1/01/1981 - 3/31/2007)

PAST PERFORMANCE IS NOT AN INDICATION OF FUTURE RESULTS. THE PERFORMANCE OF THE CURRENT RECOMMENDED ALLOCATION ON MODELS IS BASED ON SPECIFIC PASSIVE INDICES, AS DISCLOSED HEREIN, AND EXCLUDES ANY APPLICABLE 401(K) ADMINISTRATIVE AND CUSTODIAL FEES. NET OF FEE PERFORMANCE IS CALCULATED BY LOWERING THE MODEL PORTFOLIO PERFORMANCE BY THE ESTIMATED COST OF IMPLEMENTING THE PARTICULAR INVESTMENT STRATEGY (EXPENSE RATIO OF SURROGATE PASSIVE INDEX MUTUAL FUNDS PLUS 0.30% 401K INVESTMENT ADVISORY FEE). PORTFOLIO SPECIFIC ESTIMATED EXPENSE RATIO AND 401K ADVISORY FEES ARE DISCLOSED HEREIN. ADDITIONAL INFORMATION ABOUT ADVISORY FEES AND EXPENSES IS AVAILABLE UPON REQUEST.

BACKTESTED PERFORMANCE INFORMATION:

FINANCEWARE, INC. D/B/A WEALTHCARE CAPITAL MANAGEMENT (WCM) WAS FORMED IN MAY 2000. THE MODEL PORTFOLIO PERFORMANCE INFORMATION PRESENTED HERE REPRESENTS BACKTESTED RESULTS FROM JANUARY 1, 1981 THROUGH MARCH 31ST 2007, USING MONTHLY REBALANCING. THE TIME PERIODS SELECTED WERE BASED ON THE AVAILABILITY OF SELECTED INDEX DATA. THE PERFORMANCE OF THE STRATEGIC ASSET ALLOCATION WAS DERIVED BY BACKTESTING OF UNDERLYING INDEX DATA, NOT FROM ACTUAL CLIENT OR FIRM ACCOUNTS. BACKTESTING OF PERFORMANCE IS PREPARED USING A COMPUTER PROGRAM THAT STARTS WITH THE FIRST DAY OF THE GIVEN TIME PERIOD AND EVALUATES THE WEIGHTED AVERAGE PERFORMANCE OF THE RECOMMENDED INDICES BASED ON THE RECOMMENDED TARGET WEIGHTING FOR EACH PORTFOLIO, ASSUMING MONTHLY REBALANCING.

GIVEN THAT INVESTORS CAN NOT INVEST DIRECTLY IN THE PASSIVE INDICES, THE ADVISOR WILL SELECT PASSIVE INDEX MUTUAL FUNDS AS PROXIES FOR THE UNDERLYING PASSIVE INDEX TO MANAGE THE MODEL PORTFOLIOS. THE ADVISOR MAY FROM TIME TO TIME CHANGE THE SELECTION OF SURROGATE PASSIVE INDEX MUTUAL FUNDS WITHIN MODEL PORTFOLIOS WHEN IN THE BEST INTEREST OF THE CLIENT. BACKTESTED PERFORMANCE DOES NOT REPRESENT ACTUAL ACCOUNT PERFORMANCE AND SHOULD NOT BE INTERPRETED AS AN INDICATION OF SUCH PERFORMANCE. ACTUAL FUND PERFORMANCE MAY DEVIATE FROM THE UNDERLYING INDEX.

BACKTESTED PERFORMANCE DOES NOT REPRESENT THE IMPACT THAT MATERIAL ECONOMIC AND MARKET FACTORS MIGHT HAVE ON AN INVESTOR'S DECISION MAKING PROCESS IF THE INVESTOR WAS ACTUALLY INVESTED IN THE MARKET. THE BACKTESTING OF PERFORMANCE DIFFERS FROM ACTUAL ACCOUNT PERFORMANCE BECAUSE THE INVESTMENT STRATEGY MAY BE ADJUSTED AT ANY TIME FOR ANY REASON, AND MAY CONTINUE TO BE CHANGED UNTIL DESIRED OR BETTER PERFORMANCE RESULTS ARE ACHIEVED. THE RESULTS OF THE MODELS AND FUNDS REFLECT THE REINVESTMENT OF DIVIDENDS AND OTHER EARNINGS. AS WITH ANY INVESTMENT STRATEGY, THERE IS POTENTIAL FOR PROFIT AS WELL AS POSSIBILITY OF LOSS.

INVESTORS REVIEWING THIS INFORMATION SHOULD RECOGNIZE THAT PAST PERFORMANCE HAS NO RELATION TO FUTURE RESULTS.

Figure 17 Annual risk versus return for Wealthcare portfolio allocations

Wealthcare Capital Management - 401K Funds

Asset Class	Symbol	Description	Annual Expense Ratio	Returns Through 3/31/2007			
				1 Year	3 Year	5 Year	10 Year
Large Cap Equity Blend	FSMAX	**Fidelity Spartan S&P 500 Index Fund - Advantage Class**	**0.07%**	**11.78%**	**9.99%**	**6.17%**	**8.07%** [1]
		Benchmark - S&P 500 Index	*NA*	11.83%	10.06%	6.27%	8.20%
	FSTMX	**Fidelity Spartan Total Market Index Fund - Investor Shares**	**0.10%**	**11.27%**	**10.94%**	**7.54%**	**NA** [2]
		Benchmark - Dow Jones Wilshire 5000 Composite Index	*NA*	11.33%	11.04%	7.71%	8.73%
Large Cap Equity Growth	VIGRX	**Vanguard Growth Index Fund - Investor Shares**	**0.22%**	**6.80%**	**6.99%**	**3.80%**	**6.91%**
		Benchmark - Blended Large Cap Growth Index*	*NA*	6.98%	7.17%	3.95%	7.00%
		(*S&P 500/Barra Growth Index (through 5/16/2003), MSCI US Prime Market Growth Index thereafter)					
Large Cap Equity Value	VIVAX	**Vanguard Value Index Fund - Investor Shares**	**0.21%**	**17.06%**	**14.22%**	**9.45%**	**9.38%**
		Benchmark - Blended Large Cap Value Index*	*NA*	17.27%	14.39%	9.60%	9.50%
		(*S&P 500/Barra Value Index (through 5/16/2003), MSCI US Prime Market Value Index thereafter)					
Mid-Cap Equity Blend	TRBDX	**TIAA-CREF Mid-Cap Blend Index Fund - Institutional Class**	**0.08%**	**11.54%**	**15.56%**	**NA**	**NA** [3]
		Benchmark - Russell Midcap Index	*NA*	11.79%	15.72%		
Small Cap Equity Blend	TISBX	**TIAA-CREF Small-Cap Blend Index Fund - Institutional Class**	**0.08%**	**5.80%**	**11.88%**	**NA**	**NA** [3]
		Benchmark - Russell 2000	*NA*	5.91%	12.00%		
	NAESX	**Vanguard Small-Cap Index Fund - Investor Shares**	**0.23%**	**6.70%**	**13.07%**	**11.53%**	**10.97%**
		Benchmark - Blended Small-Cap Equity Index*	*NA*	6.84%	13.17%	11.46%	10.48%
		(*Russell 2000 Index through 5/16/2003, MSCI US Small-Cap 1750 thereafter)					
Foreign Large Cap Equity Blend	TCIEX	**TIAA-CREF International Equity Index Fund - Institutional Class**	**0.15%**	**20.32%**	**19.80%**	**NA**	**NA** [3]
		Benchmark - Morgan Stanley EAFE Index (Europe, Australia, Far East)	*NA*	20.68%	20.31%		

Specialty - Real Estate	VGSIX	Vanguard REIT Index Fund - Investor Shares	0.21%	21.66%	22.28%	21.62%	14.53%
		Benchmark - MSCI US REIT Index adjusted to include 2% cash position	NA	21.75%	22.37%	21.68%	14.48%
Short-Term Bond	VBISX	Vanguard Short-Term Bond Index Fund - Investor Shares	0.18%	5.61%	2.32%	3.63%	5.19%
		Benchmark - Lehman 1-5 Year Government/Credit Index	NA	5.70%	2.43%	4.10%	5.46%
Intermediate Bond	VBIIX	Vanguard Intermediate Term Bond Index Fund - Investor Shares	0.18%	6.93%	2.86%	5.90%	6.77%
		Benchmark - Lehman 5-10 Year Government/Credit Index	NA	7.00%	2.92%	6.39%	6.98%
Long-Term Bond	VBLTX	Vanguard Long-Term Bond Index Fund	0.18%	7.15%	3.98%	7.56%	8.12%
		Benchmark - Lehman US Long Government/Credit Index	NA	7.37%	4.12%	7.85%	8.13%
Money Market	VMMXX	Vanguard Prime Money Market Fund	0.29%	5.11%	3.36%	2.46%	3.76%
		Benchmark - Average Money Market Fund (Derived from Lipper data)	NA	4.43%	2.72%	1.88%	3.18%
	VMFXX	Vanguard Federal Money Market Fund - Investor Class	0.29%	5.04%	3.31%	2.42%	3.72%
		Benchmark - Average Government Money Market Fund	NA	4.48%	2.78%	1.93%	3.22%

Figure 18 Wealthcare 401(k) funds

[1] The initial offering of Fidelity's Advantage Share Class took place on October 17, 2005. Returns prior to that date are those of the Investor Class and reflect the Investors Class' higher expense ratio.

[2] Fidelity Spartan Total Market Index Fund has an inception date of November 1997

[3] TIAA-CREF funds have a October 2002 inception date

All fund performance and benchmark data is sourced from the respective fund managers' websites or Thomson Financial and is believed to be accurate but is not guaranteed as accurate by Wealthcare Capital Management.

Investors reviewing this information should recognize that past performance is not an indication of future results. As with any investment, there is potential for profit as well as the possibility of loss.

You will observe that most of the expense ratios for these funds are 0.25% a year or less and, of course, when you assemble those funds together your portfolio expenses will be in that neighborhood as well. This is probably between one-half and one-tenth the amount in expenses you are paying now. You might also notice the optional 30 basis point management fee. This optional fee is only charged to those investors who voluntarily choose to have us continuously rebalance their *portfolio and* help them, on an ongoing basis, to choose when they should change models based on *their* goals, priorities, and the markets. Even with that level of personalized, continuous, life relative advice, you see that all of the portfolios charge less than 0.50% in expenses each year for the management, advising, quarterly goal and portfolio monitoring services offered. This is our company's 401(k), and if our company can offer this high level of service with low expenses to our employees, your company could too! In fact, this portfolio sheet could be useful to you in your effort to fix your 401(k). Look at the S&P500 Index Fund expense for Fidelity Spartan. It is 7 basis points. Is your plan's S&P500 Index Fund charging double, triple, or quadruple that expense for the SAME THING?

Of course, these are just the total investment expenses. Our company's 401(k) has administration costs as well. There are plenty of vendors out there competing to provide the necessary services of record keeping, statements, website, government form filings, etc. Services like these fall into the administration category and will only be disclosed in the Summary Annual Report mentioned in chapter 1. In our company's case, we found a vendor that charges $25 a year per participant with an annual $1,500 company-wide minimum. There are several vendors in that price range and, if your benefits person would like us to refer one to you, have them call our toll-free line (1-866-261-0849) and use the code "Rip-off." With a total plan balance of about $1,800,000 for our plan, this administration cost is about 0.08% a year. Our company pays that for participants, but companies could pass this on to participants if necessary.

Finally, there is a custody charge that is 0.06% a year, because our balance is over $1 million. Our plan administrator absorbs this cost for plans with under $1 million in assets, but in our case, since we are over $1 million, this adds an annual additional cost of $1,080 FOR THE ENTIRE PLAN, not per participant. Our company pays this cost for employees as well, but it could be charged against participant balances if the company chose to do so.

Custody service charges are paid to a bank trust company for keeping track of the securities, collecting dividends, etc.

HOW DO WE KNOW THAT FEES MORE THAN 0.75% ARE TOO HIGH?

Well, we know this because even our small company is paying less. Look through the expenses starting with the model portfolios. Let's look at the WORST CASE EXPENSE with the EMPLOYER PAYING NOTHING:

	Annual Expense
Most Expensive Portfolio Expense Ratio:	0.1621%
Personalized Management, Monitoring & Consultation:	0.3000%
Administration, Record Keeping, Web Site, Gov't Filings, Testing:	0.0800%
Custody (holding the securities in trust):	0.0600%
TOTAL:	0.6021%

This is the MOST you should pay, and with it you should expect a great deal of personalized consultation and service. Now, most companies absorb some or all of the administration and custody costs as our company does. If your company would be willing to pay the $2,500 a year as ours does for those services, your portfolio and advising expenses (your total costs) would drop to 0.46% a year for the most expensive portfolio and 0.39% for the least expensive one.

Finally, if you didn't want the optional continuous monitoring, life goal advice, portfolio management, quarterly consultations, etc., you could create your own portfolios from these funds (just copy the portfolio allocations in your investment selection and make sure you rebalance), and your total expenses would be between about 0.10% and 0.17%.

THIS is why I'm asking you to pay attention to your expenses. To understand what you are paying. To encourage your employer to look for better alternatives like I did for my associates. Have your employer call me if they don't know where to start. It isn't hard to fix the 401(k) plan and make it much better.

If you are paying 0.75%–3.0% a year or more, the price to your lifestyle is huge. Look at the tables that follow and decide whether a little effort on your part might be worth thousands of dollars or years of a better retirement. This is a RIP-OFF that YOU can fix.

Using appendix tables to estimate the price of excess fees in YOUR life

We have calculated the "In Balance" and confidently supported lifestyle for 401(k) participants at various ages, current 401(k) balances, savings rates and broad asset allocation at fair total expenses. Based on that "In Balance" **base case** at fair fee levels of 0.75% a year TOTAL EXPENSE, we then calculated the price to your lifestyle of an excess 0.50% a year in TOTAL 401(k) expenses and of an excess 1.00% yearly in TOTAL 401(k) expenses.

For each scenario we then calculated the following PRICES to your LIFESTYLE of these EXCESS expenses in your 401(k):

"Additional Annual Savings Needed"

This is the additional amount you would need to save EACH YEAR until age 65 to make up for the additional excess expenses you are paying.

"Delay Retirement by This Many Years"

This is how many additional years you would need to work BEYOND age 65 to make up for the additional excess expenses you are paying.

"Reduce Annual Retirement Income By"

This is how much you would need to reduce your annual retirement spending in today's spending power (i.e,. inflation adjusted) to make up for the additional excess expenses you are paying.

"Increased Risk of Outliving Resources"

As we discussed earlier, it may not make sense to needlessly sacrifice your life for a remote risk you can adapt to if unfortunate market results or timing of those results occur. All base case plans are based on accepting this rational balance of sufficiently high confidence, yet avoiding needless sacrifice. Thus, all have some risk of outliving resources if unfortunate markets occur and nothing is done about it. The "Increased Risk of Outliving Resources" shows how much that risk increases due to EXCESS FEES. For example, if the results are 120%, the risk of outliving your money is 2.2 TIMES the risk at lower fee levels. If the results are 55%, the price to the excess fees is 1.55 TIMES the risk at lower fee levels.

"Reduction to Age 65 Portfolio Values"

*This is the price **of excess fees to the size of your retirement fund** at age 65 based on a "likely more than" number and "likely less than" number. You can think of it simply as a range of how much more money you could have at retirement if you were paying more reasonable fees. The "likely more than" number is the value that 95% of the simulations exceeded under the lower cost base case. Thus, there is a very high chance that your excess fees will cost you at least that amount. The "likely less than" number is the 5%-tile result which means you have less than a one in twenty chance of your excess fees costing you more than that figure.*

Using the tables—an example:

First, find the closest combination of your *current* age and *current* 401(k) balance based on the heading of the top of each page.

AGE 25 WITH CURRENT 401(K) BALANCE OF $25,000

Total Annual Savings	$2,500		$5,000	
Allocation: **80% Stock/20% Bonds**				
Base Comfortable "In Balance" Case:				
Maximum Fair Total Expense	0.75%		0.75%	
Retirement Income @ Age 65	$17,600		$29,100	
Age 65 Range of Portfolio Values	$206,292 to $2,313,620		$345,907 to $3,504,041	
EXCESS EXPENSE:	**0.50%**	**1.00%**	**0.50%**	**1.00%**
	(1.25% total)	(1.75% total)	(1.25% total)	(1.75% total)
COST OF EXCESS EXPENSE				
Additional Annual Savings Needed	$800	$1,800	$1,300	$2,900
Delay Retirement by	3 Years	7 Years	3 Years	6 Years
Reduce Annual Retirement Income by	$3,100	$5,700	$4,900	$9,200
Increased Risk of Outliving Resources	54%	100%	51%	99%
Reduction to Age 65 Portfolio Values:				
Likely More than:	$29,893	$56,041	$46,356	$86,285
Likely Less than:	$331,976	$631,328	$482,194	$895,018

Next, find the *column* below that heading that most closely matches your CURRENT total contribution to your 401(k) including BOTH your deferral AND your employer match.

Then, find the section with the asset allocation that most closely matches your long term planned strategic *allocation*.

Finally, find the column that most closely matches your *excess (or total)* expenses.

In the above highlights, we have a 25 year-old, who has around $25,000 in his or her 401(k) whose combined deferrals and matches are near $2,500 a year with an asset allocation that is near 80% stocks and 20% bonds and who is paying an excess fee of 0.50% a year (or 1.25% total).

THE PRICE OF EXCESS FEES:

For this person, we can see that **the price to his or her lifestyle of these excess expenses** versus the base case with more reasonable fees would require *one* of the following to make up for the fees:

Additional Annual Savings Needed: $800 a year
Delay Retirement by This Many Years: 3 years past age 65
Reduce Annual Retirement Income by: $3,100 a year (versus base of $17,600)
Increased Risk of Outliving Resources: 54% (or 1.54 TIMES the risk)
Reduction to Age 65 Portfolio Values: $29,893 to $331,976

APPENDIX A

Table of Contents

Age 25
Current 401(k) Balance: $25,000 107
Current 401(k) Balance: $75,000 109
Current 401(k) Balance: $150,000 111
Current 401(k) Balance: $250,000 113

Age 30
Current 401(k) Balance: $25,000 115
Current 401(k) Balance: $75,000 117
Current 401(k) Balance: $150,000 119
Current 401(k) Balance: $250,000 121

Age 35
Current 401(k) Balance: $25,000 123
Current 401(k) Balance: $75,000 125
Current 401(k) Balance: $150,000 127
Current 401(k) Balance: $250,000 129

Age 40
Current 401(k) Balance: $25,000 131
Current 401(k) Balance: $75,000 133
Current 401(k) Balance: $150,000 135
Current 401(k) Balance: $250,000 137

Age 45
Current 401(k) Balance: $25,000 139
Current 401(k) Balance: $75,000 141
Current 401(k) Balance: $150,000 143
Current 401(k) Balance: $250,000 145

Age 50

Current 401(k) Balance: $25,000 147
Current 401(k) Balance: $75,000 149
Current 401(k) Balance: $150,000 151
Current 401(k) Balance: $250,000 153

Age 55

Current 401(k) Balance: $25,000 155
Current 401(k) Balance: $75,000 157
Current 401(k) Balance: $150,000 159
Current 401(k) Balance: $250,000 161

Age 60

Current 401(k) Balance: $25,000 163
Current 401(k) Balance: $75,000 165
Current 401(k) Balance: $150,000 167
Current 401(k) Balance: $250,000 169

AGE 25 WITH CURRENT 401(K) BALANCE OF $25,000

Total Annual Savings	$2,500		$5,000	
Allocation: **80% Stock/20% Bonds**				
Base Comfortable "In Balance" Case:				
Maximum Fair Total Expense	0.75%		0.75%	
Retirement Income @ Age 65	$17,600		$29,100	
Age 65 Range of Portfolio Values	$206,292 to $2,313,620		$345,907 to $3,504,041	
EXCESS EXPENSE:	**0.50%**	**1.00%**	**0.50%**	**1.00%**
	(1.25% total)	(1.75% total)	(1.25% total)	(1.75% total)
COST OF EXCESS EXPENSE				
Additional Annual Savings Needed	$800	$1,800	$1,300	$2,900
Delay Retirement by	3 Years	7 Years	3 Years	6 Years
Reduce Annual Retirement Income by	$3,100	$5,700	$4,900	$9,200
Increased Risk of Outliving Resources	54%	100%	51%	99%
Reduction to Age 65 Portfolio Values:				
Likely More than:	$29,893	$56,041	$46,356	$86,285
Likely Less than:	$331,976	$631,328	$482,194	$895,018

Allocation: **60% Stock/40% Bonds**				
Base Comfortable "In Balance" Case:				
Maximum Fair Total Expense	0.75%		0.75%	
Retirement Income @ Age 65	$14,200		$23,500	
Age 65 Range of Portfolio Values	$192,515 to $1,343,585		$330,420 to $2,094,401	
EXCESS EXPENSE:	**0.50%**	**1.00%**	**0.50%**	**1.00%**
	(1.25% total)	(1.75% total)	(1.25% total)	(1.75% total)
COST OF EXCESS EXPENSE				
Additional Annual Savings Needed	$900	$1,800	$1,300	$2,700
Delay Retirement by	4 Years	7 Years	3 Years	6 Years
Reduce Annual Retirement Income by	$2,600	$4,700	$4,000	$7,400
Increased Risk of Outliving Resources	57%	121%	52%	116%
Reduction to Age 65 Portfolio Values:				
Likely More than:	$25,859	$47,340	$43,540	$78,542
Likely Less than:	$194,418	$359,874	$266,647	$516,334

Allocation: **45% Stock/55% Bonds**				
Base Comfortable "In Balance" Case:				
Maximum Fair Total Expense	0.75%		0.75%	
Retirement Income @ Age 65	$11,700		$19,800	
Age 65 Range of Portfolio Values	$181,072 to $903,914		$313,423 to $1,431,857	
EXCESS EXPENSE:	**0.50%**	**1.00%**	**0.50%**	**1.00%**
	(1.25% total)	(1.75% total)	(1.25% total)	(1.75% total)
COST OF EXCESS EXPENSE				
Additional Annual Savings Needed	$800	$1,700	$1,300	$2,700
Delay Retirement by	4 Years	7 Years	4 Years	7 Years
Reduce Annual Retirement Income by	$2,100	$3,800	$3,500	$6,300
Increased Risk of Outliving Resources	64%	144%	64%	144%
Reduction to Age 65 Portfolio Values:				
Likely More than:	$23,745	$44,127	$39,029	$71,031
Likely Less than:	$127,260	$235,784	$194,180	$360,522

Total annual savings is COMBINED annual employee AND employer contribution

AGE 25 WITH CURRENT 401(K) BALANCE OF $25,000

Total Annual Savings	$10,000		$15,000	
Allocation: **80% Stock/20% Bonds**				
Base Comfortable "In Balance" Case:				
Maximum Fair Total Expense	0.75%		0.75%	
Retirement Income @ Age 65	$51,700		$74,300	
Age 65 Range of Portfolio Values	$625,209 to $6,004,903		$904,512 to $8,437,812	
EXCESS EXPENSE:	**0.50%**	**1.00%**	**0.50%**	**1.00%**
	(1.25% total)	(1.75% total)	(1.25% total)	(1.75% total)
COST OF EXCESS EXPENSE				
Additional Annual Savings Needed	$2,300	$4,800	$3,200	$6,700
Delay Retirement by	3 Years	6 Years	3 Years	6 Years
Reduce Annual Retirement Income by	$8,500	$15,600	$12,400	$22,000
Increased Risk of Outliving Resources	47%	93%	47%	93%
Reduction to Age 65 Portfolio Values:				
Likely More than:	$77,329	$139,311	$106,239	$200,286
Likely Less than:	$800,589	$1,503,126	$1,152,010	$2,089,466

Allocation: **60% Stock/40% Bonds**				
Base Comfortable "In Balance" Case:				
Maximum Fair Total Expense	0.75%		0.75%	
Retirement Income @ Age 65	$42,500		$61,200	
Age 65 Range of Portfolio Values	$604,462 to $3,655,605		$869,623 to $5,186,829	
EXCESS EXPENSE:	**0.50%**	**1.00%**	**0.50%**	**1.00%**
	(1.25% total)	(1.75% total)	(1.25% total)	(1.75% total)
COST OF EXCESS EXPENSE				
Additional Annual Savings Needed	$2,200	$4,800	$3,100	$6,700
Delay Retirement by	3 Years	6 Years	3 Years	6 Years
Reduce Annual Retirement Income by	$6,900	$12,900	$10,000	$18,100
Increased Risk of Outliving Resources	51%	117%	51%	117%
Reduction to Age 65 Portfolio Values:				
Likely More than:	$76,130	$142,742	$107,075	$197,696
Likely Less than:	$471,163	$889,311	$667,727	$1,232,874

Allocation: **45% Stock/55% Bonds**				
Base Comfortable "In Balance" Case:				
Maximum Fair Total Expense	0.75%		0.75%	
Retirement Income @ Age 65	$35,800		$52,000	
Age 65 Range of Portfolio Values	$574,850 to $2,489,330		$828,360 to $3,544,292	
EXCESS EXPENSE:	**0.50%**	**1.00%**	**0.50%**	**1.00%**
	(1.25% total)	(1.75% total)	(1.25% total)	(1.75% total)
COST OF EXCESS EXPENSE				
Additional Annual Savings Needed	$2,200	$4,800	$3,300	$7,000
Delay Retirement by	3 Years	6 Years	4 Years	6 Years
Reduce Annual Retirement Income by	$5,900	$10,800	$8,700	$15,700
Increased Risk of Outliving Resources	63%	144%	64%	147%
Reduction to Age 65 Portfolio Values:				
Likely More than:	$68,440	$127,571	$91,096	$180,471
Likely Less than:	$317,564	$593,981	$452,844	$825,680

Total annual savings is COMBINED annual employee AND employer contribution

AGE 25 WITH CURRENT 401(K) BALANCE OF $75,000

Total Annual Savings	$2,500		$5,000	
Allocation: **80% Stock/20% Bonds**				
Base Comfortable "In Balance" Case:				
Maximum Fair Total Expense	0.75%		0.75%	
Retirement Income @ Age 65	$29,300		$41,200	
Age 65 Range of Portfolio Values	$329,353 to $4,546,624		$480,207 to $5,757,768	
EXCESS EXPENSE:	**0.50%**	**1.00%**	**0.50%**	**1.00%**
	(1.25% total)	(1.75% total)	(1.25% total)	(1.75% total)
COST OF EXCESS EXPENSE				
Additional Annual Savings Needed	$1,400	$3,000	$1,900	$4,200
Delay Retirement by	4 Years	7 Years	3 Years	7 Years
Reduce Annual Retirement Income by	$5,500	$10,100	$7,600	$13,800
Increased Risk of Outliving Resources	42%	101%	52%	99%
Reduction to Age 65 Portfolio Values:				
Likely More than:	$53,020	$95,768	$75,041	$138,935
Likely Less than:	$707,335	$1,313,590	$888,946	$1,636,250

Allocation: **60% Stock/40% Bonds**				
Base Comfortable "In Balance" Case:				
Maximum Fair Total Expense	0.75%		0.75%	
Retirement Income @ Age 65	$23,300		$33,000	
Age 65 Range of Portfolio Values	$305,795 to $2,591,061		$444,353 to $3,291,666	
EXCESS EXPENSE:	**0.50%**	**1.00%**	**0.50%**	**1.00%**
	(1.25% total)	(1.75% total)	(1.25% total)	(1.75% total)
COST OF EXCESS EXPENSE				
Additional Annual Savings Needed	$1,400	$3,000	$1,900	$4,100
Delay Retirement by	4 Years	7 Years	4 Years	7 Years
Reduce Annual Retirement Income by	$4,500	$8,200	$5,900	$11,000
Increased Risk of Outliving Resources	58%	113%	57%	119%
Reduction to Age 65 Portfolio Values:				
Likely More than:	$47,757	$88,686	$63,119	$119,869
Likely Less than:	$409,231	$753,542	$490,228	$913,381

Allocation: **45% Stock/55% Bonds**				
Base Comfortable "In Balance" Case:				
Maximum Fair Total Expense	0.75%		0.75%	
Retirement Income @ Age 65	$19,000		$26,900	
Age 65 Range of Portfolio Values	$278,245 to $1,667,339		$409,541 to $2,162,271	
EXCESS EXPENSE:	**0.50%**	**1.00%**	**0.50%**	**1.00%**
	(1.25% total)	(1.75% total)	(1.25% total)	(1.75% total)
COST OF EXCESS EXPENSE				
Additional Annual Savings Needed	$1,400	$3,000	$1,800	$3,800
Delay Retirement by	4 Years	8 Years	4 Years	7 Years
Reduce Annual Retirement Income by	$3,800	$6,800	$4,900	$9,000
Increased Risk of Outliving Resources	70%	147%	62%	144%
Reduction to Age 65 Portfolio Values:				
Likely More than:	$44,418	$80,653	$56,738	$105,091
Likely Less than:	$263,799	$482,847	$318,890	$587,846

Total annual savings is COMBINED annual employee AND employer contribution

AGE 25 WITH CURRENT 401(K) BALANCE OF $75,000

Total Annual Savings	$10,000		$15,000	
Allocation: **80% Stock/20% Bonds**				
Base Comfortable "In Balance" Case:				
Maximum Fair Total Expense	0.75%		0.75%	
Retirement Income @ Age 65	$64,600		$87,500	
Age 65 Range of Portfolio Values	$753,791 to $8,164,758		$1,037,477 to $10,511,880	
EXCESS EXPENSE:	**0.50%**	**1.00%**	**0.50%**	**1.00%**
	(1.25% total)	(1.75% total)	(1.25% total)	(1.75% total)
COST OF EXCESS EXPENSE				
Additional Annual Savings Needed	$3,000	$6,500	$3,900	$8,600
Delay Retirement by	3 Years	6 Years	3 Years	6 Years
Reduce Annual Retirement Income by	$11,400	$20,700	$14,900	$27,600
Increased Risk of Outliving Resources	53%	99%	51%	98%
Reduction to Age 65 Portfolio Values:				
Likely More than:	$107,593	$191,862	$139,067	$258,854
Likely Less than:	$1,169,195	$2,190,052	$1,446,580	$2,685,055

Allocation: **60% Stock/40% Bonds**				
Base Comfortable "In Balance" Case:				
Maximum Fair Total Expense	0.75%		0.75%	
Retirement Income @ Age 65	$51,600		$70,700	
Age 65 Range of Portfolio Values	$714,150 to $4,783,691		$991,017 to $6,282,961	
EXCESS EXPENSE:	**0.50%**	**1.00%**	**0.50%**	**1.00%**
	(1.25% total)	(1.75% total)	(1.25% total)	(1.75% total)
COST OF EXCESS EXPENSE				
Additional Annual Savings Needed	$2,800	$6,200	$3,900	$8,100
Delay Retirement by	3 Years	6 Years	3 Years	6 Years
Reduce Annual Retirement Income by	$8,900	$16,400	$12,200	$22,300
Increased Risk of Outliving Resources	51%	117%	52%	115%
Reduction to Age 65 Portfolio Values:				
Likely More than:	$89,603	$169,715	$130,620	$235,626
Likely Less than:	$678,143	$1,247,735	$799,942	$1,549,002

Allocation: **45% Stock/55% Bonds**				
Base Comfortable "In Balance" Case:				
Maximum Fair Total Expense	0.75%		0.75%	
Retirement Income @ Age 65	$42,900		$59,600	
Age 65 Range of Portfolio Values	$678,566 to $3,241,506		$940,026 to $4,295,328	
EXCESS EXPENSE:	**0.50%**	**1.00%**	**0.50%**	**1.00%**
	(1.25% total)	(1.75% total)	(1.25% total)	(1.75% total)
COST OF EXCESS EXPENSE				
Additional Annual Savings Needed	$2,600	$6,000	$3,900	$8,200
Delay Retirement by	4 Years	7 Years	4 Years	7 Years
Reduce Annual Retirement Income by	$7,100	$13,500	$10,500	$19,000
Increased Risk of Outliving Resources	63%	143%	67%	145%
Reduction to Age 65 Portfolio Values:				
Likely More than:	$87,836	$164,001	$117,087	$213,091
Likely Less than:	$450,549	$834,806	$582,539	$1,081,567

Total annual savings is COMBINED annual employee AND employer contribution

AGE 25 WITH CURRENT 401(K) BALANCE OF $150,000

Total Annual Savings	\$2,500		\$5,000	
Allocation: **80% Stock/20% Bonds**				
Base Comfortable "In Balance" Case:				
Maximum Fair Total Expense	0.75%		0.75%	
Retirement Income @ Age 65	\$47,400		\$58,700	
Age 65 Range of Portfolio Values	\$522,295 to \$7,928,625		\$658,584 to \$9,093,127	
EXCESS EXPENSE:	**0.50%**	**1.00%**	**0.50%**	**1.00%**
	(1.25% total)	(1.75% total)	(1.25% total)	(1.75% total)
COST OF EXCESS EXPENSE				
Additional Annual Savings Needed	\$2,400	\$5,300	\$2,800	\$6,100
Delay Retirement by	4 Years	8 Years	4 Years	7 Years
Reduce Annual Retirement Income by	\$9,500	\$17,300	\$11,100	\$20,200
Increased Risk of Outliving Resources	45%	99%	42%	101%
Reduction to Age 65 Portfolio Values:				
Likely More than:	\$93,767	\$171,858	\$106,039	\$191,535
Likely Less than:	\$1,291,370	\$2,375,254	\$1,414,670	\$2,627,181

Allocation: **60% Stock/40% Bonds**				
Base Comfortable "In Balance" Case:				
Maximum Fair Total Expense	0.75%		0.75%	
Retirement Income @ Age 65	\$36,900		\$46,600	
Age 65 Range of Portfolio Values	\$478,335 to \$4,325,362		\$611,591 to \$5,182,122	
EXCESS EXPENSE:	**0.50%**	**1.00%**	**0.50%**	**1.00%**
	(1.25% total)	(1.75% total)	(1.25% total)	(1.75% total)
COST OF EXCESS EXPENSE				
Additional Annual Savings Needed	\$2,300	\$4,900	\$2,700	\$6,000
Delay Retirement by	4 Years	8 Years	4 Years	7 Years
Reduce Annual Retirement Income by	\$7,400	\$13,400	\$8,900	\$16,400
Increased Risk of Outliving Resources	63%	120%	58%	113%
Reduction to Age 65 Portfolio Values:				
Likely More than:	\$82,356	\$148,845	\$95,515	\$177,372
Likely Less than:	\$701,692	\$1,290,860	\$818,463	\$1,507,085

Allocation: **45% Stock/55% Bonds**				
Base Comfortable "In Balance" Case:				
Maximum Fair Total Expense	0.75%		0.75%	
Retirement Income @ Age 65	\$29,900		\$38,000	
Age 65 Range of Portfolio Values	\$421,331 to \$2,825,736		\$556,489 to \$3,334,679	
EXCESS EXPENSE:	**0.50%**	**1.00%**	**0.50%**	**1.00%**
	(1.25% total)	(1.75% total)	(1.25% total)	(1.75% total)
COST OF EXCESS EXPENSE				
Additional Annual Savings Needed	\$2,200	\$4,900	\$2,800	\$5,900
Delay Retirement by	5 Years	9 Years	4 Years	8 Years
Reduce Annual Retirement Income by	\$6,000	\$11,100	\$7,500	\$13,600
Increased Risk of Outliving Resources	69%	153%	70%	147%
Reduction to Age 65 Portfolio Values:				
Likely More than:	\$72,379	\$131,417	\$88,834	\$161,304
Likely Less than:	\$466,888	\$853,788	\$527,599	\$965,695

Total annual savings is COMBINED annual employee AND employer contribution

AGE 25 WITH CURRENT 401(K) BALANCE OF $150,000

Total Annual Savings	$10,000		$15,000	
Allocation: **80% Stock/20% Bonds**				
Base Comfortable "In Balance" Case:				
Maximum Fair Total Expense	0.75%		0.75%	
Retirement Income @ Age 65	$82,500		$106,100	
Age 65 Range of Portfolio Values	$960,293 to $11,515,415		$1,237,144 to $13,881,116	
EXCESS EXPENSE:	**0.50%**	**1.00%**	**0.50%**	**1.00%**
	(1.25% total)	(1.75% total)	(1.25% total)	(1.75% total)
COST OF EXCESS EXPENSE				
Additional Annual Savings Needed	$3,800	$8,300	$4,900	$10,600
Delay Retirement by	3 Years	7 Years	3 Years	7 Years
Reduce Annual Retirement Income by	$15,200	$27,600	$18,900	$34,600
Increased Risk of Outliving Resources	52%	100%	51%	95%
Reduction to Age 65 Portfolio Values:				
Likely More than:	$150,082	$277,870	$179,356	$336,246
Likely Less than:	$1,777,893	$3,272,501	$1,991,857	$3,787,973

Allocation: **60% Stock/40% Bonds**				
Base Comfortable "In Balance" Case:				
Maximum Fair Total Expense	0.75%		0.75%	
Retirement Income @ Age 65	$66,100		$85,200	
Age 65 Range of Portfolio Values	$888,584 to $6,583,211		$1,155,089 to $8,061,512	
EXCESS EXPENSE:	**0.50%**	**1.00%**	**0.50%**	**1.00%**
	(1.25% total)	(1.75% total)	(1.25% total)	(1.75% total)
COST OF EXCESS EXPENSE				
Additional Annual Savings Needed	$3,800	$8,200	$4,900	$10,600
Delay Retirement by	4 Years	7 Years	4 Years	7 Years
Reduce Annual Retirement Income by	$11,900	$22,100	$15,600	$28,100
Increased Risk of Outliving Resources	58%	120%	57%	121%
Reduction to Age 65 Portfolio Values:				
Likely More than:	$126,237	$239,738	$155,155	$284,041
Likely Less than:	$980,457	$1,826,762	$1,166,509	$2,159,243

Allocation: **45% Stock/55% Bonds**				
Base Comfortable "In Balance" Case:				
Maximum Fair Total Expense	0.75%		0.75%	
Retirement Income @ Age 65	$53,900		$70,200	
Age 65 Range of Portfolio Values	$818,961 to $4,324,420		$1,086,434 to $5,423,481	
EXCESS EXPENSE:	**0.50%**	**1.00%**	**0.50%**	**1.00%**
	(1.25% total)	(1.75% total)	(1.25% total)	(1.75% total)
COST OF EXCESS EXPENSE				
Additional Annual Savings Needed	$3,600	$7,600	$4,500	$10,000
Delay Retirement by	4 Years	7 Years	4 Years	7 Years
Reduce Annual Retirement Income by	$9,900	$18,000	$12,500	$22,600
Increased Risk of Outliving Resources	63%	146%	64%	144%
Reduction to Age 65 Portfolio Values:				
Likely More than:	$113,477	$210,183	$142,473	$264,764
Likely Less than:	$637,780	$1,175,691	$763,554	$1,414,700

Total annual savings is COMBINED annual employee AND employer contribution

AGE 25 WITH CURRENT 401(K) BALANCE OF $250,000

Total Annual Savings	$2,500		$5,000	
Allocation: **80% Stock/20% Bonds**				
Base Comfortable "In Balance" Case:				
Maximum Fair Total Expense	0.75%		0.75%	
Retirement Income @ Age 65	$71,300		$83,000	
Age 65 Range of Portfolio Values	$770,592 to $12,493,600		$910,292 to $13,620,231	
EXCESS EXPENSE:	**0.50%**	**1.00%**	**0.50%**	**1.00%**
	(1.25% total)	(1.75% total)	(1.25% total)	(1.75% total)
COST OF EXCESS EXPENSE				
Additional Annual Savings Needed	$3,900	$8,000	$4,200	$9,000
Delay Retirement by	5 Years	8 Years	4 Years	8 Years
Reduce Annual Retirement Income by	$14,800	$26,600	$16,600	$30,400
Increased Risk of Outliving Resources	48%	98%	45%	99%
Reduction to Age 65 Portfolio Values:				
Likely More than:	$139,899	$257,090	$161,078	$287,534
Likely Less than:	$2,074,700	$3,812,480	$2,192,824	$4,048,204

Allocation: **60% Stock/40% Bonds**				
Base Comfortable "In Balance" Case:				
Maximum Fair Total Expense	0.75%		0.75%	
Retirement Income @ Age 65	$55,500		$65,000	
Age 65 Range of Portfolio Values	$695,289 to $6,803,729		$842,549 to $7,498,294	
EXCESS EXPENSE:	**0.50%**	**1.00%**	**0.50%**	**1.00%**
	(1.25% total)	(1.75% total)	(1.25% total)	(1.75% total)
COST OF EXCESS EXPENSE				
Additional Annual Savings Needed	$3,600	$7,600	$4,000	$8,500
Delay Retirement by	5 Years	8 Years	4 Years	8 Years
Reduce Annual Retirement Income by	$11,800	$21,100	$13,000	$23,900
Increased Risk of Outliving Resources	60%	119%	60%	117%
Reduction to Age 65 Portfolio Values:				
Likely More than:	$125,646	$227,154	$143,720	$259,787
Likely Less than:	$1,133,117	$2,083,959	$1,206,522	$2,220,636

Allocation: **45% Stock/55% Bonds**				
Base Comfortable "In Balance" Case:				
Maximum Fair Total Expense	0.75%		0.75%	
Retirement Income @ Age 65	$44,500		$52,600	
Age 65 Range of Portfolio Values	$614,540 to $4,343,084		$741,933 to $4,875,627	
EXCESS EXPENSE:	**0.50%**	**1.00%**	**0.50%**	**1.00%**
	(1.25% total)	(1.75% total)	(1.25% total)	(1.75% total)
COST OF EXCESS EXPENSE				
Additional Annual Savings Needed	$3,500	$7,700	$4,000	$8,500
Delay Retirement by	5 Years	9 Years	5 Years	8 Years
Reduce Annual Retirement Income by	$9,500	$17,000	$11,000	$19,300
Increased Risk of Outliving Resources	70%	150%	70%	152%
Reduction to Age 65 Portfolio Values:				
Likely More than:	$106,715	$198,880	$122,466	$222,605
Likely Less than:	$718,194	$1,319,017	$797,094	$1,478,844

Total annual savings is COMBINED annual employee AND employer contribution

AGE 25 WITH CURRENT 401(K) BALANCE OF $250,000

Total Annual Savings	$10,000		$15,000	
Allocation: **80% Stock/20% Bonds**				
Base Comfortable "In Balance" Case:				
Maximum Fair Total Expense	0.75%		0.75%	
Retirement Income @ Age 65	$106,300		$130,000	
Age 65 Range of Portfolio Values	$1,203,895 to $16,024,098		$1,507,347 to $18,444,190	
EXCESS EXPENSE:	0.50%	1.00%	0.50%	1.00%
	(1.25% total)	(1.75% total)	(1.25% total)	(1.75% total)
COST OF EXCESS EXPENSE				
Additional Annual Savings Needed	$5,200	$10,900	$6,100	$13,200
Delay Retirement by	4 Years	7 Years	4 Years	7 Years
Reduce Annual Retirement Income by	$20,000	$36,400	$24,300	$44,000
Increased Risk of Outliving Resources	46%	101%	52%	101%
Reduction to Age 65 Portfolio Values:				
Likely More than:	$181,416	$344,106	$231,947	$438,400
Likely Less than:	$2,527,816	$4,650,350	$2,854,169	$5,231,528

Allocation: **60% Stock/40% Bonds**				
Base Comfortable "In Balance" Case:				
Maximum Fair Total Expense	0.75%		0.75%	
Retirement Income @ Age 65	$84,200		$103,800	
Age 65 Range of Portfolio Values	$1,113,314 to $9,106,001		$1,386,429 to $10,514,590	
EXCESS EXPENSE:	0.50%	1.00%	0.50%	1.00%
	(1.25% total)	(1.75% total)	(1.25% total)	(1.75% total)
COST OF EXCESS EXPENSE				
Additional Annual Savings Needed	$4,800	$10,700	$6,000	$13,200
Delay Retirement by	4 Years	7 Years	4 Years	7 Years
Reduce Annual Retirement Income by	$16,000	$28,900	$19,100	$34,500
Increased Risk of Outliving Resources	60%	114%	59%	119%
Reduction to Age 65 Portfolio Values:				
Likely More than:	$176,241	$322,295	$200,777	$371,604
Likely Less than:	$1,419,624	$2,608,996	$1,622,791	$2,961,948

Allocation: **45% Stock/55% Bonds**				
Base Comfortable "In Balance" Case:				
Maximum Fair Total Expense	0.75%		0.75%	
Retirement Income @ Age 65	$67,900		$84,400	
Age 65 Range of Portfolio Values	$1,008,548 to $5,918,179		$1,275,778 to $6,850,442	
EXCESS EXPENSE:	0.50%	1.00%	0.50%	1.00%
	(1.25% total)	(1.75% total)	(1.25% total)	(1.75% total)
COST OF EXCESS EXPENSE				
Additional Annual Savings Needed	$4,600	$10,100	$5,500	$12,100
Delay Retirement by	4 Years	8 Years	4 Years	7 Years
Reduce Annual Retirement Income by	$13,300	$23,900	$15,400	$28,400
Increased Risk of Outliving Resources	67%	143%	64%	144%
Reduction to Age 65 Portfolio Values:				
Likely More than:	$157,507	$280,877	$179,442	$332,111
Likely Less than:	$919,550	$1,707,665	$1,030,471	$1,884,456

Total annual savings is COMBINED annual employee AND employer contribution

AGE 30 WITH CURRENT 401(K) BALANCE OF $25,000

Total Annual Savings	$2,500		$5,000	
Allocation: **80% Stock/20% Bonds**				
Base Comfortable "In Balance" Case:				
Maximum Fair Total Expense	0.75%		0.75%	
Retirement Income @ Age 65	$13,300		$21,400	
Age 65 Range of Portfolio Values	$160,661 to $1,384,456		$273,252 to $2,113,527	
EXCESS EXPENSE:	**0.50%**	**1.00%**	**0.50%**	**1.00%**
	(1.25% total)	(1.75% total)	(1.25% total)	(1.75% total)
COST OF EXCESS EXPENSE				
Additional Annual Savings Needed	$800	$1,600	$1,100	$2,400
Delay Retirement by	3 Years	6 Years	3 Years	5 Years
Reduce Annual Retirement Income by	$2,300	$4,100	$3,200	$6,000
Increased Risk of Outliving Resources	39%	91%	38%	92%
Reduction to Age 65 Portfolio Values:				
Likely More than:	$19,886	$36,449	$30,505	$56,390
Likely Less than:	$183,101	$341,576	$247,554	$475,984

Allocation: **60% Stock/40% Bonds**				
Base Comfortable "In Balance" Case:				
Maximum Fair Total Expense	0.75%		0.75%	
Retirement Income @ Age 65	$11,200		$18,500	
Age 65 Range of Portfolio Values	$157,646 to $896,444		$269,266 to $1,387,361	
EXCESS EXPENSE:	**0.50%**	**1.00%**	**0.50%**	**1.00%**
	(1.25% total)	(1.75% total)	(1.25% total)	(1.75% total)
COST OF EXCESS EXPENSE				
Additional Annual Savings Needed	$700	$1,600	$1,200	$2,500
Delay Retirement by	3 Years	6 Years	3 Years	6 Years
Reduce Annual Retirement Income by	$1,800	$3,300	$2,900	$5,300
Increased Risk of Outliving Resources	60%	120%	57%	118%
Reduction to Age 65 Portfolio Values:				
Likely More than:	$18,917	$35,312	$31,155	$57,638
Likely Less than:	$114,046	$212,993	$165,908	$309,354

Allocation: **45% Stock/55% Bonds**				
Base Comfortable "In Balance" Case:				
Maximum Fair Total Expense	0.75%		0.75%	
Retirement Income @ Age 65	$9,500		$15,900	
Age 65 Range of Portfolio Values	$150,316 to $653,618		$258,564 to $1,025,987	
EXCESS EXPENSE:	**0.50%**	**1.00%**	**0.50%**	**1.00%**
	(1.25% total)	(1.75% total)	(1.25% total)	(1.75% total)
COST OF EXCESS EXPENSE				
Additional Annual Savings Needed	$800	$1,600	$1,200	$2,500
Delay Retirement by	3 Years	6 Years	3 Years	6 Years
Reduce Annual Retirement Income by	$1,600	$2,900	$2,500	$4,700
Increased Risk of Outliving Resources	72%	154%	72%	151%
Reduction to Age 65 Portfolio Values:				
Likely More than:	$17,526	$32,943	$28,302	$52,504
Likely Less than:	$83,188	$154,121	$120,998	$228,658

Total annual savings is COMBINED annual employee AND employer contribution

AGE 30 WITH CURRENT 401(K) BALANCE OF $25,000

Total Annual Savings	$10,000		$15,000	
Allocation: **80% Stock/20% Bonds**				
Base Comfortable "In Balance" Case:				
Maximum Fair Total Expense	0.75%		0.75%	
Retirement Income @ Age 65	$38,600		$54,800	
Age 65 Range of Portfolio Values	$498,867 to $3,541,208		$729,957 to $4,924,284	
EXCESS EXPENSE:	**0.50%**	**1.00%**	**0.50%**	**1.00%**
	(1.25% total)	(1.75% total)	(1.25% total)	(1.75% total)
COST OF EXCESS EXPENSE				
Additional Annual Savings Needed	$2,100	$4,400	$2,800	$5,900
Delay Retirement by	3 Years	5 Years	2 Years	5 Years
Reduce Annual Retirement Income by	$6,100	$10,800	$7,900	$14,800
Increased Risk of Outliving Resources	37%	92%	33%	88%
Reduction to Age 65 Portfolio Values:				
Likely More than:	$52,177	$97,920	$74,974	$143,711
Likely Less than:	$426,752	$800,276	$569,085	$1,069,087

Allocation: **60% Stock/40% Bonds**				
Base Comfortable "In Balance" Case:				
Maximum Fair Total Expense	0.75%		0.75%	
Retirement Income @ Age 65	$33,100		$47,300	
Age 65 Range of Portfolio Values	$486,473 to $2,407,034		$710,602 to $3,395,754	
EXCESS EXPENSE:	**0.50%**	**1.00%**	**0.50%**	**1.00%**
	(1.25% total)	(1.75% total)	(1.25% total)	(1.75% total)
COST OF EXCESS EXPENSE				
Additional Annual Savings Needed	$2,000	$4,300	$2,800	$6,000
Delay Retirement by	3 Years	5 Years	3 Years	5 Years
Reduce Annual Retirement Income by	$5,000	$9,200	$6,900	$12,800
Increased Risk of Outliving Resources	52%	118%	50%	117%
Reduction to Age 65 Portfolio Values:				
Likely More than:	$50,597	$95,781	$73,282	$135,732
Likely Less than:	$278,421	$528,033	$385,440	$712,196

Allocation: **45% Stock/55% Bonds**				
Base Comfortable "In Balance" Case:				
Maximum Fair Total Expense	0.75%		0.75%	
Retirement Income @ Age 65	$28,300		$41,100	
Age 65 Range of Portfolio Values	$471,934 to $1,770,271		$682,500 to $2,513,084	
EXCESS EXPENSE:	**0.50%**	**1.00%**	**0.50%**	**1.00%**
	(1.25% total)	(1.75% total)	(1.25% total)	(1.75% total)
COST OF EXCESS EXPENSE				
Additional Annual Savings Needed	$2,000	$4,200	$2,900	$6,100
Delay Retirement by	3 Years	6 Years	3 Years	6 Years
Reduce Annual Retirement Income by	$4,200	$7,800	$6,300	$11,300
Increased Risk of Outliving Resources	66%	152%	64%	147%
Reduction to Age 65 Portfolio Values:				
Likely More than:	$49,352	$93,465	$68,422	$131,289
Likely Less than:	$199,800	$377,163	$278,498	$532,604

Total annual savings is COMBINED annual employee AND employer contribution

AGE 30 WITH CURRENT 401(K) BALANCE OF $75,000

Total Annual Savings	$2,500		$5,000	
Allocation: **80% Stock/20% Bonds**				
Base Comfortable "In Balance" Case:				
Maximum Fair Total Expense	0.75%		0.75%	
Retirement Income @ Age 65	$23,100		$31,700	
Age 65 Range of Portfolio Values	$260,848 to $2,752,331		$373,077 to $3,454,180	
EXCESS EXPENSE:	**0.50%**	**1.00%**	**0.50%**	**1.00%**
	(1.25% total)	(1.75% total)	(1.25% total)	(1.75% total)
COST OF EXCESS EXPENSE				
Additional Annual Savings Needed	$1,400	$3,000	$1,900	$4,100
Delay Retirement by	4 Years	7 Years	3 Years	6 Years
Reduce Annual Retirement Income by	$4,100	$7,500	$5,500	$10,100
Increased Risk of Outliving Resources	49%	96%	47%	95%
Reduction to Age 65 Portfolio Values:				
Likely More than:	$37,489	$69,721	$48,085	$87,362
Likely Less than:	$387,247	$720,505	$458,735	$855,777

Allocation: **60% Stock/40% Bonds**				
Base Comfortable "In Balance" Case:				
Maximum Fair Total Expense	0.75%		0.75%	
Retirement Income @ Age 65	$18,800		$26,500	
Age 65 Range of Portfolio Values	$245,613 to $1,689,162		$361,492 to $2,200,207	
EXCESS EXPENSE:	**0.50%**	**1.00%**	**0.50%**	**1.00%**
	(1.25% total)	(1.75% total)	(1.25% total)	(1.75% total)
COST OF EXCESS EXPENSE				
Additional Annual Savings Needed	$1,300	$2,800	$1,800	$3,800
Delay Retirement by	3 Years	7 Years	3 Years	7 Years
Reduce Annual Retirement Income by	$3,200	$6,000	$4,500	$8,200
Increased Risk of Outliving Resources	62%	121%	64%	123%
Reduction to Age 65 Portfolio Values:				
Likely More than:	$34,025	$62,230	$48,108	$85,836
Likely Less than:	$237,817	$441,134	$287,814	$539,275

Allocation: **45% Stock/55% Bonds**				
Base Comfortable "In Balance" Case:				
Maximum Fair Total Expense	0.75%		0.75%	
Retirement Income @ Age 65	$15,700		$22,200	
Age 65 Range of Portfolio Values	$235,547 to $1,201,429		$345,310 to $1,582,025	
EXCESS EXPENSE:	**0.50%**	**1.00%**	**0.50%**	**1.00%**
	(1.25% total)	(1.75% total)	(1.25% total)	(1.75% total)
COST OF EXCESS EXPENSE				
Additional Annual Savings Needed	$1,300	$2,700	$1,800	$3,800
Delay Retirement by	4 Years	7 Years	4 Years	7 Years
Reduce Annual Retirement Income by	$2,900	$5,200	$3,800	$6,900
Increased Risk of Outliving Resources	73%	156%	77%	160%
Reduction to Age 65 Portfolio Values:				
Likely More than:	$31,627	$58,990	$43,428	$81,093
Likely Less than:	$167,763	$312,058	$206,511	$385,633

Total annual savings is COMBINED annual employee AND employer contribution

AGE 30 WITH CURRENT 401(K) BALANCE OF $75,000

Total Annual Savings	$10,000		$15,000	
Allocation: **80% Stock/20% Bonds**				
Base Comfortable "In Balance" Case:				
Maximum Fair Total Expense	0.75%		0.75%	
Retirement Income @ Age 65	$47,900		$64,400	
Age 65 Range of Portfolio Values	$591,738 to $4,850,275		$819,514 to $6,340,339	
EXCESS EXPENSE:	**0.50%**	**1.00%**	**0.50%**	**1.00%**
	(1.25% total)	(1.75% total)	(1.25% total)	(1.75% total)
COST OF EXCESS EXPENSE				
Additional Annual Savings Needed	$2,700	$5,700	$3,400	$7,300
Delay Retirement by	3 Years	5 Years	3 Years	5 Years
Reduce Annual Retirement Income by	$7,500	$13,900	$9,600	$18,100
Increased Risk of Outliving Resources	38%	90%	37%	92%
Reduction to Age 65 Portfolio Values:				
Likely More than:	$67,379	$126,331	$91,517	$169,172
Likely Less than:	$593,782	$1,124,070	$742,664	$1,427,952

Allocation: **60% Stock/40% Bonds**				
Base Comfortable "In Balance" Case:				
Maximum Fair Total Expense	0.75%		0.75%	
Retirement Income @ Age 65	$41,100		$55,600	
Age 65 Range of Portfolio Values	$587,279 to $3,192,618		$807,677 to $4,161,960	
EXCESS EXPENSE:	**0.50%**	**1.00%**	**0.50%**	**1.00%**
	(1.25% total)	(1.75% total)	(1.25% total)	(1.75% total)
COST OF EXCESS EXPENSE				
Additional Annual Savings Needed	$2,700	$5,600	$3,400	$7,500
Delay Retirement by	3 Years	6 Years	3 Years	6 Years
Reduce Annual Retirement Income by	$6,500	$12,200	$8,600	$16,000
Increased Risk of Outliving Resources	63%	120%	57%	117%
Reduction to Age 65 Portfolio Values:				
Likely More than:	$68,801	$130,085	$93,465	$172,915
Likely Less than:	$400,036	$747,275	$497,721	$928,061

Allocation: **45% Stock/55% Bonds**				
Base Comfortable "In Balance" Case:				
Maximum Fair Total Expense	0.75%		0.75%	
Retirement Income @ Age 65	$34,900		$47,800	
Age 65 Range of Portfolio Values	$560,759 to $2,334,584		$775,572 to $3,077,839	
EXCESS EXPENSE:	**0.50%**	**1.00%**	**0.50%**	**1.00%**
	(1.25% total)	(1.75% total)	(1.25% total)	(1.75% total)
COST OF EXCESS EXPENSE				
Additional Annual Savings Needed	$2,600	$5,500	$3,500	$7,600
Delay Retirement by	3 Years	6 Years	3 Years	6 Years
Reduce Annual Retirement Income by	$5,600	$10,400	$7,500	$14,000
Increased Risk of Outliving Resources	71%	154%	72%	151%
Reduction to Age 65 Portfolio Values:				
Likely More than:	$63,355	$118,859	$84,906	$157,512
Likely Less than:	$289,652	$541,800	$362,992	$685,973

Total annual savings is COMBINED annual employee AND employer contribution

AGE 30 WITH CURRENT 401(K) BALANCE OF $150,000

Total Annual Savings	$2,500		$5,000	
Allocation: **80% Stock/20% Bonds**				
Base Comfortable "In Balance" Case:				
Maximum Fair Total Expense	0.75%		0.75%	
Retirement Income @ Age 65	$36,700		$46,200	
Age 65 Range of Portfolio Values	$410,117 to $4,828,576		$521,696 to $5,504,662	
EXCESS EXPENSE:	**0.50%**	**1.00%**	**0.50%**	**1.00%**
	(1.25% total)	(1.75% total)	(1.25% total)	(1.75% total)
COST OF EXCESS EXPENSE				
Additional Annual Savings Needed	$2,000	$4,700	$2,800	$6,000
Delay Retirement by	4 Years	7 Years	4 Years	7 Years
Reduce Annual Retirement Income by	$6,800	$12,200	$8,200	$14,900
Increased Risk of Outliving Resources	41%	96%	49%	96%
Reduction to Age 65 Portfolio Values:				
Likely More than:	$62,964	$119,357	$74,977	$139,441
Likely Less than:	$698,678	$1,297,631	$774,494	$1,441,010

Allocation: **60% Stock/40% Bonds**				
Base Comfortable "In Balance" Case:				
Maximum Fair Total Expense	0.75%		0.75%	
Retirement Income @ Age 65	$30,200		$37,700	
Age 65 Range of Portfolio Values	$385,243 to $2,909,969		$491,105 to $3,378,203	
EXCESS EXPENSE:	**0.50%**	**1.00%**	**0.50%**	**1.00%**
	(1.25% total)	(1.75% total)	(1.25% total)	(1.75% total)
COST OF EXCESS EXPENSE				
Additional Annual Savings Needed	$2,200	$4,500	$2,500	$5,500
Delay Retirement by	4 Years	8 Years	4 Years	7 Years
Reduce Annual Retirement Income by	$5,700	$10,400	$6,400	$12,100
Increased Risk of Outliving Resources	57%	120%	60%	120%
Reduction to Age 65 Portfolio Values:				
Likely More than:	$56,104	$106,838	$68,050	$124,460
Likely Less than:	$425,323	$789,534	$475,634	$882,268

Allocation: **45% Stock/55% Bonds**				
Base Comfortable "In Balance" Case:				
Maximum Fair Total Expense	0.75%		0.75%	
Retirement Income @ Age 65	$24,900		$31,400	
Age 65 Range of Portfolio Values	$361,014 to $2,061,452		$471,094 to $2,402,857	
EXCESS EXPENSE:	**0.50%**	**1.00%**	**0.50%**	**1.00%**
	(1.25% total)	(1.75% total)	(1.25% total)	(1.75% total)
COST OF EXCESS EXPENSE				
Additional Annual Savings Needed	$2,100	$4,400	$2,500	$5,400
Delay Retirement by	4 Years	8 Years	4 Years	7 Years
Reduce Annual Retirement Income by	$4,600	$8,500	$5,700	$10,300
Increased Risk of Outliving Resources	75%	156%	73%	156%
Reduction to Age 65 Portfolio Values:				
Likely More than:	$52,753	$97,523	$63,253	$117,981
Likely Less than:	$301,849	$560,114	$335,525	$624,114

Total annual savings is COMBINED annual employee AND employer contribution

AGE 30 WITH CURRENT 401(K) BALANCE OF $150,000

Total Annual Savings	$10,000		$15,000	
Allocation: **80% Stock/20% Bonds**				
Base Comfortable "In Balance" Case:				
Maximum Fair Total Expense	0.75%		0.75%	
Retirement Income @ Age 65	$63,400		$80,000	
Age 65 Range of Portfolio Values	$746,154 to $6,908,359		$963,723 to $8,306,496	
EXCESS EXPENSE:	**0.50%**	**1.00%**	**0.50%**	**1.00%**
	(1.25% total)	(1.75% total)	(1.25% total)	(1.75% total)
COST OF EXCESS EXPENSE				
Additional Annual Savings Needed	$3,800	$8,100	$4,700	$9,700
Delay Retirement by	3 Years	6 Years	3 Years	6 Years
Reduce Annual Retirement Income by	$11,000	$20,100	$13,500	$24,300
Increased Risk of Outliving Resources	47%	95%	40%	92%
Reduction to Age 65 Portfolio Values:				
Likely More than:	$96,171	$174,724	$119,316	$218,693
Likely Less than:	$917,468	$1,711,553	$1,098,608	$2,049,457

Allocation: **60% Stock/40% Bonds**				
Base Comfortable "In Balance" Case:				
Maximum Fair Total Expense	0.75%		0.75%	
Retirement Income @ Age 65	$53,100		$67,400	
Age 65 Range of Portfolio Values	$722,862 to $4,400,293		$945,636 to $5,378,419	
EXCESS EXPENSE:	**0.50%**	**1.00%**	**0.50%**	**1.00%**
	(1.25% total)	(1.75% total)	(1.25% total)	(1.75% total)
COST OF EXCESS EXPENSE				
Additional Annual Savings Needed	$3,500	$7,600	$4,300	$9,200
Delay Retirement by	3 Years	7 Years	3 Years	6 Years
Reduce Annual Retirement Income by	$9,100	$16,500	$10,900	$19,900
Increased Risk of Outliving Resources	64%	123%	59%	119%
Reduction to Age 65 Portfolio Values:				
Likely More than:	$96,215	$171,672	$113,507	$211,877
Likely Less than:	$575,628	$1,078,550	$684,271	$1,277,954

Allocation: **45% Stock/55% Bonds**				
Base Comfortable "In Balance" Case:				
Maximum Fair Total Expense	0.75%		0.75%	
Retirement Income @ Age 65	$44,500		$57,100	
Age 65 Range of Portfolio Values	$690,498 to $3,163,928		$901,777 to $3,921,586	
EXCESS EXPENSE:	**0.50%**	**1.00%**	**0.50%**	**1.00%**
	(1.25% total)	(1.75% total)	(1.25% total)	(1.75% total)
COST OF EXCESS EXPENSE				
Additional Annual Savings Needed	$3,600	$7,500	$4,300	$9,200
Delay Retirement by	4 Years	7 Years	3 Years	6 Years
Reduce Annual Retirement Income by	$7,600	$13,900	$9,500	$17,300
Increased Risk of Outliving Resources	77%	160%	72%	153%
Reduction to Age 65 Portfolio Values:				
Likely More than:	$86,855	$162,186	$105,161	$197,659
Likely Less than:	$413,021	$771,266	$499,127	$924,725

Total annual savings is COMBINED annual employee AND employer contribution

AGE 30 WITH CURRENT 401(K) BALANCE OF $250,000

Total Annual Savings	$2,500		$5,000	
Allocation: **80% Stock/20% Bonds**				
Base Comfortable "In Balance" Case:				
Maximum Fair Total Expense	0.75%		0.75%	
Retirement Income @ Age 65	$54,800		$64,400	
Age 65 Range of Portfolio Values	$606,654 to $7,595,338		$717,876 to $8,271,991	
EXCESS EXPENSE:	**0.50%**	**1.00%**	**0.50%**	**1.00%**
	(1.25% total)	(1.75% total)	(1.25% total)	(1.75% total)
COST OF EXCESS EXPENSE				
Additional Annual Savings Needed	$3,100	$6,700	$3,600	$8,200
Delay Retirement by	4 Years	7 Years	3 Years	7 Years
Reduce Annual Retirement Income by	$10,500	$18,900	$11,700	$21,500
Increased Risk of Outliving Resources	40%	92%	41%	97%
Reduction to Age 65 Portfolio Values:				
Likely More than:	$99,482	$184,172	$106,430	$201,535
Likely Less than:	$1,112,313	$2,065,527	$1,189,480	$2,219,101

Allocation: **60% Stock/40% Bonds**				
Base Comfortable "In Balance" Case:				
Maximum Fair Total Expense	0.75%		0.75%	
Retirement Income @ Age 65	$45,000		$53,000	
Age 65 Range of Portfolio Values	$564,738 to $4,528,970		$680,688 to $5,005,689	
EXCESS EXPENSE:	**0.50%**	**1.00%**	**0.50%**	**1.00%**
	(1.25% total)	(1.75% total)	(1.25% total)	(1.75% total)
COST OF EXCESS EXPENSE				
Additional Annual Savings Needed	$3,200	$6,800	$3,600	$7,700
Delay Retirement by	4 Years	8 Years	4 Years	7 Years
Reduce Annual Retirement Income by	$8,700	$15,800	$9,900	$17,800
Increased Risk of Outliving Resources	53%	117%	60%	121%
Reduction to Age 65 Portfolio Values:				
Likely More than:	$90,563	$167,508	$102,414	$189,840
Likely Less than:	$676,019	$1,253,925	$726,416	$1,348,903

Allocation: **45% Stock/55% Bonds**				
Base Comfortable "In Balance" Case:				
Maximum Fair Total Expense	0.75%		0.75%	
Retirement Income @ Age 65	$37,100		$43,800	
Age 65 Range of Portfolio Values	$527,191 to $3,211,588		$641,518 to $3,544,082	
EXCESS EXPENSE:	**0.50%**	**1.00%**	**0.50%**	**1.00%**
	(1.25% total)	(1.75% total)	(1.25% total)	(1.75% total)
COST OF EXCESS EXPENSE				
Additional Annual Savings Needed	$3,200	$6,900	$3,700	$7,700
Delay Retirement by	4 Years	8 Years	4 Years	8 Years
Reduce Annual Retirement Income by	$7,200	$13,000	$8,400	$14,900
Increased Risk of Outliving Resources	74%	154%	77%	160%
Reduction to Age 65 Portfolio Values:				
Likely More than:	$83,347	$152,147	$96,219	$176,307
Likely Less than:	$476,095	$883,008	$508,916	$948,168

Total annual savings is COMBINED annual employee AND employer contribution

AGE 30 WITH CURRENT 401(K) BALANCE OF $250,000

Total Annual Savings	$10,000		$15,000	
Allocation: **80% Stock/20% Bonds**				
Base Comfortable "In Balance" Case:				
Maximum Fair Total Expense	0.75%		0.75%	
Retirement Income @ Age 65	$82,000		$100,300	
Age 65 Range of Portfolio Values	$940,685 to $9,627,239		$1,171,121 to $11,009,958	
EXCESS EXPENSE:	**0.50%**	**1.00%**	**0.50%**	**1.00%**
	(1.25% total)	(1.75% total)	(1.25% total)	(1.75% total)
COST OF EXCESS EXPENSE				
Additional Annual Savings Needed	$4,800	$10,500	$6,200	$12,900
Delay Retirement by	3 Years	7 Years	3 Years	7 Years
Reduce Annual Retirement Income by	$13,700	$25,600	$17,900	$31,600
Increased Risk of Outliving Resources	49%	93%	50%	97%
Reduction to Age 65 Portfolio Values:				
Likely More than:	$132,744	$244,942	$151,827	$286,204
Likely Less than:	$1,341,829	$2,488,837	$1,473,517	$2,747,820

Allocation: **60% Stock/40% Bonds**				
Base Comfortable "In Balance" Case:				
Maximum Fair Total Expense	0.75%		0.75%	
Retirement Income @ Age 65	$68,600		$83,500	
Age 65 Range of Portfolio Values	$894,447 to $5,964,031		$1,131,526 to $6,987,202	
EXCESS EXPENSE:	**0.50%**	**1.00%**	**0.50%**	**1.00%**
	(1.25% total)	(1.75% total)	(1.25% total)	(1.75% total)
COST OF EXCESS EXPENSE				
Additional Annual Savings Needed	$4,600	$10,100	$5,600	$11,900
Delay Retirement by	4 Years	7 Years	3 Years	7 Years
Reduce Annual Retirement Income by	$11,900	$22,200	$13,900	$25,900
Increased Risk of Outliving Resources	64%	122%	64%	122%
Reduction to Age 65 Portfolio Values:				
Likely More than:	$117,063	$216,920	$145,374	$277,977
Likely Less than:	$828,445	$1,538,689	$929,407	$1,720,362

Allocation: **45% Stock/55% Bonds**				
Base Comfortable "In Balance" Case:				
Maximum Fair Total Expense	0.75%		0.75%	
Retirement Income @ Age 65	$56,700		$70,000	
Age 65 Range of Portfolio Values	$860,803 to $4,260,710		$1,078,998 to $5,028,313	
EXCESS EXPENSE:	**0.50%**	**1.00%**	**0.50%**	**1.00%**
	(1.25% total)	(1.75% total)	(1.25% total)	(1.75% total)
COST OF EXCESS EXPENSE				
Additional Annual Savings Needed	$4,400	$9,700	$5,600	$11,900
Delay Retirement by	4 Years	7 Years	4 Years	7 Years
Reduce Annual Retirement Income by	$10,000	$18,300	$12,000	$22,100
Increased Risk of Outliving Resources	73%	156%	76%	159%
Reduction to Age 65 Portfolio Values:				
Likely More than:	$114,591	$213,305	$137,786	$256,000
Likely Less than:	$587,299	$1,093,121	$671,569	$1,239,421

Total annual savings is COMBINED annual employee AND employer contribution

AGE 35 WITH CURRENT 401(K) BALANCE OF $25,000

Total Annual Savings	$2,500		$5,000	
Allocation: **80% Stock/20% Bonds**				
Base Comfortable "In Balance" Case:				
Maximum Fair Total Expense	0.75%		0.75%	
Retirement Income @ Age 65	$10,200		$16,600	
Age 65 Range of Portfolio Values	$131,176 to $988,433		$218,961 to $1,454,462	
EXCESS EXPENSE:	**0.50%**	**1.00%**	**0.50%**	**1.00%**
	(1.25% total)	(1.75% total)	(1.25% total)	(1.75% total)
COST OF EXCESS EXPENSE				
Additional Annual Savings Needed	$700	$1,500	$1,000	$2,200
Delay Retirement by	3 Years	5 Years	3 Years	4 Years
Reduce Annual Retirement Income by	$1,500	$2,800	$2,300	$4,300
Increased Risk of Outliving Resources	31%	85%	34%	87%
Reduction to Age 65 Portfolio Values:				
Likely More than:	$14,392	$25,881	$19,826	$38,023
Likely Less than:	$107,943	$207,395	$148,059	$279,878

Allocation: **60% Stock/40% Bonds**				
Base Comfortable "In Balance" Case:				
Maximum Fair Total Expense	0.75%		0.75%	
Retirement Income @ Age 65	$8,800		$14,400	
Age 65 Range of Portfolio Values	$129,494 to $659,543		$217,091 to $1,004,552	
EXCESS EXPENSE:	**0.50%**	**1.00%**	**0.50%**	**1.00%**
	(1.25% total)	(1.75% total)	(1.25% total)	(1.75% total)
COST OF EXCESS EXPENSE				
Additional Annual Savings Needed	$700	$1,500	$1,100	$2,200
Delay Retirement by	3 Years	5 Years	3 Years	5 Years
Reduce Annual Retirement Income by	$1,400	$2,500	$2,100	$3,900
Increased Risk of Outliving Resources	54%	118%	48%	111%
Reduction to Age 65 Portfolio Values:				
Likely More than:	$12,710	$24,601	$20,987	$38,128
Likely Less than:	$70,880	$133,832	$104,399	$195,664

Allocation: **45% Stock/55% Bonds**				
Base Comfortable "In Balance" Case:				
Maximum Fair Total Expense	0.75%		0.75%	
Retirement Income @ Age 65	$7,600		$12,700	
Age 65 Range of Portfolio Values	$125,436 to $496,354		$212,438 to $752,955	
EXCESS EXPENSE:	**0.50%**	**1.00%**	**0.50%**	**1.00%**
	(1.25% total)	(1.75% total)	(1.25% total)	(1.75% total)
COST OF EXCESS EXPENSE				
Additional Annual Savings Needed	$600	$1,400	$1,100	$2,300
Delay Retirement by	3 Years	6 Years	3 Years	5 Years
Reduce Annual Retirement Income by	$1,100	$2,100	$1,900	$3,400
Increased Risk of Outliving Resources	69%	152%	69%	157%
Reduction to Age 65 Portfolio Values:				
Likely More than:	$12,595	$24,022	$19,723	$36,742
Likely Less than:	$53,719	$101,321	$72,960	$138,312

Total annual savings is COMBINED annual employee AND employer contribution

AGE 35 WITH CURRENT 401(K) BALANCE OF $25,000

Total Annual Savings	$10,000		$15,000	
Allocation: **80% Stock/20% Bonds**				
Base Comfortable "In Balance" Case:				
Maximum Fair Total Expense	0.75%		0.75%	
Retirement Income @ Age 65	$29,400		$42,300	
Age 65 Range of Portfolio Values	$398,139 to $2,467,936		$572,106 to $3,441,296	
EXCESS EXPENSE:	**0.50%**	**1.00%**	**0.50%**	**1.00%**
	(1.25% total)	(1.75% total)	(1.25% total)	(1.75% total)
COST OF EXCESS EXPENSE				
Additional Annual Savings Needed	$1,700	$3,700	$2,400	$5,100
Delay Retirement by	2 Years	4 Years	2 Years	4 Years
Reduce Annual Retirement Income by	$3,900	$7,300	$5,500	$10,300
Increased Risk of Outliving Resources	32%	83%	34%	86%
Reduction to Age 65 Portfolio Values:				
Likely More than:	$34,668	$70,094	$52,615	$102,559
Likely Less than:	$250,602	$477,374	$337,971	$639,494

Allocation: **60% Stock/40% Bonds**				
Base Comfortable "In Balance" Case:				
Maximum Fair Total Expense	0.75%		0.75%	
Retirement Income @ Age 65	$25,700		$37,100	
Age 65 Range of Portfolio Values	$397,786 to $1,704,860		$577,420 to $2,436,363	
EXCESS EXPENSE:	**0.50%**	**1.00%**	**0.50%**	**1.00%**
	(1.25% total)	(1.75% total)	(1.25% total)	(1.75% total)
COST OF EXCESS EXPENSE				
Additional Annual Savings Needed	$1,800	$3,800	$2,500	$5,400
Delay Retirement by	3 Years	5 Years	3 Years	5 Years
Reduce Annual Retirement Income by	$3,600	$6,600	$5,000	$9,300
Increased Risk of Outliving Resources	48%	114%	51%	118%
Reduction to Age 65 Portfolio Values:				
Likely More than:	$34,280	$64,641	$50,618	$94,799
Likely Less than:	$158,762	$301,531	$222,040	$432,778

Allocation: **45% Stock/55% Bonds**				
Base Comfortable "In Balance" Case:				
Maximum Fair Total Expense	0.75%		0.75%	
Retirement Income @ Age 65	$22,600		$32,600	
Age 65 Range of Portfolio Values	$385,566 to $1,299,881		$562,993 to $1,844,123	
EXCESS EXPENSE:	**0.50%**	**1.00%**	**0.50%**	**1.00%**
	(1.25% total)	(1.75% total)	(1.25% total)	(1.75% total)
COST OF EXCESS EXPENSE				
Additional Annual Savings Needed	$1,800	$4,000	$2,700	$5,800
Delay Retirement by	3 Years	5 Years	3 Years	5 Years
Reduce Annual Retirement Income by	$3,100	$5,900	$4,600	$8,500
Increased Risk of Outliving Resources	63%	156%	63%	155%
Reduction to Age 65 Portfolio Values:				
Likely More than:	$32,476	$62,895	$49,283	$93,654
Likely Less than:	$122,489	$232,624	$168,877	$334,100

Total annual savings is COMBINED annual employee AND employer contribution

AGE 35 WITH CURRENT 401(K) BALANCE OF $75,000

Total Annual Savings	$2,500		$5,000	
Allocation: ***80% Stock/20% Bonds***				
Base Comfortable "In Balance" Case:				
Maximum Fair Total Expense	0.75%		0.75%	
Retirement Income @ Age 65	$17,700		$24,100	
Age 65 Range of Portfolio Values	$204,977 to $2,048,600		$304,942 to $2,499,392	
EXCESS EXPENSE:	**0.50%**	**1.00%**	**0.50%**	**1.00%**
	(1.25% total)	(1.75% total)	(1.25% total)	(1.75% total)
COST OF EXCESS EXPENSE				
Additional Annual Savings Needed	$1,300	$2,700	$1,600	$3,300
Delay Retirement by	3 Years	6 Years	3 Years	5 Years
Reduce Annual Retirement Income by	$2,800	$5,200	$3,700	$6,800
Increased Risk of Outliving Resources	39%	88%	33%	86%
Reduction to Age 65 Portfolio Values:				
Likely More than:	$23,951	$45,015	$33,739	$61,957
Likely Less than:	$242,255	$460,525	$287,432	$543,865

Allocation: ***60% Stock/40% Bonds***				
Base Comfortable "In Balance" Case:				
Maximum Fair Total Expense	0.75%		0.75%	
Retirement Income @ Age 65	$14,900		$20,800	
Age 65 Range of Portfolio Values	$210,607 to $1,288,681		$301,501 to $1,632,534	
EXCESS EXPENSE:	**0.50%**	**1.00%**	**0.50%**	**1.00%**
	(1.25% total)	(1.75% total)	(1.25% total)	(1.75% total)
COST OF EXCESS EXPENSE				
Additional Annual Savings Needed	$1,200	$2,500	$1,600	$3,600
Delay Retirement by	3 Years	6 Years	3 Years	6 Years
Reduce Annual Retirement Income by	$2,500	$4,500	$3,300	$6,000
Increased Risk of Outliving Resources	51%	114%	57%	119%
Reduction to Age 65 Portfolio Values:				
Likely More than:	$24,850	$46,677	$32,511	$60,915
Likely Less than:	$157,846	$296,540	$188,079	$353,471

Allocation: ***45% Stock/55% Bonds***				
Base Comfortable "In Balance" Case:				
Maximum Fair Total Expense	0.75%		0.75%	
Retirement Income @ Age 65	$12,500		$17,700	
Age 65 Range of Portfolio Values	$203,253 to $931,839		$290,389 to $1,225,516	
EXCESS EXPENSE:	**0.50%**	**1.00%**	**0.50%**	**1.00%**
	(1.25% total)	(1.75% total)	(1.25% total)	(1.75% total)
COST OF EXCESS EXPENSE				
Additional Annual Savings Needed	$1,200	$2,400	$1,500	$3,200
Delay Retirement by	3 Years	6 Years	3 Years	6 Years
Reduce Annual Retirement Income by	$2,000	$3,700	$2,700	$5,000
Increased Risk of Outliving Resources	58%	139%	66%	146%
Reduction to Age 65 Portfolio Values:				
Likely More than:	$24,075	$44,870	$31,547	$59,069
Likely Less than:	$113,092	$211,621	$138,466	$260,732

Total annual savings is COMBINED annual employee AND employer contribution

AGE 35 WITH CURRENT 401(K) BALANCE OF $75,000

Total Annual Savings Allocation: **80% Stock/20% Bonds**	$10,000		$15,000	
Base Comfortable "In Balance" Case:				
Maximum Fair Total Expense	0.75%		0.75%	
Retirement Income @ Age 65	$37,200		$49,900	
Age 65 Range of Portfolio Values	$481,484 to $3,411,221		$656,760 to $4,363,265	
EXCESS EXPENSE:	**0.50%** (1.25% total)	**1.00%** (1.75% total)	**0.50%** (1.25% total)	**1.00%** (1.75% total)
COST OF EXCESS EXPENSE				
Additional Annual Savings Needed	$2,400	$5,100	$3,100	$6,500
Delay Retirement by	3 Years	5 Years	3 Years	5 Years
Reduce Annual Retirement Income by	$5,300	$10,000	$7,000	$13,000
Increased Risk of Outliving Resources	32%	85%	32%	84%
Reduction to Age 65 Portfolio Values:				
Likely More than:	$46,563	$92,022	$59,475	$114,068
Likely Less than:	$364,109	$700,722	$444,176	$839,634

Allocation: **60% Stock/40% Bonds**				
Base Comfortable "In Balance" Case:				
Maximum Fair Total Expense	0.75%		0.75%	
Retirement Income @ Age 65	$32,100		$43,200	
Age 65 Range of Portfolio Values	$477,733 to $2,331,808		$651,273 to $3,013,655	
EXCESS EXPENSE:	**0.50%** (1.25% total)	**1.00%** (1.75% total)	**0.50%** (1.25% total)	**1.00%** (1.75% total)
COST OF EXCESS EXPENSE				
Additional Annual Savings Needed	$2,500	$5,200	$3,100	$6,600
Delay Retirement by	3 Years	5 Years	3 Years	5 Years
Reduce Annual Retirement Income by	$4,900	$8,900	$6,100	$11,500
Increased Risk of Outliving Resources	51%	114%	48%	111%
Reduction to Age 65 Portfolio Values:				
Likely More than:	$47,181	$90,972	$62,962	$114,383
Likely Less than:	$261,930	$483,616	$313,196	$586,991

Allocation: **45% Stock/55% Bonds**				
Base Comfortable "In Balance" Case:				
Maximum Fair Total Expense	0.75%		0.75%	
Retirement Income @ Age 65	$28,000		$38,100	
Age 65 Range of Portfolio Values	$463,039 to $1,754,237		$637,313 to $2,258,866	
EXCESS EXPENSE:	**0.50%** (1.25% total)	**1.00%** (1.75% total)	**0.50%** (1.25% total)	**1.00%** (1.75% total)
COST OF EXCESS EXPENSE				
Additional Annual Savings Needed	$2,300	$5,100	$3,100	$6,700
Delay Retirement by	3 Years	6 Years	3 Years	5 Years
Reduce Annual Retirement Income by	$3,900	$7,500	$5,600	$10,200
Increased Risk of Outliving Resources	71%	157%	69%	157%
Reduction to Age 65 Portfolio Values:				
Likely More than:	$44,947	$83,629	$59,167	$110,225
Likely Less than:	$185,598	$357,532	$218,882	$414,937

Total annual savings is COMBINED annual employee AND employer contribution

AGE 35 WITH CURRENT 401(K) BALANCE OF $150,000

Total Annual Savings	$2,500		$5,000	
Allocation: **80% Stock/20% Bonds**				
Base Comfortable "In Balance" Case:				
Maximum Fair Total Expense	0.75%		0.75%	
Retirement Income @ Age 65	$28,800		$35,500	
Age 65 Range of Portfolio Values	$320,869 to $3,589,868		$409,833 to $4,097,079	
EXCESS EXPENSE:	**0.50%**	**1.00%**	**0.50%**	**1.00%**
	(1.25% total)	(1.75% total)	(1.25% total)	(1.75% total)
COST OF EXCESS EXPENSE				
Additional Annual Savings Needed	$2,100	$4,600	$2,600	$5,400
Delay Retirement by	4 Years	7 Years	3 Years	6 Years
Reduce Annual Retirement Income by	$4,700	$8,800	$5,700	$10,500
Increased Risk of Outliving Resources	38%	86%	38%	87%
Reduction to Age 65 Portfolio Values:				
Likely More than:	$43,105	$80,548	$47,903	$90,030
Likely Less than:	$446,201	$837,988	$484,511	$921,050

Allocation: **60% Stock/40% Bonds**				
Base Comfortable "In Balance" Case:				
Maximum Fair Total Expense	0.75%		0.75%	
Retirement Income @ Age 65	$24,000		$29,800	
Age 65 Range of Portfolio Values	$323,839 to $2,228,147		$421,215 to $2,577,361	
EXCESS EXPENSE:	**0.50%**	**1.00%**	**0.50%**	**1.00%**
	(1.25% total)	(1.75% total)	(1.25% total)	(1.75% total)
COST OF EXCESS EXPENSE				
Additional Annual Savings Needed	$2,000	$4,200	$2,400	$5,000
Delay Retirement by	4 Years	7 Years	3 Years	6 Years
Reduce Annual Retirement Income by	$4,000	$7,400	$4,900	$9,000
Increased Risk of Outliving Resources	52%	109%	51%	114%
Reduction to Age 65 Portfolio Values:				
Likely More than:	$42,228	$79,076	$49,702	$93,354
Likely Less than:	$279,897	$525,845	$315,692	$593,079

Allocation: **45% Stock/55% Bonds**				
Base Comfortable "In Balance" Case:				
Maximum Fair Total Expense	0.75%		0.75%	
Retirement Income @ Age 65	$20,200		$25,100	
Age 65 Range of Portfolio Values	$319,553 to $1,587,014		$406,384 to $1,863,557	
EXCESS EXPENSE:	**0.50%**	**1.00%**	**0.50%**	**1.00%**
	(1.25% total)	(1.75% total)	(1.25% total)	(1.75% total)
COST OF EXCESS EXPENSE				
Additional Annual Savings Needed	$2,000	$4,200	$2,300	$4,700
Delay Retirement by	4 Years	7 Years	3 Years	6 Years
Reduce Annual Retirement Income by	$3,500	$6,300	$4,100	$7,500
Increased Risk of Outliving Resources	63%	146%	60%	141%
Reduction to Age 65 Portfolio Values:				
Likely More than:	$41,584	$77,805	$48,150	$89,739
Likely Less than:	$199,305	$374,604	$226,185	$423,243

Total annual savings is COMBINED annual employee AND employer contribution

AGE 35 WITH CURRENT 401(K) BALANCE OF $150,000

Total Annual Savings	$10,000		$15,000	
Allocation: **80% Stock/20% Bonds**				
Base Comfortable "In Balance" Case:				
Maximum Fair Total Expense	0.75%		0.75%	
Retirement Income @ Age 65	$48,200		$61,300	
Age 65 Range of Portfolio Values	$609,884 to $4,998,784		$786,932 to $5,930,478	
EXCESS EXPENSE:	**0.50%**	**1.00%**	**0.50%**	**1.00%**
	(1.25% total)	(1.75% total)	(1.25% total)	(1.75% total)
COST OF EXCESS EXPENSE				
Additional Annual Savings Needed	$3,200	$6,600	$3,900	$8,600
Delay Retirement by	3 Years	5 Years	3 Years	5 Years
Reduce Annual Retirement Income by	$7,300	$13,600	$9,100	$16,700
Increased Risk of Outliving Resources	33%	86%	31%	86%
Reduction to Age 65 Portfolio Values:				
Likely More than:	$67,479	$123,914	$86,351	$155,282
Likely Less than:	$574,865	$1,087,729	$647,659	$1,244,369

Allocation: **60% Stock/40% Bonds**				
Base Comfortable "In Balance" Case:				
Maximum Fair Total Expense	0.75%		0.75%	
Retirement Income @ Age 65	$41,600		$53,200	
Age 65 Range of Portfolio Values	$603,001 to $3,265,069		$776,477 to $3,956,775	
EXCESS EXPENSE:	**0.50%**	**1.00%**	**0.50%**	**1.00%**
	(1.25% total)	(1.75% total)	(1.25% total)	(1.75% total)
COST OF EXCESS EXPENSE				
Additional Annual Savings Needed	$3,200	$7,100	$4,300	$8,800
Delay Retirement by	3 Years	6 Years	3 Years	5 Years
Reduce Annual Retirement Income by	$6,500	$11,900	$8,300	$15,200
Increased Risk of Outliving Resources	57%	119%	54%	118%
Reduction to Age 65 Portfolio Values:				
Likely More than:	$65,020	$121,829	$76,259	$147,602
Likely Less than:	$376,158	$706,943	$425,284	$802,994

Allocation: **45% Stock/55% Bonds**				
Base Comfortable "In Balance" Case:				
Maximum Fair Total Expense	0.75%		0.75%	
Retirement Income @ Age 65	$35,500		$45,800	
Age 65 Range of Portfolio Values	$580,657 to $2,450,910		$752,374 to $2,977,880	
EXCESS EXPENSE:	**0.50%**	**1.00%**	**0.50%**	**1.00%**
	(1.25% total)	(1.75% total)	(1.25% total)	(1.75% total)
COST OF EXCESS EXPENSE				
Additional Annual Savings Needed	$3,000	$6,300	$3,700	$8,200
Delay Retirement by	3 Years	6 Years	3 Years	6 Years
Reduce Annual Retirement Income by	$5,500	$10,000	$6,600	$12,300
Increased Risk of Outliving Resources	67%	147%	69%	150%
Reduction to Age 65 Portfolio Values:				
Likely More than:	$63,095	$118,138	$75,570	$144,130
Likely Less than:	$276,932	$521,463	$322,313	$607,923

Total annual savings is COMBINED annual employee AND employer contribution

AGE 35 WITH CURRENT 401(K) BALANCE OF $250,000

Total Annual Savings	$2,500		$5,000	
Allocation: **80% Stock/20% Bonds**				
Base Comfortable "In Balance" Case:				
Maximum Fair Total Expense	0.75%		0.75%	
Retirement Income @ Age 65	$43,000		$50,200	
Age 65 Range of Portfolio Values	$481,768 to $5,631,026		$563,199 to $6,156,829	
EXCESS EXPENSE:	**0.50%**	**1.00%**	**0.50%**	**1.00%**
	(1.25% total)	(1.75% total)	(1.25% total)	(1.75% total)
COST OF EXCESS EXPENSE				
Additional Annual Savings Needed	$2,800	$6,600	$3,600	$8,000
Delay Retirement by	4 Years	7 Years	3 Years	7 Years
Reduce Annual Retirement Income by	$7,200	$13,300	$8,000	$15,300
Increased Risk of Outliving Resources	38%	86%	39%	88%
Reduction to Age 65 Portfolio Values:				
Likely More than:	$66,001	$125,977	$74,030	$139,167
Likely Less than:	$710,928	$1,334,367	$758,508	$1,425,093

Allocation: **60% Stock/40% Bonds**				
Base Comfortable "In Balance" Case:				
Maximum Fair Total Expense	0.75%		0.75%	
Retirement Income @ Age 65	$36,500		$41,900	
Age 65 Range of Portfolio Values	$479,033 to $3,465,980		$571,221 to $3,827,406	
EXCESS EXPENSE:	**0.50%**	**1.00%**	**0.50%**	**1.00%**
	(1.25% total)	(1.75% total)	(1.25% total)	(1.75% total)
COST OF EXCESS EXPENSE				
Additional Annual Savings Needed	$3,300	$6,900	$3,500	$7,300
Delay Retirement by	4 Years	7 Years	4 Years	7 Years
Reduce Annual Retirement Income by	$6,400	$11,900	$7,000	$12,800
Increased Risk of Outliving Resources	55%	113%	51%	111%
Reduction to Age 65 Portfolio Values:				
Likely More than:	$65,403	$123,119	$72,097	$136,411
Likely Less than:	$448,344	$840,541	$474,631	$891,220

Allocation: **45% Stock/55% Bonds**				
Base Comfortable "In Balance" Case:				
Maximum Fair Total Expense	0.75%		0.75%	
Retirement Income @ Age 65	$30,100		$35,200	
Age 65 Range of Portfolio Values	$473,156 to $2,462,291		$562,859 to $2,741,644	
EXCESS EXPENSE:	**0.50%**	**1.00%**	**0.50%**	**1.00%**
	(1.25% total)	(1.75% total)	(1.25% total)	(1.75% total)
COST OF EXCESS EXPENSE				
Additional Annual Savings Needed	$2,900	$6,200	$3,300	$7,100
Delay Retirement by	4 Years	7 Years	4 Years	7 Years
Reduce Annual Retirement Income by	$5,300	$9,600	$5,800	$10,700
Increased Risk of Outliving Resources	61%	137%	62%	143%
Reduction to Age 65 Portfolio Values:				
Likely More than:	$64,414	$120,471	$71,901	$135,144
Likely Less than:	$315,025	$590,591	$340,032	$638,296

Total annual savings is COMBINED annual employee AND employer contribution

AGE 35 WITH CURRENT 401(K) BALANCE OF $250,000

Total Annual Savings	$10,000		$15,000	
Allocation: **80% Stock/20% Bonds**				
Base Comfortable "In Balance" Case:				
Maximum Fair Total Expense	0.75%		0.75%	
Retirement Income @ Age 65	$63,600		$75,800	
Age 65 Range of Portfolio Values	$751,544 to $7,153,645		$954,870 to $8,020,945	
EXCESS EXPENSE:	**0.50%**	**1.00%**	**0.50%**	**1.00%**
	(1.25% total)	(1.75% total)	(1.25% total)	(1.75% total)
COST OF EXCESS EXPENSE				
Additional Annual Savings Needed	$4,700	$9,300	$4,900	$10,500
Delay Retirement by	3 Years	6 Years	3 Years	5 Years
Reduce Annual Retirement Income by	$10,100	$18,700	$11,400	$21,600
Increased Risk of Outliving Resources	36%	89%	31%	85%
Reduction to Age 65 Portfolio Values:				
Likely More than:	$89,491	$164,442	$105,111	$202,907
Likely Less than:	$859,076	$1,617,315	$918,971	$1,747,165

Allocation: **60% Stock/40% Bonds**				
Base Comfortable "In Balance" Case:				
Maximum Fair Total Expense	0.75%		0.75%	
Retirement Income @ Age 65	$53,500		$65,100	
Age 65 Range of Portfolio Values	$765,989 to $4,507,266		$951,963 to $5,220,966	
EXCESS EXPENSE:	**0.50%**	**1.00%**	**0.50%**	**1.00%**
	(1.25% total)	(1.75% total)	(1.25% total)	(1.75% total)
COST OF EXCESS EXPENSE				
Additional Annual Savings Needed	$4,200	$8,900	$4,800	$11,000
Delay Retirement by	3 Years	6 Years	3 Years	6 Years
Reduce Annual Retirement Income by	$8,900	$15,800	$10,000	$18,600
Increased Risk of Outliving Resources	51%	114%	53%	118%
Reduction to Age 65 Portfolio Values:				
Likely More than:	$86,740	$165,713	$108,042	$203,216
Likely Less than:	$533,688	$1,006,752	$609,129	$1,143,046

Allocation: **45% Stock/55% Bonds**				
Base Comfortable "In Balance" Case:				
Maximum Fair Total Expense	0.75%		0.75%	
Retirement Income @ Age 65	$45,300		$55,600	
Age 65 Range of Portfolio Values	$737,722 to $3,293,407		$916,110 to $3,887,146	
EXCESS EXPENSE:	**0.50%**	**1.00%**	**0.50%**	**1.00%**
	(1.25% total)	(1.75% total)	(1.25% total)	(1.75% total)
COST OF EXCESS EXPENSE				
Additional Annual Savings Needed	$3,900	$8,300	$4,600	$9,800
Delay Retirement by	3 Years	6 Years	3 Years	6 Years
Reduce Annual Retirement Income by	$7,500	$13,300	$8,500	$15,800
Increased Risk of Outliving Resources	59%	142%	63%	143%
Reduction to Age 65 Portfolio Values:				
Likely More than:	$86,745	$161,111	$104,108	$192,636
Likely Less than:	$387,513	$723,588	$438,231	$825,658

Total annual savings is COMBINED annual employee AND employer contribution

AGE 40 WITH CURRENT 401(K) BALANCE OF $25,000

Total Annual Savings	$2,500		$5,000	
Allocation: *80% Stock/20% Bonds*				
Base Comfortable "In Balance" Case:				
Maximum Fair Total Expense	0.75%		0.75%	
Retirement Income @ Age 65	$7,500		$12,100	
Age 65 Range of Portfolio Values	$101,132 to $650,685		$165,936 to $949,110	
EXCESS EXPENSE:	**0.50%**	**1.00%**	**0.50%**	**1.00%**
	(1.25% total)	(1.75% total)	(1.25% total)	(1.75% total)
COST OF EXCESS EXPENSE				
Additional Annual Savings Needed	$600	$1,400	$1,000	$2,000
Delay Retirement by	3 Years	5 Years	2 Years	4 Years
Reduce Annual Retirement Income by	$1,000	$1,900	$1,600	$2,900
Increased Risk of Outliving Resources	39%	82%	37%	80%
Reduction to Age 65 Portfolio Values:				
Likely More than:	$8,650	$16,794	$13,084	$24,179
Likely Less than:	$61,313	$116,768	$82,139	$157,963

Allocation: *60% Stock/40% Bonds*				
Base Comfortable "In Balance" Case:				
Maximum Fair Total Expense	0.75%		0.75%	
Retirement Income @ Age 65	$6,500		$10,700	
Age 65 Range of Portfolio Values	$100,394 to $455,780		$169,184 to $682,395	
EXCESS EXPENSE:	**0.50%**	**1.00%**	**0.50%**	**1.00%**
	(1.25% total)	(1.75% total)	(1.25% total)	(1.75% total)
COST OF EXCESS EXPENSE				
Additional Annual Savings Needed	$600	$1,200	$900	$2,000
Delay Retirement by	2 Years	5 Years	2 Years	4 Years
Reduce Annual Retirement Income by	$800	$1,600	$1,400	$2,600
Increased Risk of Outliving Resources	42%	106%	38%	105%
Reduction to Age 65 Portfolio Values:				
Likely More than:	$8,923	$16,877	$13,150	$25,346
Likely Less than:	$41,521	$79,788	$59,536	$113,645

Allocation: *45% Stock/55% Bonds*				
Base Comfortable "In Balance" Case:				
Maximum Fair Total Expense	0.75%		0.75%	
Retirement Income @ Age 65	$5,700		$9,400	
Age 65 Range of Portfolio Values	$102,050 to $344,786		$170,546 to $530,781	
EXCESS EXPENSE:	**0.50%**	**1.00%**	**0.50%**	**1.00%**
	(1.25% total)	(1.75% total)	(1.25% total)	(1.75% total)
COST OF EXCESS EXPENSE				
Additional Annual Savings Needed	$600	$1,300	$1,000	$2,000
Delay Retirement by	3 Years	5 Years	2 Years	5 Years
Reduce Annual Retirement Income by	$800	$1,500	$1,200	$2,300
Increased Risk of Outliving Resources	47%	118%	46%	117%
Reduction to Age 65 Portfolio Values:				
Likely More than:	$8,948	$17,012	$14,118	$26,197
Likely Less than:	$32,265	$59,824	$44,955	$84,449

Total annual savings is COMBINED annual employee AND employer contribution

AGE 40 WITH CURRENT 401(K) BALANCE OF $25,000

Total Annual Savings	$10,000		$15,000	
Allocation: **80% Stock/20% Bonds**				
Base Comfortable "In Balance" Case:				
Maximum Fair Total Expense	0.75%		0.75%	
Retirement Income @ Age 65	$21,100		$30,300	
Age 65 Range of Portfolio Values	$297,302 to $1,555,037		$430,621 to $2,192,923	
EXCESS EXPENSE:	**0.50%**	**1.00%**	**0.50%**	**1.00%**
	(1.25% total)	(1.75% total)	(1.25% total)	(1.75% total)
COST OF EXCESS EXPENSE				
Additional Annual Savings Needed	$1,600	$3,300	$2,200	$4,700
Delay Retirement by	2 Years	4 Years	2 Years	4 Years
Reduce Annual Retirement Income by	$2,500	$4,800	$3,700	$6,900
Increased Risk of Outliving Resources	33%	68%	34%	69%
Reduction to Age 65 Portfolio Values:				
Likely More than:	$20,059	$39,728	$30,266	$58,097
Likely Less than:	$127,165	$246,597	$171,106	$328,416

Allocation: **60% Stock/40% Bonds**				
Base Comfortable "In Balance" Case:				
Maximum Fair Total Expense	0.75%		0.75%	
Retirement Income @ Age 65	$18,900		$27,200	
Age 65 Range of Portfolio Values	$307,414 to $1,128,064		$442,541 to $1,579,146	
EXCESS EXPENSE:	**0.50%**	**1.00%**	**0.50%**	**1.00%**
	(1.25% total)	(1.75% total)	(1.25% total)	(1.75% total)
COST OF EXCESS EXPENSE				
Additional Annual Savings Needed	$1,600	$3,400	$2,200	$4,900
Delay Retirement by	2 Years	4 Years	2 Years	4 Years
Reduce Annual Retirement Income by	$2,300	$4,300	$3,300	$6,200
Increased Risk of Outliving Resources	35%	99%	39%	96%
Reduction to Age 65 Portfolio Values:				
Likely More than:	$23,179	$43,084	$29,169	$57,401
Likely Less than:	$92,018	$175,372	$122,030	$232,023

Allocation: **45% Stock/55% Bonds**				
Base Comfortable "In Balance" Case:				
Maximum Fair Total Expense	0.75%		0.75%	
Retirement Income @ Age 65	$16,700		$24,000	
Age 65 Range of Portfolio Values	$306,389 to $901,296		$442,520 to $1,269,782	
EXCESS EXPENSE:	**0.50%**	**1.00%**	**0.50%**	**1.00%**
	(1.25% total)	(1.75% total)	(1.25% total)	(1.75% total)
COST OF EXCESS EXPENSE				
Additional Annual Savings Needed	$1,600	$3,400	$2,200	$4,900
Delay Retirement by	2 Years	4 Years	2 Years	4 Years
Reduce Annual Retirement Income by	$2,100	$3,900	$2,900	$5,500
Increased Risk of Outliving Resources	43%	112%	46%	113%
Reduction to Age 65 Portfolio Values:				
Likely More than:	$22,603	$43,302	$32,299	$60,793
Likely Less than:	$69,089	$134,059	$95,711	$183,489

Total annual savings is COMBINED annual employee AND employer contribution

AGE 40 WITH CURRENT 401(K) BALANCE OF $75,000

Total Annual Savings	$2,500		$5,000	
Allocation: **80% Stock/20% Bonds**				
Base Comfortable "In Balance" Case:				
Maximum Fair Total Expense	0.75%		0.75%	
Retirement Income @ Age 65	$13,100		$17,800	
Age 65 Range of Portfolio Values	$165,446 to $1,322,446		$232,781 to $1,634,043	
EXCESS EXPENSE:	**0.50%**	**1.00%**	**0.50%**	**1.00%**
	(1.25% total)	(1.75% total)	(1.25% total)	(1.75% total)
COST OF EXCESS EXPENSE				
Additional Annual Savings Needed	$1,100	$2,400	$1,400	$3,100
Delay Retirement by	3 Years	5 Years	3 Years	5 Years
Reduce Annual Retirement Income by	$1,900	$3,500	$2,400	$4,500
Increased Risk of Outliving Resources	36%	80%	36%	81%
Reduction to Age 65 Portfolio Values:				
Likely More than:	$17,453	$34,030	$21,316	$40,552
Likely Less than:	$136,407	$258,995	$162,856	$303,168

Allocation: **60% Stock/40% Bonds**				
Base Comfortable "In Balance" Case:				
Maximum Fair Total Expense	0.75%		0.75%	
Retirement Income @ Age 65	$11,600		$15,700	
Age 65 Range of Portfolio Values	$166,956 to $894,724		$235,218 to $1,125,381	
EXCESS EXPENSE:	**0.50%**	**1.00%**	**0.50%**	**1.00%**
	(1.25% total)	(1.75% total)	(1.25% total)	(1.75% total)
COST OF EXCESS EXPENSE				
Additional Annual Savings Needed	$1,200	$2,500	$1,600	$3,200
Delay Retirement by	3 Years	6 Years	3 Years	5 Years
Reduce Annual Retirement Income by	$1,700	$3,300	$2,200	$4,100
Increased Risk of Outliving Resources	51%	104%	47%	103%
Reduction to Age 65 Portfolio Values:				
Likely More than:	$17,340	$33,036	$21,665	$41,717
Likely Less than:	$92,036	$174,723	$106,627	$202,916

Allocation: **45% Stock/55% Bonds**				
Base Comfortable "In Balance" Case:				
Maximum Fair Total Expense	0.75%		0.75%	
Retirement Income @ Age 65	$9,900		$13,700	
Age 65 Range of Portfolio Values	$165,045 to $668,951		$235,597 to $846,206	
EXCESS EXPENSE:	**0.50%**	**1.00%**	**0.50%**	**1.00%**
	(1.25% total)	(1.75% total)	(1.25% total)	(1.75% total)
COST OF EXCESS EXPENSE				
Additional Annual Savings Needed	$1,100	$2,400	$1,600	$3,300
Delay Retirement by	3 Years	6 Years	3 Years	6 Years
Reduce Annual Retirement Income by	$1,500	$2,700	$2,000	$3,700
Increased Risk of Outliving Resources	53%	117%	52%	118%
Reduction to Age 65 Portfolio Values:				
Likely More than:	$16,342	$31,128	$21,171	$40,160
Likely Less than:	$67,868	$128,835	$81,847	$154,451

Total annual savings is COMBINED annual employee AND employer contribution

AGE 40 WITH CURRENT 401(K) BALANCE OF $75,000

Total Annual Savings	$10,000		$15,000	
Allocation: **80% Stock/20% Bonds**				
Base Comfortable "In Balance" Case:				
Maximum Fair Total Expense	0.75%		0.75%	
Retirement Income @ Age 65	$27,300		$36,300	
Age 65 Range of Portfolio Values	$371,871 to $2,248,148		$497,809 to $2,847,331	
EXCESS EXPENSE:	**0.50%**	**1.00%**	**0.50%**	**1.00%**
	(1.25% total)	(1.75% total)	(1.25% total)	(1.75% total)
COST OF EXCESS EXPENSE				
Additional Annual Savings Needed	$2,300	$4,800	$3,000	$6,000
Delay Retirement by	2 Years	5 Years	2 Years	4 Years
Reduce Annual Retirement Income by	$3,700	$6,800	$4,800	$8,700
Increased Risk of Outliving Resources	39%	83%	37%	80%
Reduction to Age 65 Portfolio Values:				
Likely More than:	$31,958	$60,813	$39,253	$72,538
Likely Less than:	$208,136	$397,116	$246,418	$473,890

Allocation: **60% Stock/40% Bonds**				
Base Comfortable "In Balance" Case:				
Maximum Fair Total Expense	0.75%		0.75%	
Retirement Income @ Age 65	$24,000		$32,200	
Age 65 Range of Portfolio Values	$370,135 to $1,593,409		$507,432 to $2,047,065	
EXCESS EXPENSE:	**0.50%**	**1.00%**	**0.50%**	**1.00%**
	(1.25% total)	(1.75% total)	(1.25% total)	(1.75% total)
COST OF EXCESS EXPENSE				
Additional Annual Savings Needed	$2,200	$4,600	$2,800	$5,900
Delay Retirement by	3 Years	5 Years	2 Years	4 Years
Reduce Annual Retirement Income by	$3,200	$5,900	$4,100	$7,700
Increased Risk of Outliving Resources	40%	103%	37%	103%
Reduction to Age 65 Portfolio Values:				
Likely More than:	$29,299	$57,612	$39,451	$76,041
Likely Less than:	$142,555	$268,264	$178,609	$340,935

Allocation: **45% Stock/55% Bonds**				
Base Comfortable "In Balance" Case:				
Maximum Fair Total Expense	0.75%		0.75%	
Retirement Income @ Age 65	$20,900		$28,200	
Age 65 Range of Portfolio Values	$373,810 to $1,217,411		$511,639 to $1,592,342	
EXCESS EXPENSE:	**0.50%**	**1.00%**	**0.50%**	**1.00%**
	(1.25% total)	(1.75% total)	(1.25% total)	(1.75% total)
COST OF EXCESS EXPENSE				
Additional Annual Savings Needed	$2,200	$4,500	$2,800	$5,900
Delay Retirement by	3 Years	5 Years	2 Years	5 Years
Reduce Annual Retirement Income by	$2,800	$5,300	$3,600	$6,900
Increased Risk of Outliving Resources	45%	114%	46%	117%
Reduction to Age 65 Portfolio Values:				
Likely More than:	$29,069	$57,906	$42,355	$78,593
Likely Less than:	$106,781	$203,568	$134,864	$253,346

Total annual savings is COMBINED annual employee AND employer contribution

AGE 40 WITH CURRENT 401(K) BALANCE OF $150,000

Total Annual Savings			$2,500		$5,000	
Allocation: **80% Stock/20% Bonds**						
Base Comfortable "In Balance" Case:						
Maximum Fair Total Expense			0.75%		0.75%	
Retirement Income @ Age 65			$21,400		$26,200	
Age 65 Range of Portfolio Values			$257,976 to $2,350,616		$330,892 to $2,644,892	
EXCESS EXPENSE:			**0.50%**	**1.00%**	**0.50%**	**1.00%**
			(1.25% total)	(1.75% total)	(1.25% total)	(1.75% total)
COST OF EXCESS EXPENSE						
Additional Annual Savings Needed			$1,900	$4,000	$2,200	$4,700
Delay Retirement by			3 Years	6 Years	3 Years	5 Years
Reduce Annual Retirement Income by			$3,300	$6,000	$3,800	$7,000
Increased Risk of Outliving Resources			35%	82%	36%	80%
Reduction to Age 65 Portfolio Values:						
Likely More than:			$28,055	$52,987	$34,905	$68,061
Likely Less than:			$249,417	$474,828	$272,815	$517,990

Allocation: **60% Stock/40% Bonds**						
Base Comfortable "In Balance" Case:						
Maximum Fair Total Expense			0.75%		0.75%	
Retirement Income @ Age 65			$18,900		$23,300	
Age 65 Range of Portfolio Values			$260,416 to $1,574,001		$333,791 to $1,789,327	
EXCESS EXPENSE:			**0.50%**	**1.00%**	**0.50%**	**1.00%**
			(1.25% total)	(1.75% total)	(1.25% total)	(1.75% total)
COST OF EXCESS EXPENSE						
Additional Annual Savings Needed			$1,900	$4,200	$2,500	$5,100
Delay Retirement by			3 Years	6 Years	3 Years	6 Years
Reduce Annual Retirement Income by			$2,800	$5,300	$3,500	$6,600
Increased Risk of Outliving Resources			49%	101%	53%	105%
Reduction to Age 65 Portfolio Values:						
Likely More than:			$29,271	$55,569	$34,680	$66,072
Likely Less than:			$169,235	$320,808	$184,073	$349,446

Allocation: **45% Stock/55% Bonds**						
Base Comfortable "In Balance" Case:						
Maximum Fair Total Expense			0.75%		0.75%	
Retirement Income @ Age 65			$16,100		$19,800	
Age 65 Range of Portfolio Values			$259,757 to $1,168,506		$330,090 to $1,337,903	
EXCESS EXPENSE:			**0.50%**	**1.00%**	**0.50%**	**1.00%**
			(1.25% total)	(1.75% total)	(1.25% total)	(1.75% total)
COST OF EXCESS EXPENSE						
Additional Annual Savings Needed			$1,800	$3,900	$2,100	$4,700
Delay Retirement by			3 Years	6 Years	3 Years	6 Years
Reduce Annual Retirement Income by			$2,500	$4,700	$2,900	$5,400
Increased Risk of Outliving Resources			53%	120%	53%	117%
Reduction to Age 65 Portfolio Values:						
Likely More than:			$28,433	$54,186	$32,683	$62,256
Likely Less than:			$126,256	$239,234	$135,737	$257,672

Total annual savings is COMBINED annual employee AND employer contribution

AGE 40 WITH CURRENT 401(K) BALANCE OF $150,000

Total Annual Savings	$10,000		$15,000	
Allocation: *80% Stock/20% Bonds*				
Base Comfortable "In Balance" Case:				
Maximum Fair Total Expense	0.75%		0.75%	
Retirement Income @ Age 65	$35,700		$45,300	
Age 65 Range of Portfolio Values	$465,440 to $3,267,966		$606,430 to $3,903,744	
EXCESS EXPENSE:	**0.50%**	**1.00%**	**0.50%**	**1.00%**
	(1.25% total)	(1.75% total)	(1.25% total)	(1.75% total)
COST OF EXCESS EXPENSE				
Additional Annual Savings Needed	$2,800	$6,300	$3,700	$8,100
Delay Retirement by	3 Years	5 Years	3 Years	5 Years
Reduce Annual Retirement Income by	$4,900	$9,100	$6,100	$11,200
Increased Risk of Outliving Resources	35%	80%	40%	83%
Reduction to Age 65 Portfolio Values:				
Likely More than:	$42,632	$81,104	$51,901	$100,768
Likely Less than:	$325,713	$606,336	$367,877	$700,609

Allocation: *60% Stock/40% Bonds*				
Base Comfortable "In Balance" Case:				
Maximum Fair Total Expense	0.75%		0.75%	
Retirement Income @ Age 65	$31,500		$39,500	
Age 65 Range of Portfolio Values	$470,314 to $2,250,640		$601,757 to $2,734,070	
EXCESS EXPENSE:	**0.50%**	**1.00%**	**0.50%**	**1.00%**
	(1.25% total)	(1.75% total)	(1.25% total)	(1.75% total)
COST OF EXCESS EXPENSE				
Additional Annual Savings Needed	$3,200	$6,300	$3,500	$7,500
Delay Retirement by	3 Years	5 Years	3 Years	5 Years
Reduce Annual Retirement Income by	$4,500	$8,300	$5,200	$9,800
Increased Risk of Outliving Resources	48%	104%	40%	102%
Reduction to Age 65 Portfolio Values:				
Likely More than:	$43,329	$83,433	$53,540	$101,262
Likely Less than:	$213,254	$405,832	$249,123	$478,723

Allocation: *45% Stock/55% Bonds*				
Base Comfortable "In Balance" Case:				
Maximum Fair Total Expense	0.75%		0.75%	
Retirement Income @ Age 65	$27,400		$34,400	
Age 65 Range of Portfolio Values	$471,193 to $1,692,411		$612,058 to $2,068,474	
EXCESS EXPENSE:	**0.50%**	**1.00%**	**0.50%**	**1.00%**
	(1.25% total)	(1.75% total)	(1.25% total)	(1.75% total)
COST OF EXCESS EXPENSE				
Additional Annual Savings Needed	$3,100	$6,500	$3,500	$7,700
Delay Retirement by	3 Years	6 Years	3 Years	5 Years
Reduce Annual Retirement Income by	$3,900	$7,300	$4,800	$8,700
Increased Risk of Outliving Resources	52%	118%	46%	113%
Reduction to Age 65 Portfolio Values:				
Likely More than:	$42,340	$80,319	$53,691	$102,075
Likely Less than:	$163,694	$308,901	$193,591	$358,946

Total annual savings is COMBINED annual employee AND employer contribution

AGE 40 WITH CURRENT 401(K) BALANCE OF $250,000

Total Annual Savings	$2,500		$5,000	
Allocation: **80% Stock/20% Bonds**				
Base Comfortable "In Balance" Case:				
Maximum Fair Total Expense	0.75%		0.75%	
Retirement Income @ Age 65	$32,600		$37,400	
Age 65 Range of Portfolio Values	$378,895 to $3,700,618		$461,064 to $4,017,171	
EXCESS EXPENSE:	**0.50%**	**1.00%**	**0.50%**	**1.00%**
	(1.25% total)	(1.75% total)	(1.25% total)	(1.75% total)
COST OF EXCESS EXPENSE				
Additional Annual Savings Needed	$3,000	$6,200	$3,300	$7,100
Delay Retirement by	3 Years	6 Years	3 Years	6 Years
Reduce Annual Retirement Income by	$5,000	$9,500	$5,700	$10,400
Increased Risk of Outliving Resources	34%	82%	34%	79%
Reduction to Age 65 Portfolio Values:				
Likely More than:	$44,504	$84,019	$51,311	$97,729
Likely Less than:	$399,042	$756,598	$426,759	$809,583

Allocation: **60% Stock/40% Bonds**				
Base Comfortable "In Balance" Case:				
Maximum Fair Total Expense	0.75%		0.75%	
Retirement Income @ Age 65	$28,600		$33,100	
Age 65 Range of Portfolio Values	$387,662 to $2,476,925		$456,201 to $2,687,330	
EXCESS EXPENSE:	**0.50%**	**1.00%**	**0.50%**	**1.00%**
	(1.25% total)	(1.75% total)	(1.25% total)	(1.75% total)
COST OF EXCESS EXPENSE				
Additional Annual Savings Needed	$2,700	$6,400	$3,400	$7,200
Delay Retirement by	3 Years	7 Years	3 Years	6 Years
Reduce Annual Retirement Income by	$4,500	$8,300	$4,900	$9,200
Increased Risk of Outliving Resources	47%	100%	51%	102%
Reduction to Age 65 Portfolio Values:				
Likely More than:	$46,146	$87,185	$49,323	$93,554
Likely Less than:	$268,179	$508,248	$284,001	$538,654

Allocation: **45% Stock/55% Bonds**				
Base Comfortable "In Balance" Case:				
Maximum Fair Total Expense	0.75%		0.75%	
Retirement Income @ Age 65	$24,300		$28,000	
Age 65 Range of Portfolio Values	$388,752 to $1,839,842		$455,938 to $1,996,235	
EXCESS EXPENSE:	**0.50%**	**1.00%**	**0.50%**	**1.00%**
	(1.25% total)	(1.75% total)	(1.25% total)	(1.75% total)
COST OF EXCESS EXPENSE				
Additional Annual Savings Needed	$3,000	$6,100	$3,100	$6,800
Delay Retirement by	4 Years	7 Years	3 Years	6 Years
Reduce Annual Retirement Income by	$3,900	$7,100	$4,300	$8,000
Increased Risk of Outliving Resources	54%	118%	54%	119%
Reduction to Age 65 Portfolio Values:				
Likely More than:	$45,407	$85,803	$48,280	$91,729
Likely Less than:	$201,308	$382,635	$214,013	$405,608

Total annual savings is COMBINED annual employee AND employer contribution

AGE 40 WITH CURRENT 401(K) BALANCE OF $250,000

Total Annual Savings	$10,000		$15,000	
Allocation: **80% Stock/20% Bonds**				
Base Comfortable "In Balance" Case:				
Maximum Fair Total Expense	0.75%		0.75%	
Retirement Income @ Age 65	$46,800		$56,300	
Age 65 Range of Portfolio Values	$592,312 to $4,596,160		$735,309 to $5,242,840	
EXCESS EXPENSE:	**0.50%**	**1.00%**	**0.50%**	**1.00%**
	(1.25% total)	(1.75% total)	(1.25% total)	(1.75% total)
COST OF EXCESS EXPENSE				
Additional Annual Savings Needed	$4,000	$8,100	$4,500	$9,600
Delay Retirement by	3 Years	5 Years	3 Years	5 Years
Reduce Annual Retirement Income by	$6,400	$12,400	$7,700	$14,400
Increased Risk of Outliving Resources	36%	78%	36%	80%
Reduction to Age 65 Portfolio Values:				
Likely More than:	$62,106	$116,079	$74,374	$135,800
Likely Less than:	$472,514	$894,377	$507,289	$980,067

Allocation: **60% Stock/40% Bonds**				
Base Comfortable "In Balance" Case:				
Maximum Fair Total Expense	0.75%		0.75%	
Retirement Income @ Age 65	$41,400		$49,500	
Age 65 Range of Portfolio Values	$601,459 to $3,134,658		$736,601 to $3,588,075	
EXCESS EXPENSE:	**0.50%**	**1.00%**	**0.50%**	**1.00%**
	(1.25% total)	(1.75% total)	(1.25% total)	(1.75% total)
COST OF EXCESS EXPENSE				
Additional Annual Savings Needed	$4,100	$8,800	$4,700	$9,900
Delay Retirement by	3 Years	6 Years	3 Years	5 Years
Reduce Annual Retirement Income by	$6,300	$11,300	$6,700	$12,900
Increased Risk of Outliving Resources	48%	101%	47%	102%
Reduction to Age 65 Portfolio Values:				
Likely More than:	$61,016	$116,037	$67,716	$129,766
Likely Less than:	$315,136	$598,587	$344,178	$654,719

Allocation: **45% Stock/55% Bonds**				
Base Comfortable "In Balance" Case:				
Maximum Fair Total Expense	0.75%		0.75%	
Retirement Income @ Age 65	$35,600		$43,100	
Age 65 Range of Portfolio Values	$598,544 to $2,353,831		$738,291 to $2,693,751	
EXCESS EXPENSE:	**0.50%**	**1.00%**	**0.50%**	**1.00%**
	(1.25% total)	(1.75% total)	(1.25% total)	(1.75% total)
COST OF EXCESS EXPENSE				
Additional Annual Savings Needed	$4,000	$8,400	$4,600	$10,300
Delay Retirement by	3 Years	6 Years	3 Years	6 Years
Reduce Annual Retirement Income by	$5,200	$9,600	$6,200	$11,400
Increased Risk of Outliving Resources	51%	117%	51%	117%
Reduction to Age 65 Portfolio Values:				
Likely More than:	$58,602	$111,136	$66,761	$128,784
Likely Less than:	$239,259	$454,169	$256,158	$490,845

Total annual savings is COMBINED annual employee AND employer contribution

AGE 45 WITH CURRENT 401(K) BALANCE OF $25,000

Total Annual Savings	$2,500		$5,000	
Allocation: **80% Stock/20% Bonds**				
Base Comfortable "In Balance" Case:				
Maximum Fair Total Expense	0.75%		0.75%	
Retirement Income @ Age 65	$5,500		$8,700	
Age 65 Range of Portfolio Values	$76,870 to $414,961		$127,045 to $599,041	
EXCESS EXPENSE:	**0.50%**	**1.00%**	**0.50%**	**1.00%**
	(1.25% total)	(1.75% total)	(1.25% total)	(1.75% total)
COST OF EXCESS EXPENSE				
Additional Annual Savings Needed	$600	$1,200	$800	$1,700
Delay Retirement by	2 Years	4 Years	2 Years	3 Years
Reduce Annual Retirement Income by	$700	$1,300	$1,000	$1,800
Increased Risk of Outliving Resources	35%	73%	31%	76%
Reduction to Age 65 Portfolio Values:				
Likely More than:	$5,494	$10,580	$8,109	$14,904
Likely Less than:	$31,502	$60,599	$43,216	$81,207

Allocation: **60% Stock/40% Bonds**				
Base Comfortable "In Balance" Case:				
Maximum Fair Total Expense	0.75%		0.75%	
Retirement Income @ Age 65	$4,900		$7,900	
Age 65 Range of Portfolio Values	$79,614 to $299,971		$131,075 to $438,447	
EXCESS EXPENSE:	**0.50%**	**1.00%**	**0.50%**	**1.00%**
	(1.25% total)	(1.75% total)	(1.25% total)	(1.75% total)
COST OF EXCESS EXPENSE				
Additional Annual Savings Needed	$600	$1,200	$800	$1,800
Delay Retirement by	2 Years	4 Years	2 Years	4 Years
Reduce Annual Retirement Income by	$600	$1,100	$900	$1,700
Increased Risk of Outliving Resources	40%	93%	43%	93%
Reduction to Age 65 Portfolio Values:				
Likely More than:	$5,593	$11,140	$8,210	$16,350
Likely Less than:	$23,182	$44,547	$29,942	$59,655

Allocation: **45% Stock/55% Bonds**				
Base Comfortable "In Balance" Case:				
Maximum Fair Total Expense	0.75%		0.75%	
Retirement Income @ Age 65	$4,400		$7,000	
Age 65 Range of Portfolio Values	$80,197 to $242,827		$131,008 to $363,704	
EXCESS EXPENSE:	**0.50%**	**1.00%**	**0.50%**	**1.00%**
	(1.25% total)	(1.75% total)	(1.25% total)	(1.75% total)
COST OF EXCESS EXPENSE				
Additional Annual Savings Needed	$600	$1,200	$800	$1,800
Delay Retirement by	2 Years	4 Years	2 Years	4 Years
Reduce Annual Retirement Income by	$600	$1,100	$800	$1,500
Increased Risk of Outliving Resources	41%	112%	46%	112%
Reduction to Age 65 Portfolio Values:				
Likely More than:	$5,629	$11,279	$8,200	$15,488
Likely Less than:	$18,590	$35,582	$24,914	$47,950

Total annual savings is COMBINED annual employee AND employer contribution

AGE 45 WITH CURRENT 401(K) BALANCE OF $25,000

Total Annual Savings	$10,000		$15,000	
Allocation: **80% Stock/20% Bonds**				
Base Comfortable "In Balance" Case:				
Maximum Fair Total Expense	0.75%		0.75%	
Retirement Income @ Age 65	$15,400		$21,800	
Age 65 Range of Portfolio Values	$226,258 to $978,841		$323,311 to $1,356,334	
EXCESS EXPENSE:	**0.50%**	**1.00%**	**0.50%**	**1.00%**
	(1.25% total)	(1.75% total)	(1.25% total)	(1.75% total)
COST OF EXCESS EXPENSE				
Additional Annual Savings Needed	$1,500	$3,100	$2,000	$4,200
Delay Retirement by	2 Years	4 Years	2 Years	3 Years
Reduce Annual Retirement Income by	$1,700	$3,300	$2,400	$4,400
Increased Risk of Outliving Resources	40%	81%	38%	79%
Reduction to Age 65 Portfolio Values:				
Likely More than:	$13,812	$26,677	$18,895	$36,619
Likely Less than:	$63,588	$122,810	$90,334	$172,079

Allocation: **60% Stock/40% Bonds**				
Base Comfortable "In Balance" Case:				
Maximum Fair Total Expense	0.75%		0.75%	
Retirement Income @ Age 65	$13,800		$19,800	
Age 65 Range of Portfolio Values	$233,164 to $719,358		$332,132 to $1,020,595	
EXCESS EXPENSE:	**0.50%**	**1.00%**	**0.50%**	**1.00%**
	(1.25% total)	(1.75% total)	(1.25% total)	(1.75% total)
COST OF EXCESS EXPENSE				
Additional Annual Savings Needed	$1,400	$3,100	$2,100	$4,400
Delay Retirement by	2 Years	4 Years	2 Years	4 Years
Reduce Annual Retirement Income by	$1,500	$2,900	$2,200	$4,200
Increased Risk of Outliving Resources	49%	96%	50%	96%
Reduction to Age 65 Portfolio Values:				
Likely More than:	$14,180	$26,681	$18,856	$35,469
Likely Less than:	$45,004	$86,961	$63,897	$127,241

Allocation: **45% Stock/55% Bonds**				
Base Comfortable "In Balance" Case:				
Maximum Fair Total Expense	0.75%		0.75%	
Retirement Income @ Age 65	$12,400		$17,800	
Age 65 Range of Portfolio Values	$234,154 to $609,085		$335,598 to $854,822	
EXCESS EXPENSE:	**0.50%**	**1.00%**	**0.50%**	**1.00%**
	(1.25% total)	(1.75% total)	(1.25% total)	(1.75% total)
COST OF EXCESS EXPENSE				
Additional Annual Savings Needed	$1,400	$3,000	$2,000	$4,300
Delay Retirement by	2 Years	4 Years	2 Years	3 Years
Reduce Annual Retirement Income by	$1,400	$2,600	$1,900	$3,700
Increased Risk of Outliving Resources	47%	109%	50%	114%
Reduction to Age 65 Portfolio Values:				
Likely More than:	$14,292	$27,009	$20,192	$37,142
Likely Less than:	$38,237	$74,434	$55,294	$105,518

Total annual savings is COMBINED annual employee AND employer contribution

AGE 45 WITH CURRENT 401(K) BALANCE OF $75,000

Total Annual Savings	$2,500		$5,000	
Allocation: *80% Stock/20% Bonds*				
Base Comfortable "In Balance" Case:				
Maximum Fair Total Expense	0.75%		0.75%	
Retirement Income @ Age 65	$9,800		$13,200	
Age 65 Range of Portfolio Values	$131,506 to $861,817		$178,157 to $1,052,522	
EXCESS EXPENSE:	**0.50%**	**1.00%**	**0.50%**	**1.00%**
	(1.25% total)	(1.75% total)	(1.25% total)	(1.75% total)
COST OF EXCESS EXPENSE				
Additional Annual Savings Needed	$1,000	$2,200	$1,400	$3,000
Delay Retirement by	2 Years	5 Years	2 Years	4 Years
Reduce Annual Retirement Income by	$1,300	$2,400	$1,600	$3,100
Increased Risk of Outliving Resources	37%	70%	37%	72%
Reduction to Age 65 Portfolio Values:				
Likely More than:	$11,209	$21,940	$13,935	$25,705
Likely Less than:	$70,731	$135,741	$81,272	$156,022

Allocation: *60% Stock/40% Bonds*				
Base Comfortable "In Balance" Case:				
Maximum Fair Total Expense	0.75%		0.75%	
Retirement Income @ Age 65	$8,800		$11,700	
Age 65 Range of Portfolio Values	$133,789 to $617,086		$187,635 to $768,545	
EXCESS EXPENSE:	**0.50%**	**1.00%**	**0.50%**	**1.00%**
	(1.25% total)	(1.75% total)	(1.25% total)	(1.75% total)
COST OF EXCESS EXPENSE				
Additional Annual Savings Needed	$1,100	$2,300	$1,300	$2,700
Delay Retirement by	3 Years	5 Years	2 Years	4 Years
Reduce Annual Retirement Income by	$1,200	$2,200	$1,400	$2,700
Increased Risk of Outliving Resources	39%	86%	40%	90%
Reduction to Age 65 Portfolio Values:				
Likely More than:	$10,559	$20,830	$13,761	$26,542
Likely Less than:	$50,398	$96,799	$60,682	$116,540

Allocation: *45% Stock/55% Bonds*				
Base Comfortable "In Balance" Case:				
Maximum Fair Total Expense	0.75%		0.75%	
Retirement Income @ Age 65	$7,900		$10,500	
Age 65 Range of Portfolio Values	$135,415 to $486,273		$187,629 to $605,528	
EXCESS EXPENSE:	**0.50%**	**1.00%**	**0.50%**	**1.00%**
	(1.25% total)	(1.75% total)	(1.25% total)	(1.75% total)
COST OF EXCESS EXPENSE				
Additional Annual Savings Needed	$1,100	$2,300	$1,300	$2,900
Delay Retirement by	3 Years	5 Years	2 Years	4 Years
Reduce Annual Retirement Income by	$1,100	$2,000	$1,400	$2,400
Increased Risk of Outliving Resources	49%	116%	42%	113%
Reduction to Age 65 Portfolio Values:				
Likely More than:	$11,283	$21,773	$13,421	$26,309
Likely Less than:	$40,679	$78,593	$46,920	$90,131

Total annual savings is COMBINED annual employee AND employer contribution

141

AGE 45 WITH CURRENT 401(K) BALANCE OF $75,000

Total Annual Savings		$10,000		$15,000	
Allocation: *80% Stock/20% Bonds*					
Base Comfortable "In Balance" Case:					
Maximum Fair Total Expense		0.75%		0.75%	
Retirement Income @ Age 65		$19,600		$26,100	
Age 65 Range of Portfolio Values		$280,137 to $1,427,136		$381,136 to $1,797,124	
EXCESS EXPENSE:		**0.50%**	**1.00%**	**0.50%**	**1.00%**
		(1.25% total)	(1.75% total)	(1.25% total)	(1.75% total)
COST OF EXCESS EXPENSE					
Additional Annual Savings Needed		$1,900	$3,900	$2,400	$5,000
Delay Retirement by		2 Years	4 Years	2 Years	3 Years
Reduce Annual Retirement Income by		$2,300	$4,300	$2,900	$5,400
Increased Risk of Outliving Resources		33%	74%	31%	76%
Reduction to Age 65 Portfolio Values:					
Likely More than:		$19,476	$37,200	$24,327	$44,713
Likely Less than:		$101,428	$196,563	$129,650	$243,622

Allocation: *60% Stock/40% Bonds*					
Base Comfortable "In Balance" Case:					
Maximum Fair Total Expense		0.75%		0.75%	
Retirement Income @ Age 65		$17,800		$23,900	
Age 65 Range of Portfolio Values		$289,391 to $1,039,095		$392,982 to $1,315,099	
EXCESS EXPENSE:		**0.50%**	**1.00%**	**0.50%**	**1.00%**
		(1.25% total)	(1.75% total)	(1.25% total)	(1.75% total)
COST OF EXCESS EXPENSE					
Additional Annual Savings Needed		$1,800	$4,000	$2,600	$5,400
Delay Retirement by		2 Years	4 Years	2 Years	4 Years
Reduce Annual Retirement Income by		$2,100	$4,000	$2,800	$5,200
Increased Risk of Outliving Resources		39%	90%	45%	97%
Reduction to Age 65 Portfolio Values:					
Likely More than:		$19,169	$36,903	$24,631	$49,074
Likely Less than:		$75,990	$146,242	$89,827	$178,967

Allocation: *45% Stock/55% Bonds*					
Base Comfortable "In Balance" Case:					
Maximum Fair Total Expense		0.75%		0.75%	
Retirement Income @ Age 65		$15,900		$21,100	
Age 65 Range of Portfolio Values		$290,667 to $845,017		$392,902 to $1,090,991	
EXCESS EXPENSE:		**0.50%**	**1.00%**	**0.50%**	**1.00%**
		(1.25% total)	(1.75% total)	(1.25% total)	(1.75% total)
COST OF EXCESS EXPENSE					
Additional Annual Savings Needed		$2,000	$4,200	$2,400	$5,400
Delay Retirement by		2 Years	4 Years	2 Years	4 Years
Reduce Annual Retirement Income by		$1,900	$3,700	$2,400	$4,500
Increased Risk of Outliving Resources		42%	111%	45%	110%
Reduction to Age 65 Portfolio Values:					
Likely More than:		$19,651	$38,865	$24,599	$46,465
Likely Less than:		$59,695	$114,894	$74,741	$143,851

Total annual savings is COMBINED annual employee AND employer contribution

AGE 45 WITH CURRENT 401(K) BALANCE OF $150,000

Total Annual Savings	$2,500		$5,000	
Allocation: **80% Stock/20% Bonds**				
Base Comfortable "In Balance" Case:				
Maximum Fair Total Expense	0.75%		0.75%	
Retirement Income @ Age 65	$16,400		$19,700	
Age 65 Range of Portfolio Values	$211,548 to $1,555,325		$262,891 to $1,723,512	
EXCESS EXPENSE:	**0.50%**	**1.00%**	**0.50%**	**1.00%**
	(1.25% total)	(1.75% total)	(1.25% total)	(1.75% total)
COST OF EXCESS EXPENSE				
Additional Annual Savings Needed	$1,900	$3,900	$2,100	$4,500
Delay Retirement by	3 Years	5 Years	2 Years	5 Years
Reduce Annual Retirement Income by	$2,100	$4,100	$2,600	$4,800
Increased Risk of Outliving Resources	36%	74%	35%	67%
Reduction to Age 65 Portfolio Values:				
Likely More than:	$19,897	$38,033	$22,419	$43,880
Likely Less than:	$135,235	$259,234	$141,462	$271,482

Allocation: **60% Stock/40% Bonds**				
Base Comfortable "In Balance" Case:				
Maximum Fair Total Expense	0.75%		0.75%	
Retirement Income @ Age 65	$14,700		$17,700	
Age 65 Range of Portfolio Values	$213,276 to $1,089,509		$267,457 to $1,234,050	
EXCESS EXPENSE:	**0.50%**	**1.00%**	**0.50%**	**1.00%**
	(1.25% total)	(1.75% total)	(1.25% total)	(1.75% total)
COST OF EXCESS EXPENSE				
Additional Annual Savings Needed	$1,900	$4,000	$2,300	$4,600
Delay Retirement by	3 Years	5 Years	3 Years	5 Years
Reduce Annual Retirement Income by	$2,000	$3,800	$2,400	$4,500
Increased Risk of Outliving Resources	40%	90%	40%	89%
Reduction to Age 65 Portfolio Values:				
Likely More than:	$20,077	$38,368	$21,118	$41,660
Likely Less than:	$95,631	$183,190	$100,795	$193,597

Allocation: **45% Stock/55% Bonds**				
Base Comfortable "In Balance" Case:				
Maximum Fair Total Expense	0.75%		0.75%	
Retirement Income @ Age 65	$13,200		$15,900	
Age 65 Range of Portfolio Values	$219,078 to $847,761		$270,709 to $972,425	
EXCESS EXPENSE:	**0.50%**	**1.00%**	**0.50%**	**1.00%**
	(1.25% total)	(1.75% total)	(1.25% total)	(1.75% total)
COST OF EXCESS EXPENSE				
Additional Annual Savings Needed	$1,900	$4,100	$2,400	$4,600
Delay Retirement by	3 Years	6 Years	3 Years	5 Years
Reduce Annual Retirement Income by	$1,800	$3,500	$2,200	$4,100
Increased Risk of Outliving Resources	50%	119%	49%	117%
Reduction to Age 65 Portfolio Values:				
Likely More than:	$19,470	$37,498	$22,567	$43,546
Likely Less than:	$74,096	$141,924	$81,359	$157,186

Total annual savings is COMBINED annual employee AND employer contribution

AGE 45 WITH CURRENT 401(K) BALANCE OF $150,000

Total Annual Savings	$10,000		$15,000	
Allocation: **80% Stock/20% Bonds**				
Base Comfortable "In Balance" Case:				
Maximum Fair Total Expense	0.75%		0.75%	
Retirement Income @ Age 65	$26,400		$33,000	
Age 65 Range of Portfolio Values	$356,313 to $2,105,044		$461,219 to $2,489,768	
EXCESS EXPENSE:	**0.50%**	**1.00%**	**0.50%**	**1.00%**
	(1.25% total)	(1.75% total)	(1.25% total)	(1.75% total)
COST OF EXCESS EXPENSE				
Additional Annual Savings Needed	$2,700	$5,900	$3,400	$7,100
Delay Retirement by	2 Years	4 Years	2 Years	4 Years
Reduce Annual Retirement Income by	$3,200	$6,200	$3,900	$7,600
Increased Risk of Outliving Resources	37%	72%	35%	73%
Reduction to Age 65 Portfolio Values:				
Likely More than:	$27,869	$51,409	$32,965	$63,479
Likely Less than:	$162,544	$312,043	$189,012	$363,597

Allocation: **60% Stock/40% Bonds**				
Base Comfortable "In Balance" Case:				
Maximum Fair Total Expense	0.75%		0.75%	
Retirement Income @ Age 65	$23,500		$29,500	
Age 65 Range of Portfolio Values	$375,148 to $1,536,969		$477,564 to $1,799,705	
EXCESS EXPENSE:	**0.50%**	**1.00%**	**0.50%**	**1.00%**
	(1.25% total)	(1.75% total)	(1.25% total)	(1.75% total)
COST OF EXCESS EXPENSE				
Additional Annual Savings Needed	$2,600	$5,500	$3,200	$6,800
Delay Retirement by	2 Years	4 Years	2 Years	4 Years
Reduce Annual Retirement Income by	$2,900	$5,400	$3,400	$6,500
Increased Risk of Outliving Resources	36%	86%	41%	92%
Reduction to Age 65 Portfolio Values:				
Likely More than:	$27,522	$53,084	$33,559	$66,839
Likely Less than:	$121,364	$233,080	$139,090	$267,282

Allocation: **45% Stock/55% Bonds**				
Base Comfortable "In Balance" Case:				
Maximum Fair Total Expense	0.75%		0.75%	
Retirement Income @ Age 65	$21,000		$26,400	
Age 65 Range of Portfolio Values	$375,257 to $1,211,057		$481,181 to $1,456,962	
EXCESS EXPENSE:	**0.50%**	**1.00%**	**0.50%**	**1.00%**
	(1.25% total)	(1.75% total)	(1.25% total)	(1.75% total)
COST OF EXCESS EXPENSE				
Additional Annual Savings Needed	$2,600	$5,700	$3,200	$7,100
Delay Retirement by	2 Years	4 Years	2 Years	4 Years
Reduce Annual Retirement Income by	$2,700	$4,800	$3,200	$6,100
Increased Risk of Outliving Resources	42%	113%	41%	112%
Reduction to Age 65 Portfolio Values:				
Likely More than:	$26,841	$52,618	$33,775	$67,676
Likely Less than:	$93,842	$180,264	$111,543	$213,492

Total annual savings is COMBINED annual employee AND employer contribution

AGE 45 WITH CURRENT 401(K) BALANCE OF $250,000

Total Annual Savings	$2,500		$5,000	
Allocation: **80% Stock/20% Bonds**				
Base Comfortable "In Balance" Case:				
Maximum Fair Total Expense	0.75%		0.75%	
Retirement Income @ Age 65	$25,300		$28,500	
Age 65 Range of Portfolio Values	$320,274 to $2,500,480		$369,218 to $2,635,693	
EXCESS EXPENSE:	**0.50%**	**1.00%**	**0.50%**	**1.00%**
	(1.25% total)	(1.75% total)	(1.25% total)	(1.75% total)
COST OF EXCESS EXPENSE				
Additional Annual Savings Needed	$3,000	$6,200	$3,100	$6,600
Delay Retirement by	3 Years	5 Years	3 Years	5 Years
Reduce Annual Retirement Income by	$3,400	$6,500	$3,800	$7,100
Increased Risk of Outliving Resources	35%	73%	34%	69%
Reduction to Age 65 Portfolio Values:				
Likely More than:	$31,707	$60,565	$33,848	$64,733
Likely Less than:	$216,845	$416,987	$228,151	$437,395

Allocation: **60% Stock/40% Bonds**				
Base Comfortable "In Balance" Case:				
Maximum Fair Total Expense	0.75%		0.75%	
Retirement Income @ Age 65	$22,600		$25,600	
Age 65 Range of Portfolio Values	$326,125 to $1,733,569		$372,067 to $1,857,535	
EXCESS EXPENSE:	**0.50%**	**1.00%**	**0.50%**	**1.00%**
	(1.25% total)	(1.75% total)	(1.25% total)	(1.75% total)
COST OF EXCESS EXPENSE				
Additional Annual Savings Needed	$2,900	$6,400	$3,300	$6,900
Delay Retirement by	3 Years	6 Years	3 Years	5 Years
Reduce Annual Retirement Income by	$3,200	$6,000	$3,500	$6,600
Increased Risk of Outliving Resources	42%	89%	40%	90%
Reduction to Age 65 Portfolio Values:				
Likely More than:	$32,042	$60,604	$32,322	$61,858
Likely Less than:	$152,048	$291,705	$156,626	$300,716

Allocation: **45% Stock/55% Bonds**				
Base Comfortable "In Balance" Case:				
Maximum Fair Total Expense	0.75%		0.75%	
Retirement Income @ Age 65	$20,100		$23,000	
Age 65 Range of Portfolio Values	$331,578 to $1,331,759		$383,084 to $1,455,409	
EXCESS EXPENSE:	**0.50%**	**1.00%**	**0.50%**	**1.00%**
	(1.25% total)	(1.75% total)	(1.25% total)	(1.75% total)
COST OF EXCESS EXPENSE				
Additional Annual Savings Needed	$2,800	$6,200	$3,400	$7,000
Delay Retirement by	3 Years	6 Years	3 Years	6 Years
Reduce Annual Retirement Income by	$2,900	$5,400	$3,200	$6,000
Increased Risk of Outliving Resources	53%	119%	51%	123%
Reduction to Age 65 Portfolio Values:				
Likely More than:	$31,522	$60,223	$34,823	$66,582
Likely Less than:	$119,660	$229,060	$125,935	$241,271

Total annual savings is COMBINED annual employee AND employer contribution

AGE 45 WITH CURRENT 401(K) BALANCE OF $250,000

Total Annual Savings	$10,000		$15,000	
Allocation: *80% Stock/20% Bonds*				
Base Comfortable "In Balance" Case:				
Maximum Fair Total Expense	0.75%		0.75%	
Retirement Income @ Age 65	$34,900		$42,000	
Age 65 Range of Portfolio Values	$469,451 to $3,007,179		$559,410 to $3,388,079	
EXCESS EXPENSE:	**0.50%**	**1.00%**	**0.50%**	**1.00%**
	(1.25% total)	(1.75% total)	(1.25% total)	(1.75% total)
COST OF EXCESS EXPENSE				
Additional Annual Savings Needed	$3,400	$7,800	$4,500	$9,400
Delay Retirement by	2 Years	4 Years	2 Years	4 Years
Reduce Annual Retirement Income by	$4,200	$8,200	$5,300	$10,100
Increased Risk of Outliving Resources	36%	70%	36%	72%
Reduction to Age 65 Portfolio Values:				
Likely More than:	$41,420	$79,273	$41,920	$82,798
Likely Less than:	$243,449	$467,358	$271,763	$519,979

Allocation: *60% Stock/40% Bonds*				
Base Comfortable "In Balance" Case:				
Maximum Fair Total Expense	0.75%		0.75%	
Retirement Income @ Age 65	$31,500		$37,100	
Age 65 Range of Portfolio Values	$484,636 to $2,151,400		$586,381 to $2,459,887	
EXCESS EXPENSE:	**0.50%**	**1.00%**	**0.50%**	**1.00%**
	(1.25% total)	(1.75% total)	(1.25% total)	(1.75% total)
COST OF EXCESS EXPENSE				
Additional Annual Savings Needed	$4,000	$8,000	$4,000	$8,700
Delay Retirement by	3 Years	5 Years	2 Years	4 Years
Reduce Annual Retirement Income by	$4,300	$7,900	$4,600	$8,500
Increased Risk of Outliving Resources	40%	87%	38%	87%
Reduction to Age 65 Portfolio Values:				
Likely More than:	$40,134	$78,677	$42,309	$81,312
Likely Less than:	$179,413	$344,136	$189,466	$365,490

Allocation: *45% Stock/55% Bonds*				
Base Comfortable "In Balance" Case:				
Maximum Fair Total Expense	0.75%		0.75%	
Retirement Income @ Age 65	$28,200		$33,500	
Age 65 Range of Portfolio Values	$485,239 to $1,701,411		$587,354 to $1,940,187	
EXCESS EXPENSE:	**0.50%**	**1.00%**	**0.50%**	**1.00%**
	(1.25% total)	(1.75% total)	(1.25% total)	(1.75% total)
COST OF EXCESS EXPENSE				
Additional Annual Savings Needed	$3,800	$8,000	$4,300	$9,400
Delay Retirement by	3 Years	5 Years	3 Years	5 Years
Reduce Annual Retirement Income by	$3,800	$7,100	$4,300	$8,000
Increased Risk of Outliving Resources	48%	117%	46%	115%
Reduction to Age 65 Portfolio Values:				
Likely More than:	$39,609	$75,894	$42,334	$81,840
Likely Less than:	$141,701	$271,770	$153,236	$296,991

Total annual savings is COMBINED annual employee AND employer contribution

AGE 50 WITH CURRENT 401(K) BALANCE OF $25,000

Total Annual Savings	$2,500		$5,000	
Allocation: **80% Stock/20% Bonds**				
Base Comfortable "In Balance" Case:				
Maximum Fair Total Expense	0.75%		0.75%	
Retirement Income @ Age 65	$4,100		$6,300	
Age 65 Range of Portfolio Values	$59,148 to $264,454		$92,518 to $374,859	
EXCESS EXPENSE:	**0.50%**	**1.00%**	**0.50%**	**1.00%**
	(1.25% total)	(1.75% total)	(1.25% total)	(1.75% total)
COST OF EXCESS EXPENSE				
Additional Annual Savings Needed	$600	$1,200	$800	$1,700
Delay Retirement by	2 Years	3 Years	2 Years	3 Years
Reduce Annual Retirement Income by	$500	$900	$700	$1,200
Increased Risk of Outliving Resources	40%	83%	41%	84%
Reduction to Age 65 Portfolio Values:				
Likely More than:	$3,263	$6,326	$4,402	$8,567
Likely Less than:	$15,238	$29,987	$19,997	$38,885

Allocation: **60% Stock/40% Bonds**				
Base Comfortable "In Balance" Case:				
Maximum Fair Total Expense	0.75%		0.75%	
Retirement Income @ Age 65	$3,700		$5,700	
Age 65 Range of Portfolio Values	$62,753 to $199,591		$98,780 to $292,950	
EXCESS EXPENSE:	**0.50%**	**1.00%**	**0.50%**	**1.00%**
	(1.25% total)	(1.75% total)	(1.25% total)	(1.75% total)
COST OF EXCESS EXPENSE				
Additional Annual Savings Needed	$600	$1,100	$800	$1,600
Delay Retirement by	2 Years	3 Years	2 Years	3 Years
Reduce Annual Retirement Income by	$400	$800	$600	$1,100
Increased Risk of Outliving Resources	36%	92%	39%	94%
Reduction to Age 65 Portfolio Values:				
Likely More than:	$3,570	$6,926	$5,067	$9,594
Likely Less than:	$11,950	$22,960	$14,883	$28,963

Allocation: **45% Stock/55% Bonds**				
Base Comfortable "In Balance" Case:				
Maximum Fair Total Expense	0.75%		0.75%	
Retirement Income @ Age 65	$3,300		$5,200	
Age 65 Range of Portfolio Values	$63,958 to $165,948		$100,971 to $243,553	
EXCESS EXPENSE:	**0.50%**	**1.00%**	**0.50%**	**1.00%**
	(1.25% total)	(1.75% total)	(1.25% total)	(1.75% total)
COST OF EXCESS EXPENSE				
Additional Annual Savings Needed	$500	$1,000	$700	$1,600
Delay Retirement by	2 Years	3 Years	2 Years	3 Years
Reduce Annual Retirement Income by	$300	$700	$500	$1,000
Increased Risk of Outliving Resources	43%	112%	41%	115%
Reduction to Age 65 Portfolio Values:				
Likely More than:	$3,498	$6,955	$5,123	$10,037
Likely Less than:	$9,355	$18,167	$12,395	$24,116

Total annual savings is COMBINED annual employee AND employer contribution

147

AGE 50 WITH CURRENT 401(K) BALANCE OF $25,000

Total Annual Savings	$10,000		$15,000	
Allocation: **80% Stock/20% Bonds**				
Base Comfortable "In Balance" Case:				
Maximum Fair Total Expense	0.75%		0.75%	
Retirement Income @ Age 65	$10,600		$15,000	
Age 65 Range of Portfolio Values	$162,645 to $603,191		$230,620 to $824,449	
EXCESS EXPENSE:	**0.50%**	**1.00%**	**0.50%**	**1.00%**
	(1.25% total)	(1.75% total)	(1.25% total)	(1.75% total)
COST OF EXCESS EXPENSE				
Additional Annual Savings Needed	$1,300	$2,800	$1,900	$4,000
Delay Retirement by	2 Years	3 Years	2 Years	3 Years
Reduce Annual Retirement Income by	$1,000	$2,000	$1,500	$2,900
Increased Risk of Outliving Resources	39%	78%	39%	80%
Reduction to Age 65 Portfolio Values:				
Likely More than:	$7,562	$14,722	$10,476	$19,546
Likely Less than:	$28,105	$56,215	$37,504	$73,031

Allocation: **60% Stock/40% Bonds**				
Base Comfortable "In Balance" Case:				
Maximum Fair Total Expense	0.75%		0.75%	
Retirement Income @ Age 65	$9,800		$13,900	
Age 65 Range of Portfolio Values	$169,122 to $472,915		$238,973 to $647,011	
EXCESS EXPENSE:	**0.50%**	**1.00%**	**0.50%**	**1.00%**
	(1.25% total)	(1.75% total)	(1.25% total)	(1.75% total)
COST OF EXCESS EXPENSE				
Additional Annual Savings Needed	$1,200	$2,900	$1,900	$4,000
Delay Retirement by	2 Years	3 Years	2 Years	3 Years
Reduce Annual Retirement Income by	$900	$1,900	$1,400	$2,700
Increased Risk of Outliving Resources	47%	101%	51%	103%
Reduction to Age 65 Portfolio Values:				
Likely More than:	$8,021	$15,578	$10,415	$20,365
Likely Less than:	$23,677	$44,413	$29,573	$57,697

Allocation: **45% Stock/55% Bonds**				
Base Comfortable "In Balance" Case:				
Maximum Fair Total Expense	0.75%		0.75%	
Retirement Income @ Age 65	$8,900		$12,700	
Age 65 Range of Portfolio Values	$172,762 to $396,438		$244,769 to $558,068	
EXCESS EXPENSE:	**0.50%**	**1.00%**	**0.50%**	**1.00%**
	(1.25% total)	(1.75% total)	(1.25% total)	(1.75% total)
COST OF EXCESS EXPENSE				
Additional Annual Savings Needed	$1,200	$2,700	$1,800	$3,800
Delay Retirement by	1 Years	3 Years	2 Years	3 Years
Reduce Annual Retirement Income by	$900	$1,700	$1,300	$2,400
Increased Risk of Outliving Resources	45%	118%	51%	121%
Reduction to Age 65 Portfolio Values:				
Likely More than:	$7,405	$14,374	$10,656	$20,697
Likely Less than:	$17,407	$34,673	$24,429	$49,138

Total annual savings is COMBINED annual employee AND employer contribution

AGE 50 WITH CURRENT 401(K) BALANCE OF $75,000

Total Annual Savings	$2,500		$5,000	
Allocation: **80% Stock/20% Bonds**				
Base Comfortable "In Balance" Case:				
Maximum Fair Total Expense	0.75%		0.75%	
Retirement Income @ Age 65	$7,800		$10,100	
Age 65 Range of Portfolio Values	$106,109 to $576,952		$142,300 to $689,562	
EXCESS EXPENSE:	**0.50%**	**1.00%**	**0.50%**	**1.00%**
	(1.25% total)	(1.75% total)	(1.25% total)	(1.75% total)
COST OF EXCESS EXPENSE				
Additional Annual Savings Needed	$1,100	$2,200	$1,300	$2,800
Delay Retirement by	2 Years	4 Years	2 Years	4 Years
Reduce Annual Retirement Income by	$900	$1,700	$1,100	$2,100
Increased Risk of Outliving Resources	36%	80%	35%	79%
Reduction to Age 65 Portfolio Values:				
Likely More than:	$7,257	$13,947	$8,311	$16,759
Likely Less than:	$36,817	$71,737	$41,341	$80,236

Allocation: **60% Stock/40% Bonds**				
Base Comfortable "In Balance" Case:				
Maximum Fair Total Expense	0.75%		0.75%	
Retirement Income @ Age 65	$7,100		$9,100	
Age 65 Range of Portfolio Values	$113,403 to $429,270		$151,736 to $509,258	
EXCESS EXPENSE:	**0.50%**	**1.00%**	**0.50%**	**1.00%**
	(1.25% total)	(1.75% total)	(1.25% total)	(1.75% total)
COST OF EXCESS EXPENSE				
Additional Annual Savings Needed	$1,100	$2,400	$1,400	$2,900
Delay Retirement by	2 Years	4 Years	2 Years	4 Years
Reduce Annual Retirement Income by	$900	$1,600	$1,100	$2,000
Increased Risk of Outliving Resources	40%	95%	36%	94%
Reduction to Age 65 Portfolio Values:				
Likely More than:	$7,676	$14,824	$9,302	$18,147
Likely Less than:	$27,838	$53,940	$31,021	$60,179

Allocation: **45% Stock/55% Bonds**				
Base Comfortable "In Balance" Case:				
Maximum Fair Total Expense	0.75%		0.75%	
Retirement Income @ Age 65	$6,300		$8,200	
Age 65 Range of Portfolio Values	$115,013 to $343,304		$153,507 to $416,874	
EXCESS EXPENSE:	**0.50%**	**1.00%**	**0.50%**	**1.00%**
	(1.25% total)	(1.75% total)	(1.25% total)	(1.75% total)
COST OF EXCESS EXPENSE				
Additional Annual Savings Needed	$1,000	$2,200	$1,300	$2,800
Delay Retirement by	2 Years	4 Years	2 Years	4 Years
Reduce Annual Retirement Income by	$700	$1,400	$900	$1,700
Increased Risk of Outliving Resources	43%	108%	41%	108%
Reduction to Age 65 Portfolio Values:				
Likely More than:	$7,525	$14,560	$9,199	$17,507
Likely Less than:	$21,865	$42,907	$24,759	$48,034

Total annual savings is COMBINED annual employee AND employer contribution

AGE 50 WITH CURRENT 401(K) BALANCE OF $75,000

Total Annual Savings	$10,000		$15,000	
Allocation: **80% Stock/20% Bonds**				
Base Comfortable "In Balance" Case:				
Maximum Fair Total Expense	0.75%		0.75%	
Retirement Income @ Age 65	$14,500		$18,900	
Age 65 Range of Portfolio Values	$211,032 to $893,304		$277,553 to $1,124,577	
EXCESS EXPENSE:	**0.50%**	**1.00%**	**0.50%**	**1.00%**
	(1.25% total)	(1.75% total)	(1.25% total)	(1.75% total)
COST OF EXCESS EXPENSE				
Additional Annual Savings Needed	$1,800	$3,900	$2,300	$5,100
Delay Retirement by	2 Years	3 Years	2 Years	3 Years
Reduce Annual Retirement Income by	$1,400	$2,900	$1,900	$3,600
Increased Risk of Outliving Resources	40%	84%	41%	84%
Reduction to Age 65 Portfolio Values:				
Likely More than:	$11,060	$22,582	$13,204	$25,700
Likely Less than:	$50,904	$97,092	$59,991	$116,656

	$10,000		$15,000	
Allocation: **60% Stock/40% Bonds**				
Base Comfortable "In Balance" Case:				
Maximum Fair Total Expense	0.75%		0.75%	
Retirement Income @ Age 65	$13,100		$17,200	
Age 65 Range of Portfolio Values	$225,202 to $697,768		$296,217 to $878,730	
EXCESS EXPENSE:	**0.50%**	**1.00%**	**0.50%**	**1.00%**
	(1.25% total)	(1.75% total)	(1.25% total)	(1.75% total)
COST OF EXCESS EXPENSE				
Additional Annual Savings Needed	$1,800	$3,800	$2,300	$4,800
Delay Retirement by	2 Years	3 Years	2 Years	3 Years
Reduce Annual Retirement Income by	$1,300	$2,600	$1,700	$3,300
Increased Risk of Outliving Resources	35%	90%	39%	96%
Reduction to Age 65 Portfolio Values:				
Likely More than:	$12,016	$24,120	$15,199	$28,779
Likely Less than:	$37,593	$73,098	$44,651	$86,890

	$10,000		$15,000	
Allocation: **45% Stock/55% Bonds**				
Base Comfortable "In Balance" Case:				
Maximum Fair Total Expense	0.75%		0.75%	
Retirement Income @ Age 65	$12,000		$15,800	
Age 65 Range of Portfolio Values	$229,195 to $574,580		$302,671 to $730,415	
EXCESS EXPENSE:	**0.50%**	**1.00%**	**0.50%**	**1.00%**
	(1.25% total)	(1.75% total)	(1.25% total)	(1.75% total)
COST OF EXCESS EXPENSE				
Additional Annual Savings Needed	$1,900	$3,900	$2,400	$5,200
Delay Retirement by	2 Years	3 Years	2 Years	3 Years
Reduce Annual Retirement Income by	$1,300	$2,400	$1,600	$3,200
Increased Risk of Outliving Resources	42%	114%	44%	117%
Reduction to Age 65 Portfolio Values:				
Likely More than:	$12,161	$23,612	$15,369	$30,112
Likely Less than:	$32,058	$62,280	$37,183	$72,348

Total annual savings is COMBINED annual employee AND employer contribution

AGE 50 WITH CURRENT 401(K) BALANCE OF $150,000

Total Annual Savings	$2,500		$5,000	
Allocation: **80% Stock/20% Bonds**				
Base Comfortable "In Balance" Case:				
Maximum Fair Total Expense	0.75%		0.75%	
Retirement Income @ Age 65	$13,400		$15,700	
Age 65 Range of Portfolio Values	$178,764 to $1,041,173		$212,097 to $1,153,783	
EXCESS EXPENSE:	**0.50%**	**1.00%**	**0.50%**	**1.00%**
	(1.25% total)	(1.75% total)	(1.25% total)	(1.75% total)
COST OF EXCESS EXPENSE				
Additional Annual Savings Needed	$1,800	$3,900	$2,200	$4,500
Delay Retirement by	2 Years	4 Years	2 Years	4 Years
Reduce Annual Retirement Income by	$1,500	$3,000	$1,800	$3,400
Increased Risk of Outliving Resources	36%	73%	36%	79%
Reduction to Age 65 Portfolio Values:				
Likely More than:	$13,252	$25,597	$14,514	$27,894
Likely Less than:	$68,452	$132,641	$73,634	$143,475

Allocation: **60% Stock/40% Bonds**				
Base Comfortable "In Balance" Case:				
Maximum Fair Total Expense	0.75%		0.75%	
Retirement Income @ Age 65	$12,100		$14,200	
Age 65 Range of Portfolio Values	$190,302 to $769,101		$226,806 to $858,540	
EXCESS EXPENSE:	**0.50%**	**1.00%**	**0.50%**	**1.00%**
	(1.25% total)	(1.75% total)	(1.25% total)	(1.75% total)
COST OF EXCESS EXPENSE				
Additional Annual Savings Needed	$1,800	$4,000	$2,200	$4,800
Delay Retirement by	2 Years	5 Years	2 Years	4 Years
Reduce Annual Retirement Income by	$1,400	$2,700	$1,700	$3,100
Increased Risk of Outliving Resources	43%	101%	40%	95%
Reduction to Age 65 Portfolio Values:				
Likely More than:	$13,685	$26,607	$15,352	$29,648
Likely Less than:	$51,890	$100,116	$55,676	$107,880

Allocation: **45% Stock/55% Bonds**				
Base Comfortable "In Balance" Case:				
Maximum Fair Total Expense	0.75%		0.75%	
Retirement Income @ Age 65	$10,800		$12,700	
Age 65 Range of Portfolio Values	$191,653 to $608,998		$229,906 to $686,487	
EXCESS EXPENSE:	**0.50%**	**1.00%**	**0.50%**	**1.00%**
	(1.25% total)	(1.75% total)	(1.25% total)	(1.75% total)
COST OF EXCESS EXPENSE				
Additional Annual Savings Needed	$1,800	$4,000	$2,100	$4,600
Delay Retirement by	3 Years	5 Years	2 Years	4 Years
Reduce Annual Retirement Income by	$1,300	$2,500	$1,500	$2,800
Increased Risk of Outliving Resources	46%	106%	44%	108%
Reduction to Age 65 Portfolio Values:				
Likely More than:	$13,743	$26,512	$15,050	$29,122
Likely Less than:	$41,061	$79,493	$43,730	$85,814

Total annual savings is COMBINED annual employee AND employer contribution

AGE 50 WITH CURRENT 401(K) BALANCE OF $150,000

Total Annual Savings	$10,000		$15,000	
Allocation: **80% Stock/20% Bonds**				
Base Comfortable "In Balance" Case:				
Maximum Fair Total Expense	0.75%		0.75%	
Retirement Income @ Age 65	$20,200		$24,800	
Age 65 Range of Portfolio Values	$284,600 to $1,379,124		$354,644 to $1,586,482	
EXCESS EXPENSE:	**0.50%**	**1.00%**	**0.50%**	**1.00%**
	(1.25% total)	(1.75% total)	(1.25% total)	(1.75% total)
COST OF EXCESS EXPENSE				
Additional Annual Savings Needed	$2,600	$5,500	$3,300	$7,000
Delay Retirement by	2 Years	4 Years	2 Years	3 Years
Reduce Annual Retirement Income by	$2,200	$4,100	$2,700	$5,100
Increased Risk of Outliving Resources	35%	79%	39%	85%
Reduction to Age 65 Portfolio Values:				
Likely More than:	$16,621	$33,518	$19,577	$37,957
Likely Less than:	$82,683	$160,471	$91,431	$179,920

Allocation: **60% Stock/40% Bonds**				
Base Comfortable "In Balance" Case:				
Maximum Fair Total Expense	0.75%		0.75%	
Retirement Income @ Age 65	$18,200		$22,200	
Age 65 Range of Portfolio Values	$303,471 to $1,018,516		$376,521 to $1,197,543	
EXCESS EXPENSE:	**0.50%**	**1.00%**	**0.50%**	**1.00%**
	(1.25% total)	(1.75% total)	(1.25% total)	(1.75% total)
COST OF EXCESS EXPENSE				
Additional Annual Savings Needed	$2,800	$5,700	$3,100	$6,500
Delay Retirement by	2 Years	4 Years	2 Years	3 Years
Reduce Annual Retirement Income by	$2,100	$3,900	$2,400	$4,500
Increased Risk of Outliving Resources	36%	94%	36%	92%
Reduction to Age 65 Portfolio Values:				
Likely More than:	$18,602	$36,294	$21,421	$41,559
Likely Less than:	$62,043	$120,358	$71,694	$137,754

Allocation: **45% Stock/55% Bonds**				
Base Comfortable "In Balance" Case:				
Maximum Fair Total Expense	0.75%		0.75%	
Retirement Income @ Age 65	$16,500		$20,200	
Age 65 Range of Portfolio Values	$306,893 to $833,626		$383,260 to $995,203	
EXCESS EXPENSE:	**0.50%**	**1.00%**	**0.50%**	**1.00%**
	(1.25% total)	(1.75% total)	(1.25% total)	(1.75% total)
COST OF EXCESS EXPENSE				
Additional Annual Savings Needed	$2,700	$5,700	$3,100	$6,600
Delay Retirement by	2 Years	4 Years	2 Years	4 Years
Reduce Annual Retirement Income by	$1,900	$3,500	$2,200	$4,200
Increased Risk of Outliving Resources	42%	109%	40%	112%
Reduction to Age 65 Portfolio Values:				
Likely More than:	$18,398	$35,015	$20,986	$41,726
Likely Less than:	$49,518	$96,068	$56,133	$109,004

Total annual savings is COMBINED annual employee AND employer contribution

AGE 50 WITH CURRENT 401(K) BALANCE OF $250,000

Total Annual Savings	$2,500		$5,000	
Allocation: **80% Stock/20% Bonds**				
Base Comfortable "In Balance" Case:				
Maximum Fair Total Expense	0.75%		0.75%	
Retirement Income @ Age 65	$21,000		$23,300	
Age 65 Range of Portfolio Values	$274,560 to $1,673,387		$308,809 to $1,772,583	
EXCESS EXPENSE:	**0.50%**	**1.00%**	**0.50%**	**1.00%**
	(1.25% total)	(1.75% total)	(1.25% total)	(1.75% total)
COST OF EXCESS EXPENSE				
Additional Annual Savings Needed	$3,000	$6,400	$3,200	$6,900
Delay Retirement by	3 Years	5 Years	2 Years	4 Years
Reduce Annual Retirement Income by	$2,500	$4,800	$2,800	$5,100
Increased Risk of Outliving Resources	37%	74%	36%	76%
Reduction to Age 65 Portfolio Values:				
Likely More than:	$21,165	$40,867	$22,507	$43,484
Likely Less than:	$112,413	$217,826	$115,668	$224,161

Allocation: **60% Stock/40% Bonds**				
Base Comfortable "In Balance" Case:				
Maximum Fair Total Expense	0.75%		0.75%	
Retirement Income @ Age 65	$18,900		$20,900	
Age 65 Range of Portfolio Values	$290,798 to $1,223,682		$329,192 to $1,308,061	
EXCESS EXPENSE:	**0.50%**	**1.00%**	**0.50%**	**1.00%**
	(1.25% total)	(1.75% total)	(1.25% total)	(1.75% total)
COST OF EXCESS EXPENSE				
Additional Annual Savings Needed	$3,100	$6,300	$3,200	$6,900
Delay Retirement by	3 Years	5 Years	2 Years	5 Years
Reduce Annual Retirement Income by	$2,300	$4,400	$2,400	$4,700
Increased Risk of Outliving Resources	44%	99%	41%	98%
Reduction to Age 65 Portfolio Values:				
Likely More than:	$22,047	$42,577	$23,558	$45,528
Likely Less than:	$82,741	$160,218	$86,612	$167,770

Allocation: **45% Stock/55% Bonds**				
Base Comfortable "In Balance" Case:				
Maximum Fair Total Expense	0.75%		0.75%	
Retirement Income @ Age 65	$16,800		$18,800	
Age 65 Range of Portfolio Values	$295,013 to $965,391		$332,050 to $1,039,663	
EXCESS EXPENSE:	**0.50%**	**1.00%**	**0.50%**	**1.00%**
	(1.25% total)	(1.75% total)	(1.25% total)	(1.75% total)
COST OF EXCESS EXPENSE				
Additional Annual Savings Needed	$2,900	$6,200	$3,400	$7,100
Delay Retirement by	3 Years	5 Years	3 Years	5 Years
Reduce Annual Retirement Income by	$2,100	$4,000	$2,400	$4,400
Increased Risk of Outliving Resources	47%	108%	46%	109%
Reduction to Age 65 Portfolio Values:				
Likely More than:	$22,061	$42,609	$23,113	$45,111
Likely Less than:	$66,364	$128,440	$68,845	$133,329

Total annual savings is COMBINED annual employee AND employer contribution

AGE 50 WITH CURRENT 401(K) BALANCE OF $250,000

Total Annual Savings	$10,000		$15,000	
Allocation: *80% Stock/20% Bonds*				
Base Comfortable "In Balance" Case:				
Maximum Fair Total Expense	0.75%		0.75%	
Retirement Income @ Age 65	$27,700		$32,100	
Age 65 Range of Portfolio Values	$376,891 to $1,990,497		$449,396 to $2,222,463	
EXCESS EXPENSE:	**0.50%**	**1.00%**	**0.50%**	**1.00%**
	(1.25% total)	(1.75% total)	(1.25% total)	(1.75% total)
COST OF EXCESS EXPENSE				
Additional Annual Savings Needed	$3,700	$7,800	$4,000	$8,800
Delay Retirement by	2 Years	4 Years	2 Years	4 Years
Reduce Annual Retirement Income by	$3,100	$5,900	$3,400	$6,600
Increased Risk of Outliving Resources	31%	78%	34%	79%
Reduction to Age 65 Portfolio Values:				
Likely More than:	$25,332	$49,010	$28,285	$53,231
Likely Less than:	$126,958	$246,127	$133,598	$260,223

Allocation: *60% Stock/40% Bonds*				
Base Comfortable "In Balance" Case:				
Maximum Fair Total Expense	0.75%		0.75%	
Retirement Income @ Age 65	$24,900		$29,000	
Age 65 Range of Portfolio Values	$403,084 to $1,480,367		$479,923 to $1,640,647	
EXCESS EXPENSE:	**0.50%**	**1.00%**	**0.50%**	**1.00%**
	(1.25% total)	(1.75% total)	(1.25% total)	(1.75% total)
COST OF EXCESS EXPENSE				
Additional Annual Savings Needed	$3,700	$8,000	$4,500	$9,200
Delay Retirement by	2 Years	4 Years	2 Years	4 Years
Reduce Annual Retirement Income by	$2,800	$5,300	$3,200	$6,200
Increased Risk of Outliving Resources	41%	98%	36%	95%
Reduction to Age 65 Portfolio Values:				
Likely More than:	$25,553	$48,169	$28,441	$55,079
Likely Less than:	$94,827	$183,776	$100,950	$195,720

Allocation: *45% Stock/55% Bonds*				
Base Comfortable "In Balance" Case:				
Maximum Fair Total Expense	0.75%		0.75%	
Retirement Income @ Age 65	$22,500		$26,200	
Age 65 Range of Portfolio Values	$409,740 to $1,193,225		$485,757 to $1,335,598	
EXCESS EXPENSE:	**0.50%**	**1.00%**	**0.50%**	**1.00%**
	(1.25% total)	(1.75% total)	(1.25% total)	(1.75% total)
COST OF EXCESS EXPENSE				
Additional Annual Savings Needed	$3,800	$8,000	$4,400	$9,000
Delay Retirement by	2 Years	4 Years	2 Years	4 Years
Reduce Annual Retirement Income by	$2,600	$5,000	$3,000	$5,600
Increased Risk of Outliving Resources	40%	107%	40%	106%
Reduction to Age 65 Portfolio Values:				
Likely More than:	$26,805	$51,865	$29,632	$56,850
Likely Less than:	$76,207	$147,117	$80,324	$155,801

Total annual savings is COMBINED annual employee AND employer contribution

AGE 55 WITH CURRENT 401(K) BALANCE OF $25,000

Total Annual Savings	$2,500		$5,000	
Allocation: **80% Stock/20% Bonds**				
Base Comfortable "In Balance" Case:				
Maximum Fair Total Expense	0.75%		0.75%	
Retirement Income @ Age 65	$2,800		$4,200	
Age 65 Range of Portfolio Values	$44,649 to $150,039		$67,706 to $204,743	
EXCESS EXPENSE:	**0.50%**	**1.00%**	**0.50%**	**1.00%**
	(1.25% total)	(1.75% total)	(1.25% total)	(1.75% total)
COST OF EXCESS EXPENSE				
Additional Annual Savings Needed	$400	$1,000	$700	$1,600
Delay Retirement by	1 Years	2 Years	1 Years	2 Years
Reduce Annual Retirement Income by	$200	$500	$400	$800
Increased Risk of Outliving Resources	32%	74%	38%	80%
Reduction to Age 65 Portfolio Values:				
Likely More than:	$1,813	$3,550	$2,396	$4,899
Likely Less than:	$5,991	$11,736	$7,794	$15,260

Allocation: **60% Stock/40% Bonds**				
Base Comfortable "In Balance" Case:				
Maximum Fair Total Expense	0.75%		0.75%	
Retirement Income @ Age 65	$2,600		$3,800	
Age 65 Range of Portfolio Values	$46,684 to $123,897		$70,477 to $172,367	
EXCESS EXPENSE:	**0.50%**	**1.00%**	**0.50%**	**1.00%**
	(1.25% total)	(1.75% total)	(1.25% total)	(1.75% total)
COST OF EXCESS EXPENSE				
Additional Annual Savings Needed	$500	$1,100	$600	$1,500
Delay Retirement by	1 Years	3 Years	1 Years	2 Years
Reduce Annual Retirement Income by	$200	$500	$300	$600
Increased Risk of Outliving Resources	41%	93%	44%	99%
Reduction to Age 65 Portfolio Values:				
Likely More than:	$1,850	$3,699	$2,413	$4,816
Likely Less than:	$5,035	$9,870	$6,074	$12,018

Allocation: **45% Stock/55% Bonds**				
Base Comfortable "In Balance" Case:				
Maximum Fair Total Expense	0.75%		0.75%	
Retirement Income @ Age 65	$2,400		$3,500	
Age 65 Range of Portfolio Values	$47,517 to $109,721		$72,154 to $153,344	
EXCESS EXPENSE:	**0.50%**	**1.00%**	**0.50%**	**1.00%**
	(1.25% total)	(1.75% total)	(1.25% total)	(1.75% total)
COST OF EXCESS EXPENSE				
Additional Annual Savings Needed	$500	$1,100	$600	$1,400
Delay Retirement by	1 Years	3 Years	1 Years	2 Years
Reduce Annual Retirement Income by	$200	$500	$300	$600
Increased Risk of Outliving Resources	57%	114%	49%	114%
Reduction to Age 65 Portfolio Values:				
Likely More than:	$1,806	$3,603	$2,548	$5,082
Likely Less than:	$4,416	$8,690	$5,621	$11,029

Total annual savings is COMBINED annual employee AND employer contribution

AGE 55 WITH CURRENT 401(K) BALANCE OF $25,000

Total Annual Savings	$10,000		$15,000	
Allocation: **80% Stock/20% Bonds**				
Base Comfortable "In Balance" Case:				
Maximum Fair Total Expense	0.75%		0.75%	
Retirement Income @ Age 65	$6,800		$9,400	
Age 65 Range of Portfolio Values	$114,062 to $313,730		$159,352 to $424,927	
EXCESS EXPENSE:	**0.50%**	**1.00%**	**0.50%**	**1.00%**
	(1.25% total)	(1.75% total)	(1.25% total)	(1.75% total)
COST OF EXCESS EXPENSE				
Additional Annual Savings Needed	$1,100	$2,500	$1,500	$3,300
Delay Retirement by	1 Years	2 Years	1 Years	2 Years
Reduce Annual Retirement Income by	$600	$1,100	$800	$1,500
Increased Risk of Outliving Resources	32%	73%	31%	74%
Reduction to Age 65 Portfolio Values:				
Likely More than:	$3,561	$7,113	$4,545	$9,150
Likely Less than:	$10,250	$20,152	$13,205	$25,977

Allocation: **60% Stock/40% Bonds**				
Base Comfortable "In Balance" Case:				
Maximum Fair Total Expense	0.75%		0.75%	
Retirement Income @ Age 65	$6,300		$8,800	
Age 65 Range of Portfolio Values	$118,405 to $268,197		$165,860 to $365,888	
EXCESS EXPENSE:	**0.50%**	**1.00%**	**0.50%**	**1.00%**
	(1.25% total)	(1.75% total)	(1.25% total)	(1.75% total)
COST OF EXCESS EXPENSE				
Additional Annual Savings Needed	$1,100	$2,400	$1,700	$3,500
Delay Retirement by	1 Years	2 Years	1 Years	2 Years
Reduce Annual Retirement Income by	$500	$1,100	$800	$1,500
Increased Risk of Outliving Resources	45%	96%	44%	92%
Reduction to Age 65 Portfolio Values:				
Likely More than:	$3,580	$7,035	$5,154	$9,779
Likely Less than:	$8,279	$17,073	$11,166	$21,967

Allocation: **45% Stock/55% Bonds**				
Base Comfortable "In Balance" Case:				
Maximum Fair Total Expense	0.75%		0.75%	
Retirement Income @ Age 65	$5,900		$8,200	
Age 65 Range of Portfolio Values	$120,936 to $240,466		$170,158 to $327,803	
EXCESS EXPENSE:	**0.50%**	**1.00%**	**0.50%**	**1.00%**
	(1.25% total)	(1.75% total)	(1.25% total)	(1.75% total)
COST OF EXCESS EXPENSE				
Additional Annual Savings Needed	$1,300	$2,500	$1,600	$3,500
Delay Retirement by	1 Years	2 Years	1 Years	2 Years
Reduce Annual Retirement Income by	$600	$1,100	$700	$1,400
Increased Risk of Outliving Resources	54%	116%	51%	111%
Reduction to Age 65 Portfolio Values:				
Likely More than:	$3,721	$7,328	$5,041	$10,015
Likely Less than:	$7,421	$14,592	$10,421	$20,492

Total annual savings is COMBINED annual employee AND employer contribution

AGE 55 WITH CURRENT 401(K) BALANCE OF $75,000

Total Annual Savings	$2,500		$5,000	
Allocation: **80% Stock/20% Bonds**				
Base Comfortable "In Balance" Case:				
Maximum Fair Total Expense	0.75%		0.75%	
Retirement Income @ Age 65	$5,800		$7,200	
Age 65 Range of Portfolio Values	$87,593 to $339,088		$111,390 to $394,481	
EXCESS EXPENSE:	**0.50%**	**1.00%**	**0.50%**	**1.00%**
	(1.25% total)	(1.75% total)	(1.25% total)	(1.75% total)
COST OF EXCESS EXPENSE				
Additional Annual Savings Needed	$1,100	$2,300	$1,300	$2,700
Delay Retirement by	2 Years	3 Years	2 Years	3 Years
Reduce Annual Retirement Income by	$600	$1,100	$700	$1,300
Increased Risk of Outliving Resources	28%	66%	32%	67%
Reduction to Age 65 Portfolio Values:				
Likely More than:	$4,277	$8,358	$4,799	$9,639
Likely Less than:	$15,188	$29,744	$16,671	$32,610

Allocation: **60% Stock/40% Bonds**				
Base Comfortable "In Balance" Case:				
Maximum Fair Total Expense	0.75%		0.75%	
Retirement Income @ Age 65	$5,300		$6,600	
Age 65 Range of Portfolio Values	$90,461 to $275,898		$115,132 to $325,871	
EXCESS EXPENSE:	**0.50%**	**1.00%**	**0.50%**	**1.00%**
	(1.25% total)	(1.75% total)	(1.25% total)	(1.75% total)
COST OF EXCESS EXPENSE				
Additional Annual Savings Needed	$1,000	$2,200	$1,300	$2,700
Delay Retirement by	2 Years	3 Years	2 Years	3 Years
Reduce Annual Retirement Income by	$500	$1,000	$600	$1,200
Increased Risk of Outliving Resources	34%	93%	36%	90%
Reduction to Age 65 Portfolio Values:				
Likely More than:	$4,369	$8,504	$5,052	$9,885
Likely Less than:	$12,597	$24,462	$13,451	$26,357

Allocation: **45% Stock/55% Bonds**				
Base Comfortable "In Balance" Case:				
Maximum Fair Total Expense	0.75%		0.75%	
Retirement Income @ Age 65	$4,900		$6,100	
Age 65 Range of Portfolio Values	$94,017 to $238,911		$117,826 to $283,565	
EXCESS EXPENSE:	**0.50%**	**1.00%**	**0.50%**	**1.00%**
	(1.25% total)	(1.75% total)	(1.25% total)	(1.75% total)
COST OF EXCESS EXPENSE				
Additional Annual Savings Needed	$1,000	$2,200	$1,200	$2,800
Delay Retirement by	2 Years	4 Years	2 Years	3 Years
Reduce Annual Retirement Income by	$500	$900	$600	$1,100
Increased Risk of Outliving Resources	56%	113%	54%	110%
Reduction to Age 65 Portfolio Values:				
Likely More than:	$4,429	$8,807	$5,039	$9,926
Likely Less than:	$10,715	$20,983	$11,893	$23,301

Total annual savings is COMBINED annual employee AND employer contribution

AGE 55 WITH CURRENT 401(K) BALANCE OF $75,000

Total Annual Savings	$10,000		$15,000	
Allocation: **80% Stock/20% Bonds**				
Base Comfortable "In Balance" Case:				
Maximum Fair Total Expense	0.75%		0.75%	
Retirement Income @ Age 65	$10,000		$12,600	
Age 65 Range of Portfolio Values	$156,762 to $505,267		$203,118 to $614,230	
EXCESS EXPENSE:	**0.50%**	**1.00%**	**0.50%**	**1.00%**
	(1.25% total)	(1.75% total)	(1.25% total)	(1.75% total)
COST OF EXCESS EXPENSE				
Additional Annual Savings Needed	$1,800	$3,900	$2,100	$4,800
Delay Retirement by	1 Years	3 Years	1 Years	2 Years
Reduce Annual Retirement Income by	$1,000	$1,800	$1,100	$2,200
Increased Risk of Outliving Resources	35%	75%	38%	80%
Reduction to Age 65 Portfolio Values:				
Likely More than:	$6,023	$11,800	$7,188	$14,696
Likely Less than:	$19,635	$38,513	$23,382	$45,780

Allocation: **60% Stock/40% Bonds**				
Base Comfortable "In Balance" Case:				
Maximum Fair Total Expense	0.75%		0.75%	
Retirement Income @ Age 65	$9,200		$11,600	
Age 65 Range of Portfolio Values	$163,315 to $416,749		$211,187 to $516,858	
EXCESS EXPENSE:	**0.50%**	**1.00%**	**0.50%**	**1.00%**
	(1.25% total)	(1.75% total)	(1.25% total)	(1.75% total)
COST OF EXCESS EXPENSE				
Additional Annual Savings Needed	$1,800	$4,100	$2,200	$4,800
Delay Retirement by	2 Years	3 Years	1 Years	2 Years
Reduce Annual Retirement Income by	$900	$1,700	$1,100	$2,000
Increased Risk of Outliving Resources	43%	93%	40%	89%
Reduction to Age 65 Portfolio Values:				
Likely More than:	$6,472	$12,450	$7,238	$14,447
Likely Less than:	$15,487	$31,082	$18,223	$36,053

Allocation: **45% Stock/55% Bonds**				
Base Comfortable "In Balance" Case:				
Maximum Fair Total Expense	0.75%		0.75%	
Retirement Income @ Age 65	$8,400		$10,700	
Age 65 Range of Portfolio Values	$167,449 to $372,987		$216,220 to $459,789	
EXCESS EXPENSE:	**0.50%**	**1.00%**	**0.50%**	**1.00%**
	(1.25% total)	(1.75% total)	(1.25% total)	(1.75% total)
COST OF EXCESS EXPENSE				
Additional Annual Savings Needed	$1,700	$3,800	$2,100	$4,700
Delay Retirement by	1 Years	3 Years	1 Years	3 Years
Reduce Annual Retirement Income by	$700	$1,500	$1,000	$1,900
Increased Risk of Outliving Resources	52%	109%	51%	108%
Reduction to Age 65 Portfolio Values:				
Likely More than:	$6,642	$12,870	$7,644	$15,248
Likely Less than:	$14,240	$27,929	$16,861	$33,088

Total annual savings is COMBINED annual employee AND employer contribution

AGE 55 WITH CURRENT 401(K) BALANCE OF $150,000

Total Annual Savings Allocation: **80% Stock/20% Bonds**	$2,500		$5,000	
Base Comfortable "In Balance" Case:				
Maximum Fair Total Expense	0.75%		0.75%	
Retirement Income @ Age 65	$10,300		$11,600	
Age 65 Range of Portfolio Values	$150,656 to $623,482		$175,185 to $678,175	
EXCESS EXPENSE:	**0.50%**	**1.00%**	**0.50%**	**1.00%**
	(1.25% total)	(1.75% total)	(1.25% total)	(1.75% total)
COST OF EXCESS EXPENSE				
Additional Annual Savings Needed	$2,100	$4,200	$2,200	$4,500
Delay Retirement by	2 Years	4 Years	2 Years	3 Years
Reduce Annual Retirement Income by	$1,100	$2,000	$1,100	$2,200
Increased Risk of Outliving Resources	28%	65%	28%	66%
Reduction to Age 65 Portfolio Values:				
Likely More than:	$7,831	$15,296	$8,552	$16,714
Likely Less than:	$28,549	$55,907	$30,376	$59,488

Allocation: **60% Stock/40% Bonds**				
Base Comfortable "In Balance" Case:				
Maximum Fair Total Expense	0.75%		0.75%	
Retirement Income @ Age 65	$9,500		$10,700	
Age 65 Range of Portfolio Values	$157,110 to $505,456		$180,800 to $551,675	
EXCESS EXPENSE:	**0.50%**	**1.00%**	**0.50%**	**1.00%**
	(1.25% total)	(1.75% total)	(1.25% total)	(1.75% total)
COST OF EXCESS EXPENSE				
Additional Annual Savings Needed	$2,100	$4,400	$2,200	$4,600
Delay Retirement by	2 Years	4 Years	2 Years	3 Years
Reduce Annual Retirement Income by	$1,000	$1,900	$1,100	$2,100
Increased Risk of Outliving Resources	35%	86%	33%	90%
Reduction to Age 65 Portfolio Values:				
Likely More than:	$8,003	$15,744	$8,737	$17,008
Likely Less than:	$23,467	$45,940	$25,195	$48,923

Allocation: **45% Stock/55% Bonds**				
Base Comfortable "In Balance" Case:				
Maximum Fair Total Expense	0.75%		0.75%	
Retirement Income @ Age 65	$8,700		$9,900	
Age 65 Range of Portfolio Values	$162,101 to $435,212		$187,913 to $477,700	
EXCESS EXPENSE:	**0.50%**	**1.00%**	**0.50%**	**1.00%**
	(1.25% total)	(1.75% total)	(1.25% total)	(1.75% total)
COST OF EXCESS EXPENSE				
Additional Annual Savings Needed	$2,000	$4,200	$2,200	$4,600
Delay Retirement by	2 Years	4 Years	2 Years	4 Years
Reduce Annual Retirement Income by	$900	$1,700	$1,000	$1,900
Increased Risk of Outliving Resources	53%	111%	51%	105%
Reduction to Age 65 Portfolio Values:				
Likely More than:	$8,309	$16,233	$8,858	$17,614
Likely Less than:	$20,488	$40,096	$21,430	$41,966

Total annual savings is COMBINED annual employee AND employer contribution

AGE 55 WITH CURRENT 401(K) BALANCE OF $150,000

Total Annual Savings	$10,000		$15,000	
Allocation: **80% Stock/20% Bonds**				
Base Comfortable "In Balance" Case:				
Maximum Fair Total Expense	0.75%		0.75%	
Retirement Income @ Age 65	$14,400		$17,200	
Age 65 Range of Portfolio Values	$222,781 to $788,962		$267,411 to $899,748	
EXCESS EXPENSE:	**0.50%**	**1.00%**	**0.50%**	**1.00%**
	(1.25% total)	(1.75% total)	(1.25% total)	(1.75% total)
COST OF EXCESS EXPENSE				
Additional Annual Savings Needed	$2,600	$5,400	$3,100	$6,500
Delay Retirement by	2 Years	3 Years	1 Years	3 Years
Reduce Annual Retirement Income by	$1,400	$2,600	$1,600	$3,000
Increased Risk of Outliving Resources	32%	67%	33%	73%
Reduction to Age 65 Portfolio Values:				
Likely More than:	$9,599	$19,279	$10,881	$21,305
Likely Less than:	$33,341	$65,219	$35,948	$70,413

Allocation: **60% Stock/40% Bonds**				
Base Comfortable "In Balance" Case:				
Maximum Fair Total Expense	0.75%		0.75%	
Retirement Income @ Age 65	$13,200		$15,800	
Age 65 Range of Portfolio Values	$230,263 to $651,743		$279,860 to $743,141	
EXCESS EXPENSE:	**0.50%**	**1.00%**	**0.50%**	**1.00%**
	(1.25% total)	(1.75% total)	(1.25% total)	(1.75% total)
COST OF EXCESS EXPENSE				
Additional Annual Savings Needed	$2,500	$5,400	$3,000	$6,600
Delay Retirement by	2 Years	3 Years	2 Years	3 Years
Reduce Annual Retirement Income by	$1,200	$2,400	$1,400	$2,800
Increased Risk of Outliving Resources	36%	90%	39%	90%
Reduction to Age 65 Portfolio Values:				
Likely More than:	$10,104	$19,770	$11,100	$22,194
Likely Less than:	$26,903	$52,716	$30,210	$59,221

Allocation: **45% Stock/55% Bonds**				
Base Comfortable "In Balance" Case:				
Maximum Fair Total Expense	0.75%		0.75%	
Retirement Income @ Age 65	$12,300		$14,600	
Age 65 Range of Portfolio Values	$235,531 to $567,010		$284,858 to $658,085	
EXCESS EXPENSE:	**0.50%**	**1.00%**	**0.50%**	**1.00%**
	(1.25% total)	(1.75% total)	(1.25% total)	(1.75% total)
COST OF EXCESS EXPENSE				
Additional Annual Savings Needed	$2,700	$5,900	$3,100	$6,700
Delay Retirement by	2 Years	3 Years	2 Years	3 Years
Reduce Annual Retirement Income by	$1,200	$2,300	$1,400	$2,700
Increased Risk of Outliving Resources	53%	110%	55%	110%
Reduction to Age 65 Portfolio Values:				
Likely More than:	$10,079	$19,852	$10,837	$21,616
Likely Less than:	$23,787	$46,603	$26,496	$52,140

Total annual savings is COMBINED annual employee AND employer contribution

AGE 55 WITH CURRENT 401(K) BALANCE OF $250,000

Total Annual Savings	$2,500		$5,000	
Allocation: **80% Stock/20% Bonds**				
Base Comfortable "In Balance" Case:				
Maximum Fair Total Expense	0.75%		0.75%	
Retirement Income @ Age 65	$16,200		$17,600	
Age 65 Range of Portfolio Values	$233,971 to $1,009,023		$259,605 to $1,056,272	
EXCESS EXPENSE:	**0.50%**	**1.00%**	**0.50%**	**1.00%**
	(1.25% total)	(1.75% total)	(1.25% total)	(1.75% total)
COST OF EXCESS EXPENSE				
Additional Annual Savings Needed	$3,100	$6,700	$3,500	$7,100
Delay Retirement by	2 Years	4 Years	2 Years	4 Years
Reduce Annual Retirement Income by	$1,600	$3,200	$1,800	$3,400
Increased Risk of Outliving Resources	26%	62%	28%	66%
Reduction to Age 65 Portfolio Values:				
Likely More than:	$12,641	$24,684	$13,145	$25,684
Likely Less than:	$46,760	$91,559	$48,650	$95,249

Allocation: **60% Stock/40% Bonds**				
Base Comfortable "In Balance" Case:				
Maximum Fair Total Expense	0.75%		0.75%	
Retirement Income @ Age 65	$15,100		$16,200	
Age 65 Range of Portfolio Values	$243,219 to $813,860		$269,450 to $856,709	
EXCESS EXPENSE:	**0.50%**	**1.00%**	**0.50%**	**1.00%**
	(1.25% total)	(1.75% total)	(1.25% total)	(1.75% total)
COST OF EXCESS EXPENSE				
Additional Annual Savings Needed	$3,600	$7,100	$3,500	$7,200
Delay Retirement by	3 Years	5 Years	2 Years	4 Years
Reduce Annual Retirement Income by	$1,700	$3,100	$1,600	$3,200
Increased Risk of Outliving Resources	36%	89%	33%	85%
Reduction to Age 65 Portfolio Values:				
Likely More than:	$12,794	$24,988	$14,015	$27,378
Likely Less than:	$38,343	$75,050	$39,496	$77,323

Allocation: **45% Stock/55% Bonds**				
Base Comfortable "In Balance" Case:				
Maximum Fair Total Expense	0.75%		0.75%	
Retirement Income @ Age 65	$13,800		$15,000	
Age 65 Range of Portfolio Values	$252,278 to $698,105		$278,358 to $738,057	
EXCESS EXPENSE:	**0.50%**	**1.00%**	**0.50%**	**1.00%**
	(1.25% total)	(1.75% total)	(1.25% total)	(1.75% total)
COST OF EXCESS EXPENSE				
Additional Annual Savings Needed	$3,400	$7,000	$3,600	$7,400
Delay Retirement by	3 Years	5 Years	2 Years	4 Years
Reduce Annual Retirement Income by	$1,500	$2,800	$1,600	$3,000
Increased Risk of Outliving Resources	48%	108%	51%	108%
Reduction to Age 65 Portfolio Values:				
Likely More than:	$13,292	$25,960	$13,924	$27,206
Likely Less than:	$33,219	$65,005	$34,496	$67,515

Total annual savings is COMBINED annual employee AND employer contribution

AGE 55 WITH CURRENT 401(K) BALANCE OF $250,000

Total Annual Savings	$10,000		$15,000	
Allocation: **80% Stock/20% Bonds**				
Base Comfortable "In Balance" Case:				
Maximum Fair Total Expense	0.75%		0.75%	
Retirement Income @ Age 65	$20,300		$23,000	
Age 65 Range of Portfolio Values	$307,306 to $1,164,933		$353,769 to $1,279,049	
EXCESS EXPENSE:	**0.50%**	**1.00%**	**0.50%**	**1.00%**
	(1.25% total)	(1.75% total)	(1.25% total)	(1.75% total)
COST OF EXCESS EXPENSE				
Additional Annual Savings Needed	$3,800	$7,800	$4,100	$8,500
Delay Retirement by	2 Years	3 Years	2 Years	3 Years
Reduce Annual Retirement Income by	$2,000	$3,800	$2,100	$4,100
Increased Risk of Outliving Resources	29%	66%	32%	68%
Reduction to Age 65 Portfolio Values:				
Likely More than:	$14,642	$28,623	$14,952	$29,792
Likely Less than:	$50,685	$99,306	$53,322	$105,203

Allocation: **60% Stock/40% Bonds**				
Base Comfortable "In Balance" Case:				
Maximum Fair Total Expense	0.75%		0.75%	
Retirement Income @ Age 65	$18,800		$21,200	
Age 65 Range of Portfolio Values	$317,987 to $951,145		$368,111 to $1,054,077	
EXCESS EXPENSE:	**0.50%**	**1.00%**	**0.50%**	**1.00%**
	(1.25% total)	(1.75% total)	(1.25% total)	(1.75% total)
COST OF EXCESS EXPENSE				
Additional Annual Savings Needed	$4,000	$8,300	$4,000	$8,700
Delay Retirement by	2 Years	3 Years	2 Years	3 Years
Reduce Annual Retirement Income by	$1,900	$3,600	$2,000	$3,800
Increased Risk of Outliving Resources	34%	92%	37%	94%
Reduction to Age 65 Portfolio Values:				
Likely More than:	$14,795	$28,931	$16,533	$32,248
Likely Less than:	$41,510	$81,296	$45,484	$87,830

Allocation: **45% Stock/55% Bonds**				
Base Comfortable "In Balance" Case:				
Maximum Fair Total Expense	0.75%		0.75%	
Retirement Income @ Age 65	$17,400		$19,800	
Age 65 Range of Portfolio Values	$327,705 to $826,090		$376,305 to $915,228	
EXCESS EXPENSE:	**0.50%**	**1.00%**	**0.50%**	**1.00%**
	(1.25% total)	(1.75% total)	(1.25% total)	(1.75% total)
COST OF EXCESS EXPENSE				
Additional Annual Savings Needed	$3,900	$8,400	$4,500	$9,600
Delay Retirement by	2 Years	4 Years	2 Years	3 Years
Reduce Annual Retirement Income by	$1,800	$3,400	$2,000	$3,700
Increased Risk of Outliving Resources	53%	109%	52%	111%
Reduction to Age 65 Portfolio Values:				
Likely More than:	$15,755	$30,416	$16,597	$32,475
Likely Less than:	$36,379	$71,236	$39,025	$76,586

Total annual savings is COMBINED annual employee AND employer contribution

AGE 60 WITH CURRENT 401(K) BALANCE OF $25,000

Total Annual Savings Allocation: **80% Stock/20% Bonds**	$2,500		$5,000	
Base Comfortable "In Balance" Case:				
Maximum Fair Total Expense	0.75%		0.75%	
Retirement Income @ Age 65	$1,800		$2,400	
Age 65 Range of Portfolio Values	$30,994 to $81,028		$43,621 to $102,461	
EXCESS EXPENSE:	**0.50%**	**1.00%**	**0.50%**	**1.00%**
	(1.25% total)	(1.75% total)	(1.25% total)	(1.75% total)
COST OF EXCESS EXPENSE				
Additional Annual Savings Needed	$600	$1,200	$500	$1,400
Delay Retirement by	1 Years	2 Years	1 Years	2 Years
Reduce Annual Retirement Income by	$200	$300	$200	$300
Increased Risk of Outliving Resources	28%	64%	28%	60%
Reduction to Age 65 Portfolio Values:				
Likely More than:	$756	$1,496	$903	$1,836
Likely Less than:	$1,796	$3,558	$2,174	$4,307

Allocation: **60% Stock/40% Bonds**				
Base Comfortable "In Balance" Case:				
Maximum Fair Total Expense	0.75%		0.75%	
Retirement Income @ Age 65	$1,700		$2,300	
Age 65 Range of Portfolio Values	$32,470 to $71,438		$45,590 to $91,243	
EXCESS EXPENSE:	**0.50%**	**1.00%**	**0.50%**	**1.00%**
	(1.25% total)	(1.75% total)	(1.25% total)	(1.75% total)
COST OF EXCESS EXPENSE				
Additional Annual Savings Needed	$500	$1,200	$700	$1,600
Delay Retirement by	1 Years	2 Years	1 Years	2 Years
Reduce Annual Retirement Income by	$200	$300	$200	$400
Increased Risk of Outliving Resources	36%	71%	32%	71%
Reduction to Age 65 Portfolio Values:				
Likely More than:	$780	$1,544	$952	$1,870
Likely Less than:	$1,620	$3,208	$1,871	$3,706

Allocation: **45% Stock/55% Bonds**				
Base Comfortable "In Balance" Case:				
Maximum Fair Total Expense	0.75%		0.75%	
Retirement Income @ Age 65	$1,600		$2,200	
Age 65 Range of Portfolio Values	$33,240 to $65,045		$46,219 to $83,867	
EXCESS EXPENSE:	**0.50%**	**1.00%**	**0.50%**	**1.00%**
	(1.25% total)	(1.75% total)	(1.25% total)	(1.75% total)
COST OF EXCESS EXPENSE				
Additional Annual Savings Needed	$500	$1,200	$800	$1,700
Delay Retirement by	1 Years	2 Years	1 Years	2 Years
Reduce Annual Retirement Income by	$100	$300	$200	$400
Increased Risk of Outliving Resources	34%	89%	40%	92%
Reduction to Age 65 Portfolio Values:				
Likely More than:	$798	$1,578	$949	$1,893
Likely Less than:	$1,474	$2,943	$1,695	$3,357

Total annual savings is COMBINED annual employee AND employer contribution

AGE 60 WITH CURRENT 401(K) BALANCE OF $25,000

Total Annual Savings		$10,000		$15,000	
Allocation: **80% Stock/20% Bonds**					
Base Comfortable "In Balance" Case:					
Maximum Fair Total Expense		0.75%		0.75%	
Retirement Income @ Age 65		$3,700		$4,900	
Age 65 Range of Portfolio Values		$69,085 to $146,476		$93,267 to $191,168	
EXCESS EXPENSE:		**0.50%**	**1.00%**	**0.50%**	**1.00%**
		(1.25% total)	(1.75% total)	(1.25% total)	(1.75% total)
COST OF EXCESS EXPENSE					
Additional Annual Savings Needed		$1,100	$2,400	$1,100	$2,700
Delay Retirement by		1 Years	1 Years	1 Years	1 Years
Reduce Annual Retirement Income by		$300	$600	$300	$700
Increased Risk of Outliving Resources		32%	63%	31%	65%
Reduction to Age 65 Portfolio Values:					
Likely More than:		$1,276	$2,528	$1,586	$3,143
Likely Less than:		$2,576	$5,108	$3,221	$6,390

Allocation: **60% Stock/40% Bonds**					
Base Comfortable "In Balance" Case:					
Maximum Fair Total Expense		0.75%		0.75%	
Retirement Income @ Age 65		$3,500		$4,700	
Age 65 Range of Portfolio Values		$71,300 to $131,649		$96,584 to $173,573	
EXCESS EXPENSE:		**0.50%**	**1.00%**	**0.50%**	**1.00%**
		(1.25% total)	(1.75% total)	(1.25% total)	(1.75% total)
COST OF EXCESS EXPENSE					
Additional Annual Savings Needed		$900	$2,200	$1,300	$3,000
Delay Retirement by		1 Years	1 Years	1 Years	1 Years
Reduce Annual Retirement Income by		$300	$500	$300	$700
Increased Risk of Outliving Resources		38%	80%	38%	79%
Reduction to Age 65 Portfolio Values:					
Likely More than:		$1,335	$2,644	$1,598	$3,135
Likely Less than:		$2,312	$4,584	$2,892	$5,678

Allocation: **45% Stock/55% Bonds**					
Base Comfortable "In Balance" Case:					
Maximum Fair Total Expense		0.75%		0.75%	
Retirement Income @ Age 65		$3,300		$4,500	
Age 65 Range of Portfolio Values		$72,207 to $122,642		$97,718 to $161,239	
EXCESS EXPENSE:		**0.50%**	**1.00%**	**0.50%**	**1.00%**
		(1.25% total)	(1.75% total)	(1.25% total)	(1.75% total)
COST OF EXCESS EXPENSE					
Additional Annual Savings Needed		$800	$2,100	$1,500	$3,100
Delay Retirement by		1 Years	1 Years	1 Years	1 Years
Reduce Annual Retirement Income by		$200	$500	$300	$700
Increased Risk of Outliving Resources		51%	105%	43%	99%
Reduction to Age 65 Portfolio Values:					
Likely More than:		$1,305	$2,621	$1,618	$3,207
Likely Less than:		$2,181	$4,324	$2,700	$5,355

Total annual savings is COMBINED annual employee AND employer contribution

AGE 60 WITH CURRENT 401(K) BALANCE OF $75,000

Total Annual Savings	$2,500		$5,000	
Allocation: **80% Stock/20% Bonds**				
Base Comfortable "In Balance" Case:				
Maximum Fair Total Expense	0.75%		0.75%	
Retirement Income @ Age 65	$4,100		$4,800	
Age 65 Range of Portfolio Values	$68,367 to $201,376		$80,518 to $222,122	
EXCESS EXPENSE:	**0.50%**	**1.00%**	**0.50%**	**1.00%**
	(1.25% total)	(1.75% total)	(1.25% total)	(1.75% total)
COST OF EXCESS EXPENSE				
Additional Annual Savings Needed	$1,000	$2,600	$1,500	$3,400
Delay Retirement by	1 Years	3 Years	1 Years	2 Years
Reduce Annual Retirement Income by	$300	$600	$400	$800
Increased Risk of Outliving Resources	28%	63%	25%	58%
Reduction to Age 65 Portfolio Values:				
Likely More than:	$1,970	$3,894	$2,081	$4,113
Likely Less than:	$4,858	$9,617	$5,116	$10,129

Allocation: **60% Stock/40% Bonds**				
Base Comfortable "In Balance" Case:				
Maximum Fair Total Expense	0.75%		0.75%	
Retirement Income @ Age 65	$3,900		$4,500	
Age 65 Range of Portfolio Values	$71,134 to $175,914		$84,272 to $195,138	
EXCESS EXPENSE:	**0.50%**	**1.00%**	**0.50%**	**1.00%**
	(1.25% total)	(1.75% total)	(1.25% total)	(1.75% total)
COST OF EXCESS EXPENSE				
Additional Annual Savings Needed	$1,300	$2,800	$1,300	$3,200
Delay Retirement by	1 Years	3 Years	1 Years	2 Years
Reduce Annual Retirement Income by	$400	$600	$300	$700
Increased Risk of Outliving Resources	35%	69%	38%	73%
Reduction to Age 65 Portfolio Values:				
Likely More than:	$2,013	$3,978	$2,199	$4,399
Likely Less than:	$4,354	$8,616	$4,529	$8,967

Allocation: **45% Stock/55% Bonds**				
Base Comfortable "In Balance" Case:				
Maximum Fair Total Expense	0.75%		0.75%	
Retirement Income @ Age 65	$3,700		$4,300	
Age 65 Range of Portfolio Values	$73,628 to $156,638		$86,446 to $176,581	
EXCESS EXPENSE:	**0.50%**	**1.00%**	**0.50%**	**1.00%**
	(1.25% total)	(1.75% total)	(1.25% total)	(1.75% total)
COST OF EXCESS EXPENSE				
Additional Annual Savings Needed	$1,200	$2,900	$1,600	$3,400
Delay Retirement by	2 Years	3 Years	1 Years	2 Years
Reduce Annual Retirement Income by	$300	$600	$400	$700
Increased Risk of Outliving Resources	40%	87%	37%	89%
Reduction to Age 65 Portfolio Values:				
Likely More than:	$2,069	$4,089	$2,227	$4,402
Likely Less than:	$3,946	$7,807	$4,176	$8,267

Total annual savings is COMBINED annual employee AND employer contribution

AGE 60 WITH CURRENT 401(K) BALANCE OF $75,000

Total Annual Savings	$10,000		$15,000	
Allocation: **80% Stock/20% Bonds**				
Base Comfortable "In Balance" Case:				
Maximum Fair Total Expense	0.75%		0.75%	
Retirement Income @ Age 65	$6,000		$7,300	
Age 65 Range of Portfolio Values	$105,814 to $263,857		$130,740 to $307,261	
EXCESS EXPENSE:	**0.50%**	**1.00%**	**0.50%**	**1.00%**
	(1.25% total)	(1.75% total)	(1.25% total)	(1.75% total)
COST OF EXCESS EXPENSE				
Additional Annual Savings Needed	$1,500	$3,700	$1,900	$4,500
Delay Retirement by	1 Years	2 Years	1 Years	2 Years
Reduce Annual Retirement Income by	$400	$900	$500	$1,000
Increased Risk of Outliving Resources	29%	66%	28%	63%
Reduction to Age 65 Portfolio Values:				
Likely More than:	$2,436	$4,818	$2,707	$5,505
Likely Less than:	$5,632	$11,117	$6,521	$12,919

Allocation: **60% Stock/40% Bonds**				
Base Comfortable "In Balance" Case:				
Maximum Fair Total Expense	0.75%		0.75%	
Retirement Income @ Age 65	$5,700		$6,900	
Age 65 Range of Portfolio Values	$110,550 to $233,256		$136,771 to $273,729	
EXCESS EXPENSE:	**0.50%**	**1.00%**	**0.50%**	**1.00%**
	(1.25% total)	(1.75% total)	(1.25% total)	(1.75% total)
COST OF EXCESS EXPENSE				
Additional Annual Savings Needed	$1,700	$3,800	$2,000	$4,600
Delay Retirement by	1 Years	2 Years	1 Years	2 Years
Reduce Annual Retirement Income by	$400	$900	$500	$1,000
Increased Risk of Outliving Resources	33%	70%	32%	71%
Reduction to Age 65 Portfolio Values:				
Likely More than:	$2,507	$4,959	$2,856	$5,612
Likely Less than:	$5,105	$10,111	$5,612	$11,117

Allocation: **45% Stock/55% Bonds**				
Base Comfortable "In Balance" Case:				
Maximum Fair Total Expense	0.75%		0.75%	
Retirement Income @ Age 65	$5,400		$6,600	
Age 65 Range of Portfolio Values	$112,676 to $213,436		$138,657 to $251,602	
EXCESS EXPENSE:	**0.50%**	**1.00%**	**0.50%**	**1.00%**
	(1.25% total)	(1.75% total)	(1.25% total)	(1.75% total)
COST OF EXCESS EXPENSE				
Additional Annual Savings Needed	$1,700	$3,900	$2,400	$4,900
Delay Retirement by	1 Years	2 Years	1 Years	2 Years
Reduce Annual Retirement Income by	$400	$800	$500	$1,000
Increased Risk of Outliving Resources	40%	98%	40%	92%
Reduction to Age 65 Portfolio Values:				
Likely More than:	$2,613	$5,126	$2,847	$5,679
Likely Less than:	$4,609	$9,126	$5,085	$10,073

Total annual savings is COMBINED annual employee AND employer contribution

AGE 60 WITH CURRENT 401(K) BALANCE OF $150,000

Total Annual Savings	$2,500		$5,000	
Allocation: **80% Stock/20% Bonds**				
Base Comfortable "In Balance" Case:				
Maximum Fair Total Expense	0.75%		0.75%	
Retirement Income @ Age 65	$7,600		$8,300	
Age 65 Range of Portfolio Values	$123,259 to $383,380		$136,614 to $402,631	
EXCESS EXPENSE:	**0.50%**	**1.00%**	**0.50%**	**1.00%**
	(1.25% total)	(1.75% total)	(1.25% total)	(1.75% total)
COST OF EXCESS EXPENSE				
Additional Annual Savings Needed	$2,000	$5,000	$2,500	$5,600
Delay Retirement by	2 Years	3 Years	2 Years	3 Years
Reduce Annual Retirement Income by	$500	$1,100	$700	$1,300
Increased Risk of Outliving Resources	27%	60%	28%	61%
Reduction to Age 65 Portfolio Values:				
Likely More than:	$3,735	$7,369	$3,942	$7,788
Likely Less than:	$9,749	$19,295	$9,716	$19,234

Allocation: **60% Stock/40% Bonds**				
Base Comfortable "In Balance" Case:				
Maximum Fair Total Expense	0.75%		0.75%	
Retirement Income @ Age 65	$7,300		$7,800	
Age 65 Range of Portfolio Values	$129,008 to $330,523		$142,268 to $351,827	
EXCESS EXPENSE:	**0.50%**	**1.00%**	**0.50%**	**1.00%**
	(1.25% total)	(1.75% total)	(1.25% total)	(1.75% total)
COST OF EXCESS EXPENSE				
Additional Annual Savings Needed	$2,800	$5,600	$2,600	$5,600
Delay Retirement by	2 Years	3 Years	1 Years	3 Years
Reduce Annual Retirement Income by	$600	$1,200	$700	$1,200
Increased Risk of Outliving Resources	33%	69%	35%	69%
Reduction to Age 65 Portfolio Values:				
Likely More than:	$3,861	$7,628	$4,026	$7,955
Likely Less than:	$8,358	$16,541	$8,706	$17,231

Allocation: **45% Stock/55% Bonds**				
Base Comfortable "In Balance" Case:				
Maximum Fair Total Expense	0.75%		0.75%	
Retirement Income @ Age 65	$6,900		$7,400	
Age 65 Range of Portfolio Values	$133,774 to $292,977		$147,256 to $313,275	
EXCESS EXPENSE:	**0.50%**	**1.00%**	**0.50%**	**1.00%**
	(1.25% total)	(1.75% total)	(1.25% total)	(1.75% total)
COST OF EXCESS EXPENSE				
Additional Annual Savings Needed	$2,800	$5,500	$2,400	$5,700
Delay Retirement by	2 Years	3 Years	2 Years	3 Years
Reduce Annual Retirement Income by	$600	$1,200	$600	$1,200
Increased Risk of Outliving Resources	40%	88%	40%	87%
Reduction to Age 65 Portfolio Values:				
Likely More than:	$3,961	$7,825	$4,138	$8,178
Likely Less than:	$7,559	$14,955	$7,890	$15,613

Total annual savings is COMBINED annual employee AND employer contribution

AGE 60 WITH CURRENT 401(K) BALANCE OF $150,000

Total Annual Savings	$10,000		$15,000	
Allocation: **80% Stock/20% Bonds**				
Base Comfortable "In Balance" Case:				
Maximum Fair Total Expense	0.75%		0.75%	
Retirement Income @ Age 65	$9,600		$10,800	
Age 65 Range of Portfolio Values	$161,036 to $444,244		$185,966 to $486,167	
EXCESS EXPENSE:	**0.50%**	**1.00%**	**0.50%**	**1.00%**
	(1.25% total)	(1.75% total)	(1.25% total)	(1.75% total)
COST OF EXCESS EXPENSE				
Additional Annual Savings Needed	$3,000	$6,800	$3,200	$7,200
Delay Retirement by	1 Years	2 Years	1 Years	2 Years
Reduce Annual Retirement Income by	$800	$1,500	$800	$1,600
Increased Risk of Outliving Resources	25%	58%	28%	64%
Reduction to Age 65 Portfolio Values:				
Likely More than:	$4,162	$8,227	$4,541	$8,979
Likely Less than:	$10,231	$20,259	$10,777	$21,344

Allocation: **60% Stock/40% Bonds**				
Base Comfortable "In Balance" Case:				
Maximum Fair Total Expense	0.75%		0.75%	
Retirement Income @ Age 65	$9,100		$10,400	
Age 65 Range of Portfolio Values	$168,423 to $390,155		$194,579 to $428,388	
EXCESS EXPENSE:	**0.50%**	**1.00%**	**0.50%**	**1.00%**
	(1.25% total)	(1.75% total)	(1.25% total)	(1.75% total)
COST OF EXCESS EXPENSE				
Additional Annual Savings Needed	$3,000	$6,800	$4,000	$8,000
Delay Retirement by	1 Years	2 Years	1 Years	2 Years
Reduce Annual Retirement Income by	$700	$1,500	$900	$1,700
Increased Risk of Outliving Resources	35%	72%	36%	75%
Reduction to Age 65 Portfolio Values:				
Likely More than:	$4,399	$8,799	$4,684	$9,263
Likely Less than:	$9,059	$17,934	$9,721	$19,249

Allocation: **45% Stock/55% Bonds**				
Base Comfortable "In Balance" Case:				
Maximum Fair Total Expense	0.75%		0.75%	
Retirement Income @ Age 65	$8,600		$9,700	
Age 65 Range of Portfolio Values	$172,891 to $353,163		$199,316 to $390,147	
EXCESS EXPENSE:	**0.50%**	**1.00%**	**0.50%**	**1.00%**
	(1.25% total)	(1.75% total)	(1.25% total)	(1.75% total)
COST OF EXCESS EXPENSE				
Additional Annual Savings Needed	$3,200	$6,700	$3,300	$7,300
Delay Retirement by	1 Years	2 Years	1 Years	2 Years
Reduce Annual Retirement Income by	$700	$1,400	$700	$1,500
Increased Risk of Outliving Resources	37%	89%	39%	94%
Reduction to Age 65 Portfolio Values:				
Likely More than:	$4,452	$8,802	$4,787	$9,468
Likely Less than:	$8,354	$16,535	$8,843	$17,656

Total annual savings is COMBINED annual employee AND employer contribution

Appendix A

AGE 60 WITH CURRENT 401(K) BALANCE OF $250,000

Total Annual Savings	$2,500		$5,000	
Allocation: **80% Stock/20% Bonds**				
Base Comfortable "In Balance" Case:				
Maximum Fair Total Expense	0.75%		0.75%	
Retirement Income @ Age 65	$12,400		$13,000	
Age 65 Range of Portfolio Values	$196,222 to $626,152		$210,036 to $645,131	
EXCESS EXPENSE:	**0.50%**	**1.00%**	**0.50%**	**1.00%**
	(1.25% total)	(1.75% total)	(1.25% total)	(1.75% total)
COST OF EXCESS EXPENSE				
Additional Annual Savings Needed	$3,900	$8,600	$4,000	$8,900
Delay Retirement by	2 Years	4 Years	2 Years	3 Years
Reduce Annual Retirement Income by	$1,000	$2,000	$1,000	$2,000
Increased Risk of Outliving Resources	24%	57%	25%	60%
Reduction to Age 65 Portfolio Values:				
Likely More than:	$6,091	$12,030	$6,361	$12,565
Likely Less than:	$16,078	$31,821	$16,333	$32,326

Allocation: **60% Stock/40% Bonds**				
Base Comfortable "In Balance" Case:				
Maximum Fair Total Expense	0.75%		0.75%	
Retirement Income @ Age 65	$11,700		$12,300	
Age 65 Range of Portfolio Values	$206,335 to $536,567		$219,473 to $558,146	
EXCESS EXPENSE:	**0.50%**	**1.00%**	**0.50%**	**1.00%**
	(1.25% total)	(1.75% total)	(1.25% total)	(1.75% total)
COST OF EXCESS EXPENSE				
Additional Annual Savings Needed	$4,200	$9,000	$4,500	$9,000
Delay Retirement by	2 Years	4 Years	2 Years	3 Years
Reduce Annual Retirement Income by	$1,000	$1,900	$1,000	$2,000
Increased Risk of Outliving Resources	35%	72%	33%	71%
Reduction to Age 65 Portfolio Values:				
Likely More than:	$6,326	$12,495	$6,490	$12,864
Likely Less than:	$13,753	$27,216	$14,020	$27,746

Allocation: **45% Stock/55% Bonds**				
Base Comfortable "In Balance" Case:				
Maximum Fair Total Expense	0.75%		0.75%	
Retirement Income @ Age 65	$11,100		$11,600	
Age 65 Range of Portfolio Values	$214,956 to $475,489		$227,851 to $495,252	
EXCESS EXPENSE:	**0.50%**	**1.00%**	**0.50%**	**1.00%**
	(1.25% total)	(1.75% total)	(1.25% total)	(1.75% total)
COST OF EXCESS EXPENSE				
Additional Annual Savings Needed	$4,300	$8,900	$4,100	$8,900
Delay Retirement by	2 Years	4 Years	2 Years	3 Years
Reduce Annual Retirement Income by	$900	$1,900	$900	$1,900
Increased Risk of Outliving Resources	39%	88%	40%	90%
Reduction to Age 65 Portfolio Values:				
Likely More than:	$6,574	$12,986	$6,657	$13,153
Likely Less than:	$12,424	$24,580	$12,680	$25,089

Total annual savings is COMBINED annual employee AND employer contribution

AGE 60 WITH CURRENT 401(K) BALANCE OF $250,000

Total Annual Savings	$10,000		$15,000	
Allocation: **80% Stock/20% Bonds**				
Base Comfortable "In Balance" Case:				
Maximum Fair Total Expense	0.75%		0.75%	
Retirement Income @ Age 65	$14,300		$15,600	
Age 65 Range of Portfolio Values	$236,367 to $684,882		$259,393 to $726,495	
EXCESS EXPENSE:	**0.50%**	**1.00%**	**0.50%**	**1.00%**
	(1.25% total)	(1.75% total)	(1.25% total)	(1.75% total)
COST OF EXCESS EXPENSE				
Additional Annual Savings Needed	$4,500	$9,600	$5,200	$11,000
Delay Retirement by	2 Years	3 Years	1 Years	2 Years
Reduce Annual Retirement Income by	$1,100	$2,200	$1,200	$2,400
Increased Risk of Outliving Resources	29%	62%	27%	60%
Reduction to Age 65 Portfolio Values:				
Likely More than:	$6,682	$13,204	$6,824	$13,488
Likely Less than:	$16,365	$32,398	$16,880	$33,423

Allocation: **60% Stock/40% Bonds**				
Base Comfortable "In Balance" Case:				
Maximum Fair Total Expense	0.75%		0.75%	
Retirement Income @ Age 65	$13,500		$14,800	
Age 65 Range of Portfolio Values	$246,016 to $597,863		$271,954 to $637,107	
EXCESS EXPENSE:	**0.50%**	**1.00%**	**0.50%**	**1.00%**
	(1.25% total)	(1.75% total)	(1.25% total)	(1.75% total)
COST OF EXCESS EXPENSE				
Additional Annual Savings Needed	$4,500	$9,900	$5,200	$11,200
Delay Retirement by	1 Years	3 Years	1 Years	2 Years
Reduce Annual Retirement Income by	$1,100	$2,200	$1,200	$2,400
Increased Risk of Outliving Resources	34%	70%	33%	69%
Reduction to Age 65 Portfolio Values:				
Likely More than:	$6,756	$13,352	$7,196	$14,178
Likely Less than:	$14,512	$28,708	$15,179	$30,048

Allocation: **45% Stock/55% Bonds**				
Base Comfortable "In Balance" Case:				
Maximum Fair Total Expense	0.75%		0.75%	
Retirement Income @ Age 65	$12,800		$14,000	
Age 65 Range of Portfolio Values	$253,791 to $534,053		$279,290 to $576,236	
EXCESS EXPENSE:	**0.50%**	**1.00%**	**0.50%**	**1.00%**
	(1.25% total)	(1.75% total)	(1.25% total)	(1.75% total)
COST OF EXCESS EXPENSE				
Additional Annual Savings Needed	$4,500	$10,000	$5,200	$11,200
Delay Retirement by	2 Years	3 Years	1 Years	3 Years
Reduce Annual Retirement Income by	$1,100	$2,000	$1,100	$2,200
Increased Risk of Outliving Resources	39%	90%	36%	88%
Reduction to Age 65 Portfolio Values:				
Likely More than:	$7,002	$13,840	$7,309	$14,448
Likely Less than:	$13,305	$26,328	$13,769	$27,252

Total annual savings is COMBINED annual employee AND employer contribution

APPENDIX B

FINANCEWARE, INC. 401(K) PLAN

Contract Number 4-43730
Date of Birth: ▮▮▮▮▮
Date of Employment: 05/07/1999

DAVID B LOEPER

Identification Number
XXX-XX-▮▮▮▮

*Here is a summary of retirement account information from **January 1, 2005** to **December 31, 2005**.*

ACCOUNT BALANCE	TOTAL ACCOUNT BALANCE BY RISK CATEGORY

TOTAL ACCOUNT BALANCE
$120,687.46

VESTED ACCOUNT BALANCE
$120,687.46

$98,627.07
82%

$22,060.39
18%

■ Moderate
■ Dynamic

PERSONALIZED RATE OF RETURN

For the report period 01/01/2005 – 12/31/2005 = 8.02%

This is the percentage change, weighted for transactions, of individual investment options and this retirement plan portfolio over the time period of this report. It takes into consideration deposits, transfers, withdrawals, fees, and unit value changes or interest credited at the time of the calculation. Past results do not predict future results.

Please see page three of this statement for performance information on each of the investment options you have available. For more details about these investment options, including comparisons to benchmarks, portfolio holdings, etc., visit The Principal Retirement Service Center® at www.principal.com.

MESSAGE BOARD

· You will notice some recent changes to your statement. We responded to your valuable feedback and have added a column to the Account Activity by Investment Option to display the Investment Advisor. The Investment Advisor is the company that manages the investment option. Your awareness of the strong business relationships we have with these Investment Advisors is important to us as we help you reach your retirement goals. The amounts which were previously displayed in the Transfers column have been combined in the Additions/Transfers In and Withdrawals/Transfers Out columns.

· Sign up today to view your retirement plan statements online! By accessing your statement online, you'll be able to easily and quickly retrieve desired information about the employer's retirement plan with the click of a mouse. You will also have access to an archive of past statements, as well as the many other tools available through The Principal Retirement Service Center®. Visit www.principal.com to sign up!

*Please review this statement and notify us of any discrepancies within
90 days. After 90 days, corrections will be made on a current basis.*

WE UNDERSTAND WHAT
YOU'RE WORKING FOR®

Principal
*Financial
Group*

ACCOUNT SUMMARY AS OF 12/31/2005

	EMPLOYER	EMPLOYEE DEFERRAL	TOTAL
Account Balance By Contribution Type	$22,367.32	$98,320.14	$120,687.46
Contributions Received 01/01/2005 – 12/31/2005 Since You Entered the Plan	$3,500.00 $16,583.33	$14,000.00 $71,000.00	$17,500.00 $87,583.33
Vesting Percent*	100.00%	100.00%	

*Your vesting percent is calculated based on the assumption that you are employed through the end date of this statement. Vesting will be verified when your benefit payment is processed.

ACCOUNT ACTIVITY BY INVESTMENT OPTION AS OF 12/31/2005

INVESTMENT ADVISOR	INVESTMENT OPTION	Beginning Balance	Additions/ Transfers In¹	*Net Earnings	Withdrawals/ Expenses/ Transfers Out²	Ending Balance	Ending Units/Shares
Principal Global Investors	Moderate Total Market Stk Idx Sep Acct+	$79,413.38	$14,875.12	$4,336.57	$0.00	$98,627.07	8820.3711
Principal Global Investors	Dynamic Diversified Intl Sep Acct+	$13,069.14	$2,274.95	$3,515.85	$0.00	$18,859.94	382.1098
Principal Global Investors	Intl Emerging Mkts Sep Acct+	$2,048.72	$349.93	$801.80	$0.00	$3,200.45	95.9583
TOTALS		$94,531.24	$17,500.00	$8,656.22	$0.00	$120,687.46	

Detailed transaction activity is available on the web at www.principal.com.
¹May include deposits and transfers.
*Net earnings reflect plan expenses as well as the timing and amount of deposits to the account.
²May include withdrawals, transfers, and expenses.

INVESTMENT DIRECTION BY INVESTMENT OPTION AS OF 12/31/2005

INVESTMENT ADVISOR	INVESTMENT OPTION	EMPLOYER	ELECTIVE DEFERRAL
Principal Global Investors	Moderate Total Market Stk Idx Sep Acct+	85.00%	85.00%
Principal Global Investors	Dynamic Diversified Intl Sep Acct+	13.00%	13.00%
Principal Global Investors	Intl Emerging Mkts Sep Acct+	2.00%	2.00%

USE YOUR WINDFALL TO PLAN FOR A RAINY DAY

Many people will get a tax refund this year, and most will consider this extra cash as a "windfall." Before you spend it on a vacation, bills, or any impulse item, consider this: the money in your tax refund is not found money, but simply money you overpaid the government throughout the year. It is not an "extra bonus" but money you could have been using instead all year long.

If you're getting a large tax refund, consider adjusting your deductions on your paycheck for next year. While you may not get a large check when you file taxes, you will have a little more in your paycheck each month. More importantly, if you invest that small amount in a retirement or other savings plan, the difference could really add up over time.

In the meantime, consider investing any tax refund you do receive. Its a simple way to put a dent in retirement savings – and end up with something that will last longer than a vacation or impulse item!

Appendix B

YOUR FUTURE INVESTMENT DIRECTION BY RISK CATEGORY

This is how your future contributions/deposits will be directed to the plan as of 12/31/2005.

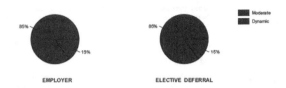

■ Moderate
■ Dynamic

85%   15%
EMPLOYER

85%   15%
ELECTIVE DEFERRAL

INVESTMENT PERFORMANCE THROUGH 12/31/2005

While past performance does not predict future results, this section helps you compare investment options. This history shows the rate of return that would have been earned from a sum of money invested on the first day of the period and left until the last day of the period, with no other transactions. Returns marked with an asterisk (*) reflect performance since the inception date of the investment option. Returns shown for periods of less than one year are not annualized. All returns displayed here are after Total Investment Expense, but before any plan expenses of the investment option.

INVESTMENT ADVISOR	INVESTMENT OPTION	YTD	Last Calendar Quarter	1 Yr	3 Yr	5 Yr	10 Yr or *Since Inception	Inception Date	NAV/ Unit Value
	Stable								
	Guaranteed 5 year	3.05	---	---	---	---	---	---	---
Principal Global Investors	Money Market Sep Acct+	2.72	0.87	2.72	1.45	1.96	3.64	12/10/1980	45.3369531
	Conservative								
Principal Global Investors	Bond and Mtg Sep Acct+	2.48	0.62	2.48	4.12	6.04	6.30	02/01/1983	735.7602015
	Moderate								
American Century Inv. Mgmt.	LgCap Value II SA+	5.83	1.61	5.83	---	---	*5.81	12/31/2004	10.5826814
Principal Global Investors	Lg Cap Stk Idx Sep Acct+	4.58	2.00	4.58	13.99	0.16	8.66	01/01/1990	47.0805293
Principal Global Investors	Total Market Stk Idx Sep Acct+	5.33	2.03	5.33	14.83	1.05	*1.81	09/28/1999	11.1817384
	Aggressive								
American Century Inv. Mgmt.	LgCap Growth II Sep Acct+	4.50	3.31	4.58	12.91	-2.63	*-2.62	12/29/2000	8.7541287
Mazama Capital Management	SmCap Growth III Sep Acct+	12.50	8.04	12.50	---	---	*13.31	06/01/2004	12.1930230
Mellon Equity	MidCap Growth I Sep Acct+	13.43	4.18	13.43	20.43	-5.15	*-10.49	12/31/1999	19.6066484
Principal Global Investors	Mid-Cap Stk Idx Sep Acct+	12.20	3.23	12.20	20.63	8.11	*10.90	08/31/1999	19.2818973
Principal Global Investors	Small Co Growth Sep Acct+	4.35	2.64	4.35	22.22	1.61	6.00	06/01/1995	19.2785040
Principal Global Investors	Sm-Cap Stk Idx Sep Acct+	7.29	0.29	7.29	21.09	10.27	*11.66	08/31/1999	20.1305345
	Dynamic								
Principal Global Investors	Diversified Intl Sep Acct+	24.14	5.75	24.14	26.17	5.16	8.53	05/20/1987	49.3574051
Principal Global Investors	Intl Emerging Mkts Sep Acct+	35.09	7.54	35.09	38.94	18.87	11.99	01/01/1995	33.3525171

These results are for the investment options selected by your company's plan, and may be different from the results for other plans.
+For more information about this investment option, including its full name, please visit The Principal Retirement Service Center® at www.principal.com or call ▮▮▮▮▮▮ for assistance from a retirement specialist.
The Guaranteed Interest Account rate is as of the statement effective date.

TAKE NOTE

· View account information online and find the educational tools you need to help plan your retirement. Go to www.principal.com, click "Login," enter your username and password. New to this site? First time users can click on "Establish your new username and password" at the "Login" screen.

· Start planning for a more secure financial future today by following the simplified, step-by-step planning guide found exclusively at The Principal Retirement Service Center®. Log in today to find out what you can do to be on track to saving for your retirement. Visit www.principal.com/PlanGuide to get started!

· Introducing Spotlight: We're excited to announce another resource available through The Principal Retirement Service Center®. Our new Spotlight Section will focus on innovative services that are being added to The Principal Retirement Service Center®, along with specific and customized alerts for you to review. Log in today to see what Spotlight is all about!

RETHINKING YOUR SAVING HABITS

We've become a nation of spendthrifts – the result of living in an age where credit cards offer free gifts, and ATM machines dispense quick money. Consequently, many live paycheck–to–paycheck. If it's time to rethink your saving habits, here are three financial resolutions to consider.

Track your cash. Start by getting a clearer picture of where your paycheck really goes. There are several things you can do to keep a closer eye on your spending:

· Keep a diary – record every purchase and how you pay. This will help you develop a new spending plan.
· Use automatic transfers to pay bills, ensuring bills are paid on time, without late fees.
· Quit using credit – you won't buy as much, and will avoid high finance charges.
· Only use an ATM once per week – and withdraw only what you need.

Cut spending. Here are a couple ways to save:

· Consider raising your deductibles on insurance policies. You'll pay more out of your own pocket if you make a claim, but may save more than 10 percent off your premium.
· Also, consider prepaying your mortgage. Every dollar paid towards the principal reduces interest.

Save money. There are several simple ways you can save money.

· Instead of spending right away, put your next bonus or raise towards a specific savings goal.
· When you come to the end of a debt payment, put the same amount each month into your investment plan.
· Open an account to cover three to six months of living expense and automatically deposit a set amount from each paycheck.

APPENDIX C

CGS2339   ANNUITY CONTRACT NUMBER 4-43730   DISTRIBUTION 23   559-SPEARSB   07/03/06

SUMMARY ANNUAL REPORT

This is a summary of the annual report for

FINANCEWARE, INC. 401(K) PLAN

EIN 51▮▮▮▮▮▮▮
for January 1, 2005, through December 31, 2005. The annual report has been filed with the Employee Benefits Security Administration, as required under the Employee Retirement Income Security Act of 1974 (ERISA).

BASIC FINANCIAL STATEMENT

Benefits under the plan are provided by a combination of funding arrangements. Plan expenses were $46,230. These expenses included $0 in administrative expenses and $34,926 in benefits paid to participants and beneficiaries, and $11,304 in other expenses. A total of 25 persons were participants in or beneficiaries of the plan at the end of the plan year, although not all of these persons had yet earned the right to receive benefits.

The value of plan assets, after subtracting liabilities of the plan, was $1,341,870 as of December 31, 2005, compared to $1,013,895 as of January 1, 2005. During the plan year, the plan experienced an increase in its net assets of $327,975. This increase includes unrealized appreciation or depreciation in the value of the plan assets; that is, the difference between the value of plan's assets at the end of the year and the value of the assets at the beginning of the year or cost of assets acquired during the year. The plan had total income of $374,205, including employer contributions of $42,614, employee contributions of $221,624, gains of $0, from the sale of assets, and earnings from investments of $109,967.

YOUR RIGHTS TO ADDITIONAL INFORMATION

You have the right to receive a copy of the full annual report, or any part thereof, on request. The items listed below are included in that report:
- Financial information
- Insurance information including sales commissions paid by insurance carriers
- Information regarding any common or collective trusts, pooled separate accounts; master trusts or 103-12 investment entities in which the plan participates

To obtain a copy of the full annual report, or any part thereof, write or call
FINANCEWARE, INC.
▮▮▮▮▮▮▮▮▮▮▮▮▮▮▮▮▮▮▮▮▮▮▮▮▮▮▮
RICHMOND, VA 23220-5048
▮▮▮▮▮▮▮▮▮

The charge to cover copying costs will be $1.00 for the full annual report, or $.10 per page for any part thereof.

CGS2339   ANNUITY CONTRACT NUMBER 4-43730   DISTRIBUTION 23   559-SPEARSB   07/03/06

You also have the right to receive from the plan administrator, on request and at no charge, a statement of the assets and liabilities of the plan and accompanying notes, or a statement of income and expenses of the plan and accompanying notes, or both. If you request a copy of the full annual report from the plan administrator, these two statements and accompanying notes will be included as part of that report. The charge to cover copying costs given above does not include a charge for the copying of these portions of the report because these portions are furnished without charge.

You also have the legally protected right to examine the annual report at the main office of the plan ██

RICHMOND, VA 23220-5048

and at the U.S. Department of Labor in Washington, D.C., or to obtain a copy from the U.S. Department of Labor upon payment of copying costs. Requests to the Department should be addressed to: Public Disclosure Room, Room N1513, Employee Benefits Security Administration, U.S. Department of Labor, 200 Constitution Avenue, N.W., Washington, D.C. 20210.

This plan is not required to attach an accountant's report because it satisfies all of the conditions to qualify for a waiver of the audit requirement.

APPENDIX D

Form **5500**	**Annual Return/Report of Employee Benefit Plan**	Official Use Only
	This form is required to be filed under sections 104 and 4065 of the Employee	OMB Nos. 1210 – 0110
Department of the Treasury Internal Revenue Service	Retirement Income Security Act of 1974 (ERISA) and sections 6047(e),	1210 – 0089
Department of Labor Employee Benefits Security Administration	6057(b), and 6058(a) of the Internal Revenue Code (the Code).	**2005**
	▶ Complete all entries in accordance with	**This Form is Open to**
Pension Benefit Guaranty Corporation	the instructions to the Form 5500.	**Public Inspection.**

Part I   Annual Report Identification Information

For the calendar plan year 2005 or fiscal plan year beginning _____ and ending _____

A This return/report is for: **(1)** ☐ a multiemployer plan;   **(3)** ☐ a multiple–employer plan; or

(2) ☒ a single–employer plan (other than a   **(4)** ☐ a DFE (specify) _____

multiple–employer plan);

B This return/report is: **(1)** ☐ the first return/report filed for the plan;   **(3)** ☐ the final return/report filed for the plan;

(2) ☐ an amended return/report;   **(4)** ☐ a short plan year return/report (less than 12 months).

C If the plan is a collectively–bargained plan, check here .... ▶

D If filing under an extension of time or the DFVC program, check box and attach required information. (see instructions) .... ▶

Part II   Basic Plan Information —enter all requested information.

1a Name of plan	**1b** Three–digit
FINANCEWARE, INC. 401(K) PLAN	plan number (PN) ▶ 001
	1c Effective date of plan (mo., day, yr.) 07/01/2000

2a Plan sponsor's name and address (employer, if for a single–employer plan)	**2b** Employer Identification Number (EIN)
(Address should include room or suite no.)	51- ████
FINANCEWARE, INC.	**2c** Sponsor's telephone number 804- ████
	2d Business code (see instructions) 523900

RICHMOND   VA   23220-5048

Caution: A penalty for the late or incomplete filing of this return/report will be assessed unless reasonable cause is established.

Under penalties of perjury and other penalties set forth in the instructions, I declare that I have examined this return/report, including accompanying schedules, statements and attachments, as well as the electronic version of this return/report if it is being filed electronically, and to the best of my knowledge and belief, it is true, correct and complete.

SIGN HERE

_____   _____   _____
Signature of plan administrator   Date   Type or print name of individual signing as plan administrator

SIGN HERE

_____   _____   _____
Signature of employer/plan sponsor/DFE   Date   Type or print name of individual signing as employer, plan sponsor or DFE

For Paperwork Reduction Act Notice and OMB Control Numbers, see the instructions for Form 5500.   v8.2   Form **5500** (2005)

0 2 0 5 6 7 0 1 0 L

Form 5500 (2005)   Page **2**

Official Use Only

3a Plan administrator's name and address (If same as plan sponsor, enter "Same") SAME	**3b** Administrator's EIN	
	3c Administrator's telephone number	

4   If the name and/or EIN of the plan sponsor has changed since the last return/report filed for this plan, enter the name, EIN and the plan number from the last return/report below:

   a Sponsor's name   **b** EIN

                                                                 c PN

5   Preparer information (optional)   **a**   Name (including firm name, if applicable) and address   **b** EIN

                                                               c Telephone number

6	Total number of participants at the beginning of the plan year	**6**	28
7	Number of participants as of the end of the plan year (welfare plans complete only lines **7a, 7b, 7c,** and **7d**)		
a	Active participants	**7a**	21
b	Retired or separated participants receiving benefits	**7b**	
c	Other retired or separated participants entitled to future benefits	**7c**	3
d	Subtotal. Add lines **7a, 7b,** and **7c**	**7d**	24
e	Deceased participants whose beneficiaries are receiving or are entitled to receive benefits	**7e**	1
f	Total. Add lines **7d** and **7e**	**7f**	25
g	Number of participants with account balances as of the end of the plan year (only defined contribution plans complete this item)	**7g**	23
h	Number of participants that terminated employment during the plan year with accrued benefits that were less than 100% vested	**7h**	3
i	If any participant(s) separated from service with a deferred vested benefit, enter the number of separated participants required to be reported on a Schedule SSA (Form 5500)	**7i**	1

8   Benefits provided under the plan (complete **8a** and **8b** as applicable)

   a ☒ Pension benefits (check this box if the plan provides pension benefits and enter the applicable pension feature codes from the List of Plan Characteristics Codes printed in the instructions): | 2E | | 2F | | 2G | | 2J | | 2K | | 3E | | ☐ | | ☐ | | ☐ |

   b ☐ Welfare benefits (check this box if the plan provides welfare benefits and enter the applicable welfare feature codes from the List of Plan Characteristics Codes printed in the instructions): | ☐ | | ☐ | | ☐ | | ☐ | | ☐ | | ☐ | | ☐ | | ☐ | | ☐ |

9a Plan funding arrangement (check all that apply)	**9b** Plan benefit arrangement (check all that apply)
(1) ☒ Insurance	**(1)** ☒ Insurance
(2) ☐ Code section 412(i) insurance contracts	**(2)** ☐ Code section 412(i) insurance contracts
(3) ☒ Trust	**(3)** ☒ Trust
(4) ☐ General assets of the sponsor	**(4)** ☐ General assets of the sponsor

0   2   0   5   6   7   0   2   0   M

Appendix D

Form 5500 (2005)   Page **3**

Official Use Only

10   Schedules attached (Check all applicable boxes and, where indicated, enter the number attached. See instructions.)

a   **Pension Benefit Schedules**

(1)	☒	**R**	(Retirement Plan Information)
(2)	☐	**B**	(Actuarial Information)
(3)	☐	**E**	(ESOP Annual Information)
(4)	☒	**SSA**	(Separated Vested Participant Information)

b   **Financial Schedules**

(1)	☐		**H**	(Financial Information)
(2)	☒		**I**	(Financial Information -- Small Plan)
(3)	☒	1	**A**	(Insurance Information)
(4)	☐		**C**	(Service Provider Information)
(5)	☒		**D**	(DFE/Participating Plan Information)
(6)	☐		**G**	(Financial Transaction Schedules)
(7)	☒	1	**P**	(Trust Fiduciary Information)

0 2 0 5 6 7 0 3 0 N

179

Stop the 401(k) Rip-off!

SCHEDULE A (Form 5500) Department of the Treasury Internal Revenue Service Department of Labor Employee Benefits Security Administration Pension Benefit Guaranty Corporation	**Insurance Information** This schedule is required to be filed under section 104 of the Employee Retirement Income Security Act of 1974. ▶ **File as an attachment to Form 5500.** ▶ Insurance companies are required to provide this information pursuant to ERISA section 103(a)(2).	Official Use Only OMB No. 1210–0110 **2005** **This Form is Open to Public Inspection.**

For calendar plan year 2005 or fiscal plan year beginning , and ending ,

A Name of plan FINANCEWARE, INC. 401(K) PLAN	B Three–digit plan number ▶	001
C Plan sponsor's name as shown on line 2a of Form 5500 FINANCEWARE, INC.	D **Employer Identification Number** 51-	

Part I Information Concerning Insurance Contract Coverage, Fees, and Commissions

Provide information for each contract on a separate Schedule A. Individual contracts grouped as a unit in Parts II and III can be reported on a single Schedule A.

1 Coverage:

(a) Name of insurance carrier

PRINCIPAL LIFE INSURANCE COMPANY

(b) EIN	(c) NAIC code	(d) Contract or identification number	(e) Approximate number of persons covered at end of policy or contract year	Policy or contract year	
				(f) From	(g) To
42-0127290	61271	4-43730	25	01/01/2005	12/31/2005

2 Insurance fees and commissions paid to agents, brokers and other persons. Enter the total fees and total commisions below and list agents, brokers and other persons individually in descending order of the amount paid in the items on the following page(s) in Part I.

Totals

Total amount of commissions paid	Total fees paid / amount
3811	202

For Paperwork Reduction Act Notice and OMB Control Numbers, see the Instructions for Form 5500.   v8.2   Schedule A (Form 5500) 2005

0 6 0 5 6 7 0 1 0 P

Appendix D

Schedule A (Form 5500) 2005   Page **2**

Official Use Only

(a) Name and address of the agents, brokers or other persons to whom commissions or fees were paid

MARK ▮▮▮▮▮

RICHMOND   VA   23225-0000

(b) Amount of commissions paid	Fees paid		**(e)** Organization code
	(c) Amount	**(d)** Purpose	
		SERVICE FEE	
3811	202		3

(a) Name and address of the agents, brokers or other persons to whom commissions or fees were paid

(b) Amount of commissions paid	Fees paid		**(e)** Organization code
	(c) Amount	**(d)** Purpose	

(a) Name and address of the agents, brokers or other persons to whom commissions or fees were paid

(b) Amount of commissions paid	Fees paid		**(e)** Organization code
	(c) Amount	**(d)** Purpose	

0 6 0 5 6 7 0 2 0 Q

181

Schedule A (Form 5500) 2005   Page **3**

Official Use Only

Part II   **Investment and Annuity Contract Information**

Where individual contracts are provided, the entire group of such individual contracts with each carrier may be treated as a unit for purposes of this report.

3	Current value of plan's interest under this contract in the general account at year end	1728
4	Current value of plan's interest under this contract in separate accounts at year end	1303120

5   Contracts With Allocated Funds

a   State the basis of premium rates ▶ _____

b   Premiums paid to carrier ....

c   Premiums due but unpaid at the end of the year...

d   If the carrier, service, or other organization incurred any specific costs in connection with the acquisition
or retention of the contract or policy, enter amount ....
Specify nature of costs ▶ _____

e   Type of contract   **(1)** ☐ individual policies   **(2)** ☐ group deferred annuity
    (3) ☐ other (specify) ▶

f   If contract purchased, in whole or in part, to distribute benefits from a terminating plan check here ....▶ ☐

6   Contracts With Unallocated Funds (Do not include portions of these contracts maintained in separate accounts)

a   Type of contract   **(1)** ☐ deposit administration   **(2)** ☐ immediate participation guarantee
    (3) ☐ guaranteed investment   **(4)** ☒ other (specify below)
      ▶ FLEXIBLE INVESTMENT ANNUITY

b	Balance at the end of the previous year	1669
c	Additions: (1) Contributions deposited during the year 244	
	(2) Dividends and credits	
	(3) Interest credited during the year 57	
	(4) Transferred from separate account	
	(5) Other (specify below)	
	▶ _____	
	(6) Total additions	301
d	Total of balance and additions (add **b** and **c**(6))	1970
e	Deductions:	
	(1) Disbursed from fund to pay benefits or purchase annuities during year	
	(2) Administration charge made by carrier............................... 28	
	(3) Transferred to separate account	
	(4) Other (specify below) 214	
	▶ LOAN WITHDRAWAL , MKT VALUE CHANGE	
	(5) Total deductions	242
f	Balance at the end of the current year (subtract **e**(5) from **d**)	1728

```
0   6   0   5   6   7   0   3   0   R
```

Appendix D

Official Use Only

Part III   **Welfare Benefit Contract Information**

If more than one contract covers the same group of employees of the same employer(s) or members of the same employee organization(s), the information may be combined for reporting purposes if such contracts are experience–rated as a unit. Where individual contracts are provided, the entire group of such individual contracts with each carrier may be treated as a unit for purposes on this report.

7   Benefit and contract type (check all applicable boxes)

a ☐ Health (other than dental or vision)	**b** ☐ Dental	**c** ☐ Vision	**d** ☐ Life Insurance
e ☐ Temporary disability (accident and sickness)	**f** ☐ Long–term disability	**g** ☐ Supplemental unemployment	**h** ☐ Prescription drug
i ☐ Stop loss (large deductible)	**j** ☐ HMO contract	**k** ☐ PPO contract	**l** ☐ Indemnity contract
m ☐ Other (specify) ▶			

8   Experience–rated contracts

a   Premiums: (1) Amount received . . . .

(2) Increase (decrease) in amount due but unpaid . . . .

(3) Increase (decrease) in unearned premium reserve . . . .

(4) Earned ((1) + (2) – (3)) . . . .

b   Benefit charges: (1) Claims paid . . . .

(2) Increase (decrease) in claim reserves . . . .

(3) Incurred claims (add (1) and (2)) . . . .

(4) Claims charged . . . .

c   Remainder of premium: (1) Retention charges (on an accrual basis) --

(A) Commissions . . . .

(B) Administrative service or other fees . . . .

(C) Other specific acquisition costs . . . .

(D) Other expenses . . . .

(E) Taxes . . . .

(F) Charges for risks or other contingencies . . . .

(G) Other retention charges . . . .

(H) Total retention . . . .

(2) Dividends or retroactive rate refunds. (These amounts were ☐ paid in cash, or ☐ credited.) . . . .

d   Status of policyholder reserves at end of year: (1) Amount held to provide benefits after retirement . . . .

(2) Claim reserves . . . .

(3) Other reserves . . . .

e   Dividends or retroactive rate refunds due. (Do not include amount entered in c(2).) . . . .

9   Nonexperience–rated contracts:

a   Total premiums or subscription charges paid to carrier . . . .

b   If the carrier, service, or other organization incurred any specific costs in connection with the acquisition

or retention of the contract or policy, other than reported in Part I, item 2 above, report amount . . . .

Specify nature of costs ▶

0   6   0   5   6   7   0   4   0   S

Stop the 401(k) Rip-off!

<table>
<tr><td rowspan="3">SCHEDULE D
(Form 5500)

Department of the Treasury
Internal Revenue Service

Department of Labor
Employee Benefits Security Administration</td><td>DFE/Participating Plan Information

This schedule is required to be filed under section 104 of the Employee Retirement Income Security Act of 1974 (ERISA).

▶ File as an attachment to Form 5500.</td><td>Official Use Only

OMB No. 1210–0110

2005

This Form is Open to Public Inspection.</td></tr>
</table>

For calendar plan year 2005 or fiscal plan year beginning , and ending ,

A Name of plan or DFE
FINANCEWARE, INC. 401(K) PLAN

B Three–digit plan number ▶ 001

C Plan or DFE sponsor's name as shown on line 2a of Form 5500
FINANCEWARE, INC.

D Employer Identification Number
51

Part I Information on interests in MTIAs, CCTs, PSAs, and 103–12 IEs (to be completed by plans and DFEs)

(a) Name of MTIA, CCT, PSA, or 103–12IE PRIN PTR LG-CAP GR II SEP ACCT

(b) Name of sponsor of entity listed in (a) PRINCIPAL LIFE INSURANCE COMPANY

(c) EIN–PN 42-0127290-067 **(d)** Entity code P **(e)** Dollar value of interest in MTIA, CCT, PSA, or 103–12IE at end of year (see instructions) 122382

(a) Name of MTIA, CCT, PSA, or 103–12IE PRINCIPAL MONEY MKT SEP ACCT

(b) Name of sponsor of entity listed in (a) PRINCIPAL LIFE INSURANCE COMPANY

(c) EIN–PN 42-0127290-024 **(d)** Entity code P **(e)** Dollar value of interest in MTIA, CCT, PSA, or 103–12IE at end of year (see instructions) 65196

(a) Name of MTIA, CCT, PSA, or 103–12IE PRINCIPAL BOND AND MTG SEP ACC

(b) Name of sponsor of entity listed in (a) PRINCIPAL LIFE INSURANCE COMPANY

(c) EIN–PN 42-0127290-005 **(d)** Entity code P **(e)** Dollar value of interest in MTIA, CCT, PSA, or 103–12IE at end of year (see instructions) 110369

(a) Name of MTIA, CCT, PSA, or 103–12IE PRIN PTR SM-CP GR III SEP ACCT

(b) Name of sponsor of entity listed in (a) PRINCIPAL LIFE INSURANCE COMPANY

(c) EIN–PN 42-0127290-097 **(d)** Entity code P **(e)** Dollar value of interest in MTIA, CCT, PSA, or 103–12IE at end of year (see instructions) 9469

For Paperwork Reduction Act Notice and OMB Control Numbers, see the instructions for Form 5500. v8.2 Schedule D (Form 5500) 2005

1 2 0 5 6 7 0 1 0 M

Appendix D

Official Use Only

(a) Name of MTIA, CCT, PSA, or 103–12IE   PRIN PTNRS LG-CAP VALUE II SA

(b) Name of sponsor of entity listed in (a)   PRINCIPAL LIFE INSURANCE COMPANY

(c) EIN–PN 42-0127290-100   **(d)** Entity code P   **(e)** Dollar value of interest in MTIA, CCT, PSA, or 103–12IE at end of year (see instructions)   59072

(a) Name of MTIA, CCT, PSA, or 103–12IE   PRIN LG CP STK IDX SEP ACCT

(b) Name of sponsor of entity listed in (a)   PRINCIPAL LIFE INSURANCE COMPANY

(c) EIN–PN 42-0127290-016   **(d)** Entity code P   **(e)** Dollar value of interest in MTIA, CCT, PSA, or 103–12IE at end of year (see instructions)   171636

(a) Name of MTIA, CCT, PSA, or 103–12IE   PRIN TOT MKT STK IDX SEP ACCT

(b) Name of sponsor of entity listed in (a)   PRINCIPAL LIFE INSURANCE COMPANY

(c) EIN–PN 42-0127290-033   **(d)** Entity code P   **(e)** Dollar value of interest in MTIA, CCT, PSA, or 103–12IE at end of year (see instructions)   191459

(a) Name of MTIA, CCT, PSA, or 103–12IE   PRIN MID CAP STK IDX SEP ACCT

(b) Name of sponsor of entity listed in (a)   PRINCIPAL LIFE INSURANCE COMPANY

(c) EIN–PN 42-0127290-023   **(d)** Entity code P   **(e)** Dollar value of interest in MTIA, CCT, PSA, or 103–12IE at end of year (see instructions)   113200

(a) Name of MTIA, CCT, PSA, or 103–12IE   PRIN SM CAP STK IDX SEP ACCT

(b) Name of sponsor of entity listed in (a)   PRINCIPAL LIFE INSURANCE COMPANY

(c) EIN–PN 42-0127290-028   **(d)** Entity code P   **(e)** Dollar value of interest in MTIA, CCT, PSA, or 103–12IE at end of year (see instructions)   204077

(a) Name of MTIA, CCT, PSA, or 103–12IE   PRINCIPAL SM CO GRWTH SEP ACCT

(b) Name of sponsor of entity listed in (a)   PRINCIPAL LIFE INSURANCE COMPANY

(c) EIN–PN 42-0127290-030   **(d)** Entity code P   **(e)** Dollar value of interest in MTIA, CCT, PSA, or 103–12IE at end of year (see instructions)   6630

1 2 0 5 6 7 0 2 0 N

185

Schedule D (Form 5500) 2005   Page **2**

(a) Name of MTIA, CCT, PSA, or 103–12IE <u>PRINCIPAL INTL EM MKT SEP ACCT</u>

(b) Name of sponsor of entity listed in (a) <u>PRINCIPAL LIFE INSURANCE COMPANY</u>

(c) EIN–PN <u>42-0127290-013</u> **(d)** Entity code <u>P</u> **(e)** Dollar value of interest in MTIA, CCT, PSA, or 103–12IE at end of year (see instructions) <u>102204</u>

(a) Name of MTIA, CCT, PSA, or 103–12IE <u>PRINCIPAL DIVERS INTL SEP ACCT</u>

(b) Name of sponsor of entity listed in (a) <u>PRINCIPAL LIFE INSURANCE COMPANY</u>

(c) EIN–PN <u>42-0127290-015</u> **(d)** Entity code <u>P</u> **(e)** Dollar value of interest in MTIA, CCT, PSA, or 103–12IE at end of year (see instructions) <u>123882</u>

(a) Name of MTIA, CCT, PSA, or 103–12IE <u>AMER CENT ULTRA (ADV) SEP ACCT</u>

(b) Name of sponsor of entity listed in (a) <u>PRINCIPAL LIFE INSURANCE COMPANY</u>

(c) EIN–PN <u>42-0127290-041</u> **(d)** Entity code <u>P</u> **(e)** Dollar value of interest in MTIA, CCT, PSA, or 103–12IE at end of year (see instructions) <u>0</u>

(a) Name of MTIA, CCT, PSA, or 103–12IE <u>AMER CT INC&GR (ADV) SP ACCT</u>

(b) Name of sponsor of entity listed in (a) <u>PRINCIPAL LIFE INSURANCE COMPANY</u>

(c) EIN–PN <u>42-0127290-044</u> **(d)** Entity code <u>P</u> **(e)** Dollar value of interest in MTIA, CCT, PSA, or 103–12IE at end of year (see instructions) <u>0</u>

(a) Name of MTIA, CCT, PSA, or 103–12IE <u>FID ADV EQUITY GROWTH SEP ACCT</u>

(b) Name of sponsor of entity listed in (a) <u>PRINCIPAL LIFE INSURANCE COMPANY</u>

(c) EIN–PN <u>42-0127290-045</u> **(d)** Entity code <u>P</u> **(e)** Dollar value of interest in MTIA, CCT, PSA, or 103–12IE at end of year (see instructions) <u>0</u>

(a) Name of MTIA, CCT, PSA, or 103–12IE <u>INVESCO SMALL CO GR SEP ACCT</u>

(b) Name of sponsor of entity listed in (a) <u>PRINCIPAL LIFE INSURANCE COMPANY</u>

(c) EIN–PN <u>42-0127290-058</u> **(d)** Entity code <u>P</u> **(e)** Dollar value of interest in MTIA, CCT, PSA, or 103–12IE at end of year (see instructions) <u>0</u>

1 2 0 5 6 7 0 2 0 N

Appendix D

Page **2**

Official Use Only

(a) Name of MTIA, CCT, PSA, or 103–12IE PRIN PTR MD-CP GR I SEP ACCT

(b) Name of sponsor of entity listed in (a) PRINCIPAL LIFE INSURANCE COMPANY

(c) EIN–PN 42-0127290-056 **(d)** Entity code P **(e)** Dollar value of interest in MTIA, CCT, PSA, or 103–12IE at end of year (see instructions) 23542

(a) Name of MTIA, CCT, PSA, or 103–12IE JANUS ADV CAP APPR SEP ACCT

(b) Name of sponsor of entity listed in (a) PRINCIPAL LIFE INSURANCE COMPANY

(c) EIN–PN 42-0127290-057 **(d)** Entity code P **(e)** Dollar value of interest in MTIA, CCT, PSA, or 103–12IE at end of year (see instructions) 0

(a) Name of MTIA, CCT, PSA, or 103–12IE

(b) Name of sponsor of entity listed in (a)

(c) EIN–PN **(d)** Entity code **(e)** Dollar value of interest in MTIA, CCT, PSA, or 103–12IE at end of year (see instructions)

(a) Name of MTIA, CCT, PSA, or 103–12IE

(b) Name of sponsor of entity listed in (a)

(c) EIN–PN **(d)** Entity code **(e)** Dollar value of interest in MTIA, CCT, PSA, or 103–12IE at end of year (see instructions)

(a) Name of MTIA, CCT, PSA, or 103–12IE

(b) Name of sponsor of entity listed in (a)

(c) EIN–PN **(d)** Entity code **(e)** Dollar value of interest in MTIA, CCT, PSA, or 103–12IE at end of year (see instructions)

(a) Name of MTIA, CCT, PSA, or 103–12IE

(b) Name of sponsor of entity listed in (a)

(c) EIN–PN **(d)** Entity code **(e)** Dollar value of interest in MTIA, CCT, PSA, or 103–12IE at end of year (see instructions)

1 2 0 5 6 7 0 2 0 N

Stop the 401(k) Rip-off!

SCHEDULE I **(Form 5500)** Department of the Treasury Internal Revenue Service Department of Labor Employee Benefits Security Administration Pension Benefit Guaranty Corporation	**Financial Information –– Small Plan** This schedule is required to be filed under Section 104 of the Employee Retirement Income Security Act of 1974 (ERISA) and section 6058(a) of the Internal Revenue Code (the Code). ▶ **File as an attachment to Form 5500.**	Official Use Only OMB No. 1210–0110 **2005** **This Form is Open to Public Inspection.**

For calendar year 2005 or fiscal plan year beginning , and ending ,

A Name of plan FINANCEWARE, INC. 401(K) PLAN	**B** Three–digit plan number ▶ 001
C Plan sponsor's name as shown on line 2a of Form 5500 FINANCEWARE, INC.	**D** Employer Identification Number 51

Complete Schedule I if the plan covered fewer than 100 participants as of the beginning of the plan year. You may also complete Schedule I if you are filing as a small plan under the 80–120 participant rule (see instructions). Complete Schedule H if reporting as a large plan or DFE.

Part I   Small Plan Financial Information

Report below the current value of assets and liabilities, income, expenses, transfers and changes in net assets during the plan year. Combine the value of plan assets held in more than one trust. Do not enter the value of the portion of an insurance contract that guarantees during this plan year to pay a specific dollar benefit at a future date. Include all income and expenses of the plan including any trust(s) or separately maintained fund(s) and any payments/receipts to/from insurance carriers. **Round off amounts to the nearest dollar.**

1	**Plan Assets and Liabilities:**		(a) Beginning of Year	(b) End of Year
a	Total plan assets	1a	1013895	1341870
b	Total plan liabilities	1b		
c	Net plan assets (subtract line 1b from line 1a)	1c	1013895	1341870
2	**Income, Expenses, and Transfers for this Plan Year:**		(a) Amount	(b) Total
a	Contributions received or receivable			
	(1) Employers	2a(1)	42614	
	(2) Participants	2a(2)	221624	
	(3) Others (including rollovers)	2a(3)		
b	Noncash contributions	2b		
c	Other income	2c	109967	
d	Total income (add lines 2a(1), 2a(2), 2a(3), 2b, and 2c)	2d		374205
e	Benefits paid (including direct rollovers)	2e	34926	
f	Corrective distributions (see instructions)	2f		
g	Certain deemed distributions of participant loans (see instructions)	2g		
h	Other expenses	2h	11304	
i	Total expenses (add lines 2e, 2f, 2g, and 2h)	2i		46230
j	Net income (loss) (subtract line 2i from line 2d)	2j		327975
k	Transfers to (from) the plan (see instructions)	2k		

3   **Specific Assets:** If the plan held assets at anytime during the plan year in any of the following categories, check "Yes" and enter the current value of any assets remaining in the plan as of the end of the plan year. Allocate the value of the plan's interest in a commingled trust containing the assets of more than one plan on a line–by–line basis unless the trust meets one of the specific exceptions described in the instructions.

			Yes	No	Amount
a	Partnership/joint venture interests	3a		X	
b	Employer real property	3b		X	

For Paperwork Reduction Act Notice and OMB Control Numbers, see the instructions for Form 5500.   v8.2   Schedule I (Form 5500) 2005

2 0 0 5 6 7 0 1 0 L

Appendix D

Schedule I (Form 5500) 2005   Page **2**

Official Use Only

			Yes	No	Amount
3c	Real estate (other than employer real property)	3c		X	
d	Employer securities	3d		X	
e	Participant loans	3e	X		29789
f	Loans (other than to participants)	3f		X	
g	Tangible personal property	3g		X	

Part II   Transactions During Plan Year

			Yes	No	Amount
4	During the plan year:				
a	Did the employer fail to transmit to the plan any participant contributions within the time period described in 29 CFR 2510.3–102? (See instructions and DOL's Voluntary Fiduciary Correction Program)	4a		X	
b	Were any loans by the plan or fixed income obligations due the plan in default as of the close of the plan year or classified during the year as uncollectible? Disregard participant loans secured by the participants' account balance	4b		X	
c	Were any leases to which the plan was a party in default or classified during the year as uncollectible?	4c		X	
d	Were there any nonexempt transactions with any party–in–interest? (Do not include transactions reported on line 4a.)	4d		X	
e	Was the plan covered by a fidelity bond?	4e	X		140000
f	Did the plan have a loss, whether or not reimbursed by the plan's fidelity bond, that was caused by fraud or dishonesty?	4f		X	
g	Did the plan hold any assets whose current value was neither readily determinable on an established market nor set by an independent third party appraiser?	4g		X	
h	Did the plan receive any noncash contributions whose value was neither readily determinable on an established market nor set by an independent third party appraiser?	4h		X	
i	Did the plan at any time hold 20% or more of its assets in any single security, debt, mortgage, parcel of real estate, or partnership/joint venture interest?	4i		X	
j	Were all the plan assets either distributed to participants or beneficiaries, transferred to another plan, or brought under the control of the PBGC?	4j		X	
k	Are you claiming a waiver of the annual examination and report of an independent qualified public accountant (IQPA) under 29 CFR 2520.104–46? If no, attach the IQPA's report or 2520.104–50 statement. (See instructions on waiver eligibility and conditions.)	4k	X		

5a Has a resolution to terminate the plan been adopted during the plan year or any prior plan year? If yes, enter the amount of any plan assets that reverted to the employer this year .... ☐ Yes ☒ No   Amount _____

5b If during this plan year, any assets or liabilities were transferred from this plan to another plan(s), identify the plan(s) to which assets or liabilities were transferred. (See instructions.)

5b(1) Name of plan(s)   **5b(2)** EIN(s)   **5b(3)** PN(s)

2 0 0 5 6 7 0 2 0 M

189

Stop the 401(k) Rip-off!

SCHEDULE P (FORM 5500)	**Annual Return of Fiduciary of Employee Benefit Trust**	Official Use Only
	This schedule may be filed to satisfy the requirements under section 6033(a) for an annual information return from every section 401(a) organization exempt from tax under section 501(a).	OMB No. 1210–0110
	Filing this form will start the running of the statute of limitations under section 6501(a) for any trust described in section 401(a) that is exempt from tax under section 501(a).	**2005**
Department of the Treasury Internal Revenue Service	▶ **File as an attachment to Form 5500 or 5500–EZ.**	This Form is Open to Public Inspection.

For trust calendar year 2005 or fiscal year beginning   03/15/2005 ,   and ending   12/31/2005

1a Name of trustee or custodian

█████████████

b Number, street, and room or suite no. (If a P.O. box, see the instructions for Form 5500 or 5500–EZ.)

███████████████████████

c City or town, state, and ZIP code

RICHMOND   VA   23220-5048

2a Name of trust

FINANCEWARE, INC. 401(K) PLAN

b Trust's employer identification number   42-0127290

3 Name of plan if different from name of trust

4 Have you furnished the participating employee benefit plan(s) with the trust financial information required
to be reported by the plan(s)? .... ☒ **Yes**   ☐ **No**

5 Enter the plan sponsor's employer identification number as shown on Form 5500
or 5500–EZ. .... ▶   ██████████

Under penalties of perjury, I declare that I have examined this schedule, and to the best of my knowledge and belief it is true, correct, and complete.

SIGN HERE   Signature of fiduciary ▶ _____   Date ▶ _____

For the Paperwork Reduction Notice and OMB Control Numbers,   v8.2   Schedule P (Form 5500) 2005
see the instructions for Form 5500 or 5500–EZ.

2 6 0 5 6 7 0 1 0 R

Appendix D

```
SCHEDULE R        Retirement Plan Information              Official Use Only
(Form 5500)
Department of the Treasury    This schedule is required to be filed under sections 104 and 4065 of the   OMB No. 1210-0110
Internal Revenue Service      Employee Retirement Security Act of 1974 (ERISA) and section 6058(a) of the
Department of Labor           Internal Revenue Code (the Code).                                            2005
Employee Benefits Security
Administration
Pension Benefit Guaranty Corporation   ► File as an Attachment to Form 5500.            This Form is Open to
                                                                                         Public Inspection.
```

For calendar year 2005 or fiscal plan year beginning   , and ending   ,

A Name of plan
FINANCEWARE, INC. 401(K) PLAN

B Three-digit plan number ► 001

C Plan sponsor's name as shown on line 2a of Form 5500
FINANCEWARE, INC.

D Employer Identification Number

Part I Distributions

All references to distributions relate only to payments of benefits during the plan year.

1 Total value of distributions paid in property other than in cash or the forms of property specified in the instructions .... **1** $

2 Enter the EIN(s) of payor(s) who paid benefits on behalf of the plan to participants or beneficiaries during the year (if more than two, enter EINs of the two payors who paid the greatest dollar amounts of benefits). _____   _____

Profit-sharing plans, ESOPs, and stock bonus plans, skip line 3.

3 Number of participants (living or deceased) whose benefits were distributed in a single sum, during the plan year **3**

Part II Funding Information (If the plan is not subject to the minimum funding requirements of section 412 of the Internal Revenue Code or ERISA section 302, skip this Part)

4 Is the plan administrator making an election under Code section 412(c)(8) or ERISA section 302(c)(8)? .... ☐ Yes ☐ No ☐ N/A

If the plan is a defined benefit plan, go to line 7.

5 If a waiver of the minimum funding standard for a prior year is being amortized in this plan year, see instructions, and enter the date of the ruling letter granting the waiver .... ► Month_____ Day_____ Year_____

If you completed line 5, complete lines 3, 9, and 10 of Schedule B and do not complete the remainder of this schedule.

6a Enter the minimum required contribution for this plan year .... **6a** $

b Enter the amount contributed by the employer to the plan for this plan year .... **6b** $

c Subtract the amount in line 6b from the amount in line 6a. Enter the result (enter a minus sign to the left of a negative amount) .... **6c** $

If you completed line 6c, do not complete the remainder of this schedule.

7 If a change in actuarial cost method was made for this plan year pursuant to a revenue procedure providing automatic approval for the change or a class ruling letter, does the plan sponsor or plan administrator agree with the change?.... ☐ Yes ☐ No ☐ N/A

Part III Amendments

8 If this is a defined benefit pension plan, were any amendments adopted during this plan year that increased or decreased the value of benefits? If yes, check the appropriate box(es). If no, check the "No" box. (See instructions.)... ☐ Increase ☐ Decrease ☐ No

Part IV Coverage (See instructions.)

9 Check the box for the test this plan used to satisfy the coverage requirements .... ☐ the ratio percentage test ☐ average benefit test

For Paperwork Reduction Act Notice and OMB Control Numbers, see the instructions for Form 5500.   v8.2   Schedule R (Form 5500) 2005

2 2 0 5 6 7 0 1 0 N

Stop the 401(k) Rip-off!

SCHEDULE SSA (Form 5500)	Annual Registration Statement Identifying Separated Participants With Deferred Vested Benefits	Official Use Only
	Under Section 6057(a) of the Internal Revenue Code	OMB No. 1210–0110
	▶ File as an attachment to Form 5500 unless box 1 is checked.	**2005**
Department of the Treasury Internal Revenue Service		This Form is NOT Open to Public Inspection.

For calendar year 2005 or fiscal plan year beginning , and ending ,

A Name of plan
FINANCEWARE, INC. 401(K) PLAN

B Three–digit plan number ▶ 001

C Plan sponsor's name as shown on line 2a of Form 5500
FINANCEWARE, INC.

D Employer Identification Number
████████

1 ☐ Check here if plan is a government, church or other plan that elects to voluntarily file Schedule SSA. If so, complete lines 2 through 3c, and the signature area.

2 Plan sponsor's address (number, street, and room or suite no.) (If a P.O. box, see the instructions for line 2.)

City or town, state, and ZIP code

3a Name of plan administrator (if other than sponsor)

3b Administrator's EIN

3c Number, street, and room or suite no. (If a P.O. box, see the instructions for line 2.)

City or town, state, and ZIP code

Under penalties of perjury, I declare that I have examined this report, and to the best of my knowledge and belief, it is true, correct, and complete.

SIGN HERE Signature of plan administrator ▶

Phone number of plan administrator ▶ _____ Date ▶ _____

For Paperwork Reduction Act Notice and OMB Control Numbers, see the instructions for Form 5500. v7.2 **Schedule SSA (Form 5500) 2005**

3 0 0 5 6 7 0 1 0 M

192

Appendix D

Schedule SSA (Form 5500) 2005   Page **2**

Official Use Only

4   Enter one of the following Entry Codes in column (a) for each separated participant with deferred vested benefits that:

Code A — has not previously been reported.

Code B — has previously been reported under the above plan number but requires revisions to the information previously reported.

Code C — has previously been reported under another plan number but will be receiving their benefits from the plan listed above instead.

Code D — has previously been reported under the above plan number but is no longer entitled to those deferred vested benefits.

		Use with entry code "A", "B", "C", or "D"			Use with entry code "A" or "B"		
(a) Entry Code	**(b)** Social Security Number	**(c)** Name of Participant (First)	(M.I.)	(Last)	Enter code for nature and form of benefit **(d)** Type of annuity	**(e)** Payment frequency	Amount of vested benefit **(f)** Defined benefit plan — periodic payment
■■■■■■■■■■	■■■■■■■■■■	■■■■■■■■■■			A	A	

		Use with entry code "A" or "B"			Use with entry code "C"	
(a) Entry Code	Amount of vested benefit — Defined contribution plan **(g)** Units or shares	Share indicator	**(h)** Total value of account		**(i)** Previous sponsor's employer identification number	**(j)** Previous plan number

3 0 0 5 6 7 0 2 0 N

INDEX

Misc.
12b-1, 21, 54

A
administrative expense(s), 13
"AGE" Based Investing, 90
annual saving(s), xiii, 32, 102, 104
Asset Allocation, ix, xxiv, 18, 58, 72, 76-78, 88, 92, 102, 104
assumed rate(s), 29

B
Bait and Switch, 57, 61, 70
Bankrate.com, 19
Basic Financial Statement(s), 13
benefit risk(s), xi-xiii
Boston College, xiii, 59
Brinson, Beebower & Hood, 78
broker, 18, 39-40, 43, 56-59, 71, 72
brokerage, 18-19, 21-23, 41-42, 62, 72-73, 77

C
Campanale, Frank, xvii
CDSC, 20
Center for Retirement Research, xiii
Certified Wealthcare Analyst™, 62
chance of outliving your resources, xiii
CNBC, 72
comfort, 34-35, 66-67
comfort zone, 34-35
conflicted, xxiv, 43, 57-58, 63, 68
compound return, 27, 29-30, 72
conservative assumption(s), 31-32
consultant, 18
custody, 18, 42, 100-101
contingent deferred sales charge, 20
continuous process, xxiv
correlation coefficient, 74
Crash of '29, 28, 32-33, 35-36, 87

D
defined benefit, xi, xiii-xiv
defined benefit pension plan, xi
Deeply Hidden Expense(s), ix, 17, 24
dream(s), i, xxii-xxiii, 36, 61, 63-65, 69

E
Employee Fiduciary Corp, i, xviii
Employer Identification Number, 59
ETF, 22, 93
ethical, 1, 6, 14, 51
Expense Ratio, 6-8, 11, 14-15, 20-22, 54, 75, 101
expense saving dividend, xxiii

F
fiduciary obligation(s), xxi
Financeware, iv, xvii
Five Steps, ix, xv, xix, xxii-xxiii
float, 23-24
Form 5500, ix, 58
free help, xx
Fund of fund, xiii, xx-xxii, 4, 6-8, 11, 14-16, 19-23, 27-28, 31-33, 40-41, 49, 54-57, 62, 68, 72-77, 90-91, 100, 103
fund rating(s), xxii, 75

G
Galt, John, xviii
gambling, 41, 63-64, 70, 90-91
Government Accountability Office, xiv, 51, 59
Great Depression, 27, 31-33, 35-36

H
hidden cost(s), xv, xviii, 21, 23

I

Index Fund, 6, 14, 54, 75, 100
informed choice(s), xxiii-xxiv
investment risk, xi-xii, xxii, 32-33, 35-
   36, 47, 53, 64-65, 69, 78, 82, 90

K

kickback(s), 13-16, 39, 45, 57

L

Labor Department, xiv, 17, 51-52, 53,
   59-60
lifecycle fund, 20
Life Relative Allocation, 91

M

macro asset classes, 42
Make the Most of My Life, ix, 25, 61
Making the Most of Your Life, xxii, 61-
   62, 68, 71
market lottery, 34, 91
materially underperformed, 74
misclassified, 75
Morningstar, 7, 55, 76
M&E, 19
mutual fund(s), xi, 18-22, 26, 72-74,
   77, 93
Miller, George, xiv
Multi-Discipline Account(s), 18
Multi-Manager Account(s), 18

N

NASD, 26, 72
needless sacrifice(s), 32-37, 58, 103
no load, 4, 54

P

Payson, Parker, i, xviii
past performance, xxii, 26, 40, 55-56,
   72-73
peer group, 69, 75
pension plan, xi-xii
performance report, 69
plan expense(s), xiv, xix, xxii, 4, 6, 11,
   13-15, 40, 42-43
powers that be, xxi, 40, 47-48, 50, 52
privately held companies, xii

product vendor(s), xiii, xxii, 31, 33, 41, 69
prudent fiduciary, xiv, 53, 55-56
public companies, xii, 1

R

Rallying Your Troops, ix, xx, 47
Rand, Ayn, vii, xviii
Reinhart, Len, i, xvii
retirement benefit(s), xi-xii
retirement plan(s), i, xi-xii, xx, xxii, 20,
   25, 45, 53, 56, 65
revenue sharing, 13-14, 39, 57

S

sacrifice, 32-37, 58, 63, 71, 103
sales pitch, 62, 74
savings shortfall, 26, 32
saving too much, xxiii, 26, 32
scare tactic(s), 31
Schwab, 23
self-directed brokerage account, 42
SEC, 19
simulation, 31-32, 34, 37
soup line(s), 31, 34
stable value fund, 23
SAI, 21
Summary Annual Report, ix, 11-13, 15,
   40, 42, 59, 100
surrender charge(s), 20

T

target fund(s), 21, 90-91
too much uncertainty, 34, 37
Total Market Index Fund, 6, 14, 75
Total Investment Expense, 6-7
treasury bill, 22-23

U

uncertainty, 26-28, 30, 32-34, 37, 68,
   70-71
universe rank(s), 75

V

vacationing too little, xxiii
variable annuities, 19, 40

W

Wall Street, 63-64, 69, 71, 77-78, 92
Wealthcare, xxiv, 42-43, 62, 86, 88-90, 95, 97, 99
working too long, xxiii
wrap fee(s), 18

Y

Yahoo, 7, 76

Z

Zero Alpha Group, 22